A STUDENT'S MANUAL
OF BIBLIOGRAPHY

*The Library Association Series
of Library Manuals I*

A STUDENT'S MANUAL
OF BIBLIOGRAPHY

BY ARUNDELL ESDAILE

Late of the British Museum
Sandars Reader in Bibliography in the
University of Cambridge 1926–27
Lecturer in Bibliography in the University of London
School of Librarianship 1919–1939

REVISED BY ROY STOKES

Head of the Library School, Loughborough College

Qui scit ubi sit scientia, scienti est
proximus.
Wer das kleine tut als sei es etwas
grosse, dem gibt Gott die Gnade,
dass er das grosse tue als sei es
etwas kleine.

LONDON
GEORGE ALLEN & UNWIN LTD
& THE LIBRARY ASSOCIATION

First Published in 1931
Second Edition 1932
Third Revised Edition 1954

Printed in Great Britain
in 12pt. Caslon type by
Messrs. Butler & Tanner Ltd.
Frome and London

GENERAL INTRODUCTION TO THE SERIES

The publication of a systematic series of authoritative Manuals of Library Work, which shall survey Library polity and practice in their latest aspects, is a requirement of which administrators, librarians and students have long been conscious, and is much overdue.

The Library Act of 1919 marked the end of one long epoch and the beginning of a new. The removal of the rate limit paved the way for remarkable extensions and innovations, both in buildings and service. The great work of the Carnegie Trustees in fostering the development of urban Public Libraries has been largely diverted into fresh channels, and County Library Systems now cover the country from Land's End to John o' Groats. The public demand for, and the appreciation of, Libraries have increased enormously. The evolution of Commercial and Technical Libraries and the development of Business and Works Libraries would amply suffice to indicate this progress, but, during the last decade or so, the entire field of Library service has been subjected to review and experiment, and little, in administration or routine, remains unchanged.

It will, therefore, be obvious that old textbooks on practice can no longer serve, and there is a need for new manuals, written by persons of experience and authority, and treating of the new conditions in a full and practical manner. These Manuals are designed to fill the void, and the fact that they are issued by Messrs. George Allen and Unwin Ltd., in conjunction with the Library Association, should afford adequate proof of the qualifications of the authors to treat of the subjects upon which they will write.

GENERAL INTRODUCTION

The volumes will be supplied with bibliographical references throughout, and will be illustrated when necessary. No effort will be spared to make the series an essential tool for all those who are engaged in Library work, or who intend to embrace Librarianship as a profession.

WILLIAM E. DOUBLEDAY
General Editor until 1949

To Mr. Doubleday's general introduction, written more than twenty years ago, it need only be added that the plan and purpose of these Manuals remain unchanged.

DUNCAN GRAY
General Editor

PREFACE TO THIRD EDITION

The stock of the current (the second) edition of this
book was "blitzed" in the City in 1941. It was not
till after the war that the publishers could contem-
plate a new edition. Mere reprinting seemed unworthy, in view of the mass of bibliographical work
that had appeared since its publication. I had retired
from the staff of the British Museum in 1940, and
was, as I am, living in the country. Eventually it
proved possible for Mr. Roy Stokes to undertake the
considerable work of revision, and very well he has
done it. I trust that new generations of students may
find it useful, and may realise that bibliography is
not at all a dull subject.

ARUNDELL ESDAILE

PREFACE TO FIRST EDITION

The function of a preface is defined on page 99 as to be
"useful for the author's afterthoughts, for first-aid to reviewers,
and for those acknowledgments to helpers which can so easily be
overdone". These last were once described by the late Sir Walter
A. Raleigh as "a tombstone which is only read by the departed".
That to this volume exists also for the author's self-exculpation.

It is hoped that the book may be of use to foreign as well as to
English students. The former are asked to remember that it was
based on lectures delivered to the latter, and that therefore the
examples cited to illustrate principles are largely derived from
English books, and that the select lists of books in Chapters IX
and X are confined to those produced in Great Britain and the
four countries whose literatures are most read here, the United
States, France, Germany, and Italy. Similar lists for other countries would have weighted the burden on the student's memory,
and can easily be supplied by teachers. Many can be found in
Dr. Wilhelm Krabbe's little handbook for Berlin students,
Bibliographie.

Orientalia, Slavonica, maps, and music are left on one side as
being special studies.

I have had much help from friends whom I would thank.
Mr. A. F. Johnson, Mr. Norman Parley, Mr. H. M. Hake,
Mr. Douglas Cockerell, and Mr. P. B. James have read chapters
in proof, and saved me from some errors into which I had fallen.
Messrs. Unwin Brothers' Reader also has made valuable suggestions on the passages in which I, an amateur, describe the art
in which he is a professional. I am relieved that my errors here
were not more numerous.

My debt to my fellow members of the Bibliographical Society,
and notably to Dr. Pollard, Dr. Greg and Dr. McKerrow, is
such that I no longer know when I am quoting their words and
when I am not.

Miss Katherine Leathem and Miss Paule de Lépervanche

have checked the titles of the books mentioned in Chapters IX and X.

If the price of the volume was to be kept within the reach of students, illustrations, which ideally should be numerous in any book on bibliography, had to be confined to a few which could be borrowed. My publishers and I are indebted to Messrs. Bernard Quaritch, Ltd., for Plates III, IV, and V; to Messrs. Ellis for Plate VI; to Messrs. Tregaskis for Plate I; to the Trustees of the British Museum for Figures 3–8 and 12; to Dr. R. B. McKerrow and the Clarendon Press for Figures 2, 10 and 11; and to Mr. Douglas Cockerell and the Clarendon Press for Figure 9.

Plates II, VII, and VIII are reproduced by permission of Messrs. Kegan Paul & Co. from H. P. Horne's *The Binding of Books*.

FOREWORD

The arrangement of this book has not altered in any important respect from the previous editions. The plan is, that after a discussion on the nature of bibliography, the history and make-up of the book itself are dealt with. Having thus, as it were, created the physical form of the book, it is then analysed for the purposes of collation and description. The survey ends with some small discussion on certain important bibliographical works and a glance at the problems of the arrangement of bibliographies.

A reading list is appended to each chapter, divided into two parts. "List A" contains those books, articles or chapters which, it is suggested, the student should read as first priority. "List B" contains further important works on the subject of the chapter of which the student should be aware, and which he will need to consult a little later on in his studies. The lists do not attempt to be full bibliographies. Every effort has been made to keep them down to a few titles which, it is hoped, will be readily available to most students.

To my colleagues at the Loughborough Library School, both staff and students, my thanks are due for the help of their friendly advice and criticism. Above all, Mr. F. C. Francis, of the Department of Printed Books in the British Museum, has given me the benefit of his experience with that generosity which is natural to him and no acknowledgment can sufficiently express my gratitude.

ROY STOKES

CONTENTS

ILLUSTRATIONS

PLATES

FIGURES IN THE TEXT

I

INTRODUCTORY

DEFINITION

Bibliography is an art and also a science. The art is that of recording books; the science, necessary to it, is that of the making of books and of their extant record.

This may be made clearer by a little examination. The ultimate aim is to record books. It may be thought that all books are recorded, but this is very far from being the case. When his *Repertorium Bibliographicum ad annum MD.* was published in 1826–1838, the bibliographer Ludwig Hain recorded some sixteen thousand incunabula or books printed before the end of the fifteenth century. When the English bibliographer, W. A. Copinger, published his supplement to Hain in 1895–1902, he added nearly six thousand entries for books not referred to by Hain. Today, the number known, though not yet all registered in any single list, must total nearly three times Hain's original figure. In sale catalogues the word "unrecorded" is of frequent occurrence, and, even if a book be recorded, the record is often inaccurate or inadequate to its main purposes of showing what is in the book and distinguishing it from other books. The modern solution of some bibliographical problems, to which reference will be made later, provides ample evidence of the need to make the record accurate and complete.

Bibliography in its idea is concerned with writings surviving in manuscript as much as with those which have been multiplied by print. The written book is as much a book as the printed book; the early printer, by his mechanical invention, merely gave the book-buyer more cheaply and abundantly a commodity like in all its aspects to that to which he was accustomed; and the principles of examining and recording both are the same in essentials. But the bibliography of manuscript, and especially of pre-Gutenberg book-manuscript, has unfortunately been in modern practice severed from that of print. The present author has not the knowledge to justify him in attempting to include palæography. I would merely refer the beginner, in the first place, to Falconer Madan's *Books in Manuscript*.

The record of books may take different forms. The first need for all who deal with books is that of a bare registration of their having been printed at a specific place and date, with the author's name and the distinctive title. In modern times, that is within the last century or less, the organized book trade of each civilized country produces current lists which do this, though nowhere exhaustively. But these lists are scattered and an entry must be hunted through many volumes. Clearly, if the student is to find his book, which is the aim of bibliography, there must be something simpler. In the seventeenth and eighteenth centuries attempts were made at more or less universal bibliographies. But these were at once too universal, in the sense that they aimed at what was impracticable, and not universal enough, in the sense that they disregarded popular and fugitive literature. The modern historian recognizes the value of what is thought to be, and in fact often is, ephemeral when it is new. G. K. Chesterton observed in his *Heretics* that "good books can tell us the mind of one man; bad books can tell us the mind of many men". Under the modern Copyright Acts of this country, and corresponding laws elsewhere, a high proportion of the recent output of the press is preserved in the national libraries and can be traced in the catalogues of those libraries, which thus became the largest contributions to world bibliography. But of the output of the earlier centuries, not indeed so profuse, a far lower proportion is recorded and accessible.

It is difficult to make any estimate of the total number of editions of books actually in existence. In 1911, in *Bulletin de l' Institut International de Bibliographie*, Iwinski put the figure at twenty-five million at the lowest guess; and fugitive sheets and pieces of all kinds, often of great interest and always of extreme rarity, are innumerable. In the same collection of statistics, Iwinski calculated that world book production had doubled in the period between 1858 to 1898. Moreover, a huge quantity of printed matter in modern times, and increasingly from year to year, appears in periodical literature, and is mostly not separately registered in catalogues. Much of this material is ephemeral; but for the man of science a

catalogue or bibliography containing separately published books only can be but of small service, since
practically all original scientific work makes its first
appearance in Journals, Transactions, Memoirs, Reports, and the like, and is only reproduced in ordinary
books when there is the danger of its being at the
point of supersession. In the same way, the shorter
pieces of many modern men of letters first appear in
literary magazines and have to be collected and collated by their editors when the authors are eminent
enough to be deemed worth editing.

In all this enormous accumulation of material the
student would lose his way, wasting years before
finding even part of what he needed, were it not
for bibliography. It has been absurdly stated that
bibliography comprehends all sciences; some bibliographers, and many more who know nothing of the
matter, have looked to bibliographers for the criticism and selection of books. But it is obvious that no
one but a chemist can assign their relative values to
rival books or papers on chemistry, and that the
bibliographer who attempts any such task, even by
collating expert criticism, is straying outside his pro-
vince. A librarian has to do this, but not in his
capacity of bibliographer. Fortunately for the latter
he is concerned not with opinion but with fact; his
task is simply to show what has been written. In
accepting this limitation, he has no need for humility;
if he builds honestly, his work is founded on a rock
and will endure.

Students of librarianship, for whom this book is

written, are sometimes victims of the delusion that bibliography is confined to a knowledge of title-pages. If this book is not a sufficient refutation of that opinion, they may be referred to Dr. R. B. McKerrow's book, *An Introduction to Bibliography*, in which the relationship of the examination of the book to the study of literature is expounded. This work is of supreme importance to the student, and constant reference must be made to it. In 1948, a reviewer wrote in *The Times Literary Supplement* that "nothing is more salutary for any man who thinks he has discovered something or formed some theory or reached some conclusion in almost any department of bibliography than a reference to McKerrow, where (ten to one) he will find the essence of it set down with quiet but august precision". Such, indeed, is the standing of this remarkable book.

Another general delusion is that the aims of the librarian or student and of the book-collector are widely different, that the serious and practical interests of the former are to be contrasted with the frivolity of the latter. Now it cannot be denied that, in book-collecting, as in other pursuits, there are people who simply follow fashion; these buy the famous books that everyone else buys and about which everything is known. Books, contrary to a common notion, are very little bought for mere rarity; it is rarity combined with interest which gives them their market value. But the real collector is also a librarian and uses his books accordingly, just as the librarian is also a collector for his library. Both are

21

bibliographers and so arrange, study and describe their collections as to reveal new interest and importance. The best results are generally achieved by selecting some special field of which little is known. Such collections as the Baron James de Rothschild's of early French literature, the Prince d'Essling's of early illustrated Venetian books, John Scott's of Mary Queen of Scots, James Young's of chemistry and alchemy, Sir William Osler's of medicine, Paul Hirsch's of music, or Mr. Michael Sadleir's of nineteenth-century fiction, by means of the catalogues published of their contents, are foundations of the study of those branches of knowledge. It is to be regretted that, in too many instances, the only monument of a great collection is the sale catalogue which records its dispersal.

BIBLIOGRAPHICAL METHOD

A certain amount of difficulty is often caused owing to a misunderstanding of the word "bibliography". The wide use of the word to mean simply a list of books has obscured the real issue. Dr. W. W. (now, Sir Walter) Greg in his chapter on "Bibliography— a retrospect", in *The Bibliographical Society, 1892– 1942*, defined the subject as follows.

To avoid ambiguity I would define "bibliography" to mean the study of books as material objects. The qualification is important. It is a sort of *filioque* clause directed against a particular heresy; one which is or has been widespread, is still popular, but is in my opinion none the less damnable. It seems obvious that I may study the Book of Genesis, or the *Odyssey*, or *The Laws of Ecclesiastical Polity*, or *The Origin of Species*, or *The Bad Child's Book of Beasts,* and never come within a hundred miles of bibliography, because bibliography has nothing whatever to do with the subject or literary content of the book.

In another notable paper read before the Bibliographical Society in 1932 (*Transactions,* 4th series, Vol. xiii), Dr. Greg made the purpose of bibliography clear in two sentences. "At the root of all literary criticism lies the question of transmission, and it is bibliography that enables us to deal with the problem." "Books are the material means by which literature is transmitted; therefore bibliography, the study of books, is essentially the science of the transmission of literary documents." From this it follows that books must be studied in order that their part in the transmission process is understood and that, following such an investigation, their salient features may be recorded. Thus, bibliographical method falls into two reasonably distinct halves. The first is *analytical or critical,* the second *systematic.*

ANALYTICAL OR CRITICAL BIBLIOGRAPHY

In all sciences laboratory work on the specimen precedes classification. Before entries of books can be rationally assembled, we must be able to make those entries individually, in other words to describe books. When a volume comes into a bibliographer's hands, he asks himself, and has to answer, certain questions. *First:* What work, or works, does this volume contain? *Second:* What edition of that work is this? *Third:* Is this copy perfect? The briefest library catalogue entry must answer these questions, and the difference between it and the standard description in a full-dress historical bibliography is only one of degree of detail.

All this sounds easy enough; but it is often only by much experience and research that the authorship, order of edition, date, place of printing, and perfection of copy can be satisfactorily established, where the book does not bear these facts on its face. Their importance will emerge when we come, in a later chapter, to deal with the collation and description of books. Anyone setting out to take charge of or to describe a collection of pottery and porcelain, in order to describe the pieces exactly and lucidly, and to classify them in their countries, periods, and styles, must acquaint himself with the elements at least of many mysteries; the technique of clays, of painting and firing, of glazes and marks. And so with any other art—and so too with books. The technique of "book-building" must be understood in order to establish the facts required. Moreover, to establish them for a book and to record at the same time the details of its production in typography, decoration, and so forth, is to lay a secure foundation for placing and dating other books of the same class or period. Every book printed is a monument, great or small, of the civilization of its time and place; in the aggregate, therefore, a knowledge of the books of a generation is a large part of the knowledge of that generation's mind. It is perhaps a lesser merit, yet not a negligible one, that by assembling such historical book-descriptions we help to write the history of the arts of the book-writing, printing, illuminating, engraving and binding.

HISTORICAL BIBLIOGRAPHY

A further stage in the study of the book, commonly called historical bibliography, is beyond the scope of an elementary handbook. It has very close connections with critical bibliography, and some idea must be given of its great importance, of its development, and of the revolution it is working in literary history and in the editing of older authors. As Dr. Greg said, "strictly bibliographical investigation is three-fourths of textual criticism".

Just as the examination of the book may be called its anatomy, so the study of books as objects of art may be called their biology. The book is the genus; the country or town is the family of which all books produced there are members; the printing press is the species; the edition is the sub-species; the copy is the specimen of all this. As the book-arts evolve, we can follow them just as biologists follow the evolution of the species of living creatures.

You may dissect and you may describe [says Dr. Greg], but until your anatomy becomes comparative you will never arrive at the principle of evolution. You may name and classify the colours of your sweet peas and produce nothing but a florist's catalogue; it is only when you begin grouping them according to their genetic origin that you will arrive at Mendel's formula.

This fertilizing idea, commonly known as the

"natural history method" of bibliography, is a product of the same development of thought as culminated in Darwinism; it is, in fact, Darwinism applied by analogy to a human activity. It was first applied to the historical classification of books by Henry Bradshaw, Librarian of Cambridge University (1831–1886), following the lead which had been given by J. W. Holtrop. On May 10, 1866, Bradshaw wrote to Holtrop,

We cannot afford to lose our master yet; for I always look on you and speak of you as the chief of my department—the *département des incunables*—for, indeed, there is no one connected with any English library, still less in Paris, who has the leisure and inclination to study our subject scientifically.

Bradshaw's work was carried on in Cambridge by Francis Jenkinson (1853–1923), who, being a distinguished entomologist as well as a scholar, was prepared to appreciate the idea. But it was first worked out on a large scale by a younger bibliographer, Robert Proctor (1868–1903), who examined and arranged under their countries, towns, and presses, and in the last resort chronologically, all the incunabula, then numbering some eight thousand, in the British Museum. Of early printed books very many give no indication of either place, or printer, or date, and some of none of these. By working, as all science must, from the known to the unknown, that is to say, by classifying those books which bear these facts on them, and then comparing the types, the ornaments and the signs of printers' technical development, Proctor succeeded in attributing to their true printers nearly all the unassigned books in this great collection. Later and more detailed research, culminating in the still incomplete *Catalogue of Fifteenth Century Printed Books*, has failed to upset his conclusions very materially, though it has largely added to them. All this he achieved by a genius for detail and for fact, aided by a wonderful visual memory.

Though, as we know, analogy is not argument, Bradshaw's analogy has changed the face of historical bibliography. Its influence can be measured by a comparison between the admirable author-list of all incunabula then known, Hain's *Repertorium Bibliographicum* (1826–1838), already mentioned, and Proctor's *Index of Early Printed Books*, the fruit of his work at the Museum, or the *Catalogue of Fifteenth Century Printed Books*.

A very notable example of this method is the establishment of Caxton's claim to be the first printer in England. The first book from his Westminster press which bears a date is the *Dictes or sayengis of the philosophres* of 1477, though an indulgence of the previous year has now been identified in the Public Record Office. But there is a book, the *Expositio S. Hieronymi in Symbolum Apostolorum*, from the Oxford press of Theodoric Rood, bearing the date 1468; on its face this gives Oxford and Rood a long priority, and many bibliographers once accepted it. But the natural history method shows that, not only are there no books from Rood's press bearing dates between 1468 and 1479, but that his books of those two years represent exactly the same stage of typographical development. Now anyone who has worked on incunabula by the new method knows that no printer at so early a period remained for eleven years at the same level of accomplishment, since the art was then in the pioneer stage and rapidly advancing. The only possible explanation of the date 1468 (M.CCCC.lxviii. xvij die decembris) is that an *x* has dropped out of the colophon, and that the date is 1478—a misprint for which there are exact parallels.[1] This explanation is now universally accepted, and Caxton is acknowledged as our first printer, though at a painful sacrifice to scientific integrity on the part of patriotic Oxford bibliographers.

Later periods are not so full of "unassigned" books as the fifteenth century; but there are great numbers, nevertheless, of secretly printed books with false imprints, and other mysteries, which await the Proctors of the future.

The placing and dating of books is of value not only to the historian of civilization; it is specially valuable to the literary editor, in that it enables him to settle the order of editions, and to explain mysteries shrouding the transmission of the text. An author's books cannot be properly edited, nor can his life, so far as it is in his books, be properly written, without our first distinguishing, describing, arranging in their right order and making available in libraries, first the original editions of all his works, then all the later editions in which authentic altera-

[1] Notably Jenson's edition of the *Decor puellarum*, Venice, 1461 [1471], which once was thought to give Jenson priority in Italian printing.

made. First editions, which are
bibliophiles.

ideally in the same person. Comp

classics have been so edited, yet without this sort of
editing there is no security that we are reading what
the author wished us to read.

The best way in which it can be made clear that a
close examination of a book may prove of value in
determining the origin, date, and textual authority of
a particular edition is by showing how it did so in one
very notable instance.

Of the forty or more quarto editions of separate
plays by, or once attributed to, Shakespeare which
appeared before the publication of his collected plays
in one folio volume in 1623, there are nine, of which,
as A. W. Pollard noticed, several sets are known
bound or at least till recently bound together. In
some cases the bindings are very little later than the
date of issue and there is therefore some reason to
suppose that they were put on the market together.
But the plays are not all dated in the same year; three
are dated 1600, two 1608, three 1619, while one has
no date. They have marked typographical similarity
which differentiates them all from other Shakespeare
quartos, the chief of which is the absence from all of
them of a publisher's address, showing where the

A more recent example of the same kind of bibliographical investigation on books of a later period can be found in John Carter and Graham Pollard's two books, *An Enquiry into the Nature of certain Nineteenth Century Pamphlets* (1934) and *The Firm of Charles Ottley, Landon & Co.* (1948).

By methods which included minute examination of types and paper the authors proved a number of small books by nineteenth-century English writers which had appeared in the rare book market to have been printed many years later than the dates on their title-pages, and therefore to be forgeries. These two works should be studied carefully by any student who wishes to understand this aspect of the subject. The bibliographer, in the seclusion of libraries, is not the dusty and bloodless creature he is often thought to be, but a detective engaged in a thrilling kind of hunt. The method is now universal but not practised widely except in the United States of America; but we may take a legitimate pride in the fact that our countrymen were among its first masters.

SYSTEMATIC BIBLIOGRAPHY

The further stage, any necessary examination of the individual books being done, is to assemble the resulting entries, simple or elaborate as the case may require, into logical and useful arrangements for reference and study. The need for this kind of work has always been obvious, if books were to be findable, with the result that for long it monopolized the word "bibliography", much as one virtue monopolized the word Virtue.

Clearly the first need is of a general repertory, by which the student who knows of the existence of a book can locate a copy. The catalogues of the great national libraries cover some of the ground but this is not sufficient. Many notable attempts have been made in the past to provide bibliographies and catalogues on a large scale but many of them have been left incomplete or are moving with disheartening slowness. One of the most interesting developments in this sphere of recent years has been the Unesco-Library of Congress Bibliographical Survey. Although this was designed to stimulate national effort rather than to attempt the provision of a general repertory, it holds out a hope for the realization of some long-standing plans.

Out of the whole body of written and printed material it is the work of the bibliographer to collect and arrange the titles of books and writings which deal with his chosen subject. While a very great quantity of this work has been done, as may be seen from such books as Henri Stein's, W. P. Courtney's and Theodore Besterman's lists of bibliographies, there remains much more to do. Every student may hope to add to the store a bibliography of permanent value on any subject which he will make his own. If he be engaged in a library, let him not be afraid to have a special subject. If the nature of the library point out his subject to him, so much the better, but special knowledge of any

B   33

reasonable subject is sure to come in useful some time.

In the absence of exhaustive repertories the bibliographer must be acquainted with many scattered sources. Let us take two very simple cases. Is he making a bibliography of English verse of the seventeenth century? He may expect to use the *Cambridge Bibliography of English Literature*; Pollard and Redgrave's *Short-title Catalogue*; Wing's *Short-title Catalogue*; the British Museum's catalogue of the Thomason Civil War and Commonwealth Tracts; the two series of transcripts of the *Stationers' Register*, Arber's for 1557–1640, and Eyre's for 1641–1709; the *Term Catalogues* for 1668–1709; and for each poet listed, the heading under his name in the printed catalogues of the great libraries. He will then go on to fill up the gaps from sale catalogues and from every kind of special source. The bibliographer of a modern subject will have to make an extensive search through the bibliographies of modern books, through publishers' lists and library catalogues, through journals which publish reviews on the subject, through abstracting journals, and through an enormous quantity of periodicals to the problem of which much bibliographical energy is now being applied.

CLASSIFICATION AND ARRANGEMENT

The natural arrangement for the great primary repertories is by the alphabetical order of authors' names or by chronology. But this is almost useless in a special bibliography, where the material must be arranged in such a way as to make the entries illuminate each other by collocation. Every subject has a guiding principle and it is the business of the bibliographer at the outset to discover that principle and to make it the key to his arrangement, using the alphabet secondarily, in his index, for quick reference. General schemes for the classification of knowledge, and as a corollary, of books, both on library shelves and in catalogues, have been devised in plenty. Of modern schemes, one of the first important stages was reached in 1876 when Melvil Dewey, then Librarian of Amherst College, Massachusetts, developed the idea that by the use of decimals the component classes of a scheme could be indefinitely sub-divided and any new subjects which might spring up could be intercalated into their logical places without disturbance to the rest. The brilliant simplicity of this idea is limited in its application by the fact that new or minor subjects may prove major and that new knowledge may upset the relationships of various subjects. It was early seen that Dewey's scheme was inadequate for international use, and the Brussels Institute obtained the inventor's permission to expand and develop it. The resulting scheme is held by many to be far superior both to the original Dewey scheme and to the successive enlargements and modifications of the original which have been produced.

The present century has seen an important proliferation of classification schemes many of which have had important practical advantages and have added to the growth of the theory of this subject. The classification of the Library of Congress at Washington has been frequently hailed as the only really adequate one for use in considerable libraries. The work of Henry Evelyn Bliss is regarded by very many competent critics to be the outstanding scheme of modern times, while the brilliant theorizing of Dr. Ranganathan has added immeasurably to our understanding of the problems of classification.

But however excellent any of these general schemes of classification may be, the bibliographer of a special subject will always find them inadequate. Subjects which, for his purposes, are closely allied will frequently be widely sundered. He must always expect to plan the arrangement of his material for himself and not be able to inherit a ready-made answer from any of the classifiers.

At the risk of seeming too serious I will add seven commandments to bibliographers:

1. Be proud, and think highly of your calling.
2. Be humble, and do not despise details.
3. Be accurate, in small things as in great.
4. Be brief.
5. Be clear.
6. Take nothing on trust, except in necessity, and even then not without saying so. There have been many bad bibliographers and it is human to err.
7. Never guess. You are sure to be found out, and then you will be written down as one of the

bad bibliographers, than which there is no more terrible fate.

It would be easy to write a discourse on each of these heads, enriched with many notable warnings and examples; but their truth will be borne in on the student by experience. They come in the mass to no more than an amplification of our old friend the copy-book motto, that honesty is the best policy. And indeed the real bibliographer, like the real scholar in whatever field, must be intellectually honest, for his task is to seek truth and ensue it.

READING LIST

LIST A

> CHAMBERS' ENCYCLOPEDIA. Articles on "Bibliography" and "Book Collecting".
>
> ENCYCLOPEDIA BRITANNICA. Articles on "Bibliography" and "Book-collecting".
>
> GREG, W. W. Bibliography—a retrospect, in The Bibliographical Society, "The Bibliographical Society, 1892–1942". 1945.

LIST B

> BESTERMAN, Theodore. The beginnings of systematic bibliography. 1935.
>
> CARTER, John. ABC for book-collectors. 1952.
>
> CARTER, John. Taste and technique in book collecting. 1948.
>
> CHAPMAN, R. W. *and others*. Four talks on book collecting. 1950.
>
> McKERROW, R. B. An introduction to bibliography for literary students. 1928.

A STUDENT'S MANUAL OF BIBLIOGRAPHY

MUIR, P. H. Talks on book collecting. 1952.
SCHNEIDER, Georg. History and theory of bibliography. *Translated by* R. R. Shaw. 1934.
VAN HOESEN, H. B. *and* Walter, F. K. Bibliography: practical, enumerative, historical. 1928.

Students should also read: *The Library: the transactions of the Bibliographical Society*, which is published quarterly.

II

PAPYRUS, PARCHMENT, VELLUM, PAPER

The first writing material was stone, the first writing an inscription, and the first pen a chisel. When it became necessary to record minor transactions and to set down ceremonials, rituals, dedications, etc., in something lighter and more portable than stone blocks, the Sumerians incised clay tablets and hardened them by baking. Then skins were used, the use of them for writing purposes being known in Egypt as early as 1500 B.C. and possibly even earlier. But these took second place to the celebrated material papyrus (βύβλος), from which come our words paper and Bible.

PAPYRUS

Papyrus is manufactured from the stem of a river plant that grew freely, and still grows sparsely, in the Nile. Strips were cut and laid side by side; a second layer of strips was laid transversely over the first and the sheet beaten, pressed and polished. There is still some doubt as to whether these layers were pasted or not but the latest opinion suggests that they were not. It was written on in ink with a reed quill, and is the material of practically all the books of antiquity. As we see it today, it is a frail-looking brown substance which can only be handled between sheets of glass,

39

but no doubt when new it was strong, white and pleasant to the eye. When necessary, one sheet would be pasted to another to form a continuous roll, sufficient for the length of the book or the section of the book; for example, an ancient copy of Homer's *Iliad* would have been not in one roll but in twenty-four. References suggest that wooden rollers were frequently attached to the ends of the rolls and ornamented with projecting knobs (*cornua*, or *umbilici*). To these could be attached tickets bearing the titles. The whole was kept rolled up on the handles and in pigeon-holes. From the Latin word for a roll, *volumen*, comes our word volume. The writing was in columns, usually on one side only, the side on which the strips ran horizontally. If text was written on both sides, then the roll is known as an *opisthograph*. The columns of text crossed the roll, whereas in the skin rolls, used during the later Middle Ages for accounts and chronicles, the writing was in a single immense column down the whole length of the roll. It was impossible to refer quickly to any passage in a *volumen*. It is therefore natural that the earliest books to be found in codex form (the modern form of book) are exactly those books to which rapid reference was most required—the law digests (called *par excellence* the Codices) and the Bible. The word codex means block of wood, probably from the wooden covers.

The codex form of manuscript is associated chiefly with vellum, and the changes in form and material proceed side by side. There are, however, examples of papyrus codices; the most notable of them being

40

the eleven Chester Beatty Biblical papyri whose dates are estimated to range from the second to the fourth or fifth centuries A.D.

Papyrus was used in Egypt from the third millenium at the latest and there is a considerable body of papyrus rolls extant which date from about 2000 B.C. onwards. It continued in use as late as the eleventh century but in diminishing quantity, perhaps because of some failure in the supply of the plant. In any case, it was driven out by parchment and vellum. The other vegetable materials which served similar purposes, such as the Oriental palm-leaf and the birch-bark of the American Indian, do not affect the history of the book as known in Europe, but it is worth remarking that the Latin *liber* originally meant the inner bark of trees.

PARCHMENT AND VELLUM

Both these terms are used for the prepared skins of animals and are frequently so loosely used as to be almost interchangeable. Strictly speaking, parchment is made from the skins of sheep or goats while vellum is made from calf-skin. Parchment was known, and probably used, as early as 1500 B.C. but was not used extensively until the beginning of the Christian era. There is a tradition that Eumenes II, King of Pergamum in Asia Minor (197–159 B.C.), incurred the displeasure of the King of Egypt, who thereupon forebade the export of papyrus. The people of Pergamum then reverted to the use of skins as writing material and, perfecting the methods of treatment, produced a more durable substance than papyrus, although heavier and more expensive. Pergamum, from which parchment took its name, was probably the centre of the trade and by the end of the third or beginning of the fourth century it had become the leading material in Europe. Vellum, taking its name from the animal whose skin was employed, had a much finer and whiter surface than parchment and was used for some of the choicest examples of manuscript decorative art. The finest of all vellums, known as "uterine" vellum, is believed to have been the skin of the unborn or stillborn calf.

Parchment and vellum were made up into books in the codex form by cutting the prepared skins into rectangular pieces that, when folded, made two leaves of the size required. Paper, on the other hand, is brought by successive foldings to the smaller book sizes. The parchment or vellum sheets were so arranged that the pages of each opening were of the same texture, both being either the fine "flesh" side or the "hair" side which was spotted with the roots of the hair. This fact is often of use in determining obscure questions as to the make-up of particular manuscript volumes.

Paper

Paper is of a great antiquity. There is no reason to doubt the tradition that it was invented in China; and Sir Aurel Stein discovered in Chinese Turkestan pieces which can be dated to the second century of our era. The Arabs brought it into the Near East about the eighth century, and to them is believed to be due the use of cotton. With the Moslem power and civilization, then much greater than the Christian, the use of paper moved west and crossed the Mediterranean into Spain. The earliest example in Europe is a document in the Escorial dated 1009; there is one of exactly a century later at Palermo. According to M. Charles Briquet, the watermark appears first in Western papers of the thirteenth century. Oriental papers did not bear marks until two or three centuries later. The latter have always been of a thicker, creamier, and more vellum-like make than ours. The spread of paper was very slow. It appears with increasing frequency in archives, but was not really made in quantity till the manufacture was stimulated by the invention of printing. It is significant that of the very earliest books many copies survive printed on vellum, but of books of half a century later very few indeed, while in England its use in printing was rare from the first.

The first paper mill in this country was set up with royal aid by John Tate the Younger in Hertfordshire in 1495, and paper made by him was used in that year by Wynkyn de Worde, who calls attention to it in the often-quoted *prohemium* to his English edition of Bartholomæus (Glanville) Anglicus *On the Properties of Things*. Tate's enterprise seems to have been short-lived. The study of the history of paper-making is still in an embryonic state and much investigation is yet to be done.

MATERIALS OF PAPER

To the downward succession of the Ages of Gold, Silver, and Iron must now be added the Age of Paper, in which we live. Paper has become the most ubiquitous and obtrusive of all the stuffs of daily life. The huge use of it, and the diminishing resources of material, make it important that we should know enough of it to use it appropriately, consuming temporary paper on temporary uses and thus economizing permanent paper for permanent preservation of books and written matter of value in our libraries and archives.

Paper is vegetable fibre disintegrated and reintegrated in water; this distinguishes it from vellum and parchment, which are animal skins, and from papyrus, which is vegetable leaf not disintegrated but simply dressed by drying, rolling, and polishing. In practice printing papers are made of four main groups of material:

    (*a*) rag; linen and cotton, generally mixed;
    (*b*) chemical wood, in which the cellulose fibres are released by chemical action;
    (*c*) esparto grass and straw;
    (*d*) mechanical wood, in which the wood is disintegrated by passing it between coarse grinders.

The final quality of the paper will depend upon a number of combined characteristics of the basic materials, but no individual feature is more important than the fibres themselves. The fibres must be long, tough, flexible and easy to separate from the raw bulk of which they should form a high percentage. The durability of the paper is in inverse ratio to the amount of chemical action needed to separate the fibres from the inter-cellular matter of the plant. In addition to this, it has to be remembered that the strength and longevity of the fibres will vary considerably according to the plant of their origin and the care with which they are treated during manufacture.

Since cotton is an extremely pure form of cellulose and since flax is one of the strongest and hardest of fibres, it follows that rag paper, which is usually a mixture of these two fibres, stands as the most durable of papers. They were the only materials used in earlier centuries and since such papers are found today in perfect condition, white and strong, it is only of them that we can state from experience that they reach what may be called absolute permanence. Certain newspapers, including *The Times*, print a special issue on an all-rag or part-rag paper so that it may be preserved without difficulty. The best of the non-rag papers is chemical wood, which, if carefully manufactured, makes a paper standing the tests well. Papers manufactured from esparto grass, which is imported from North Africa and Southern Spain, have, when well made, only little less lasting power than chemical wood. Esparto grass is a fine and tough fibre but, when specially beaten, can bulk out considerably and was largely used in the manufacture of "featherweight" papers. It is also preferred for

45

the body of art-paper. Mechanical wood, which is ground up instead of being chemically disintegrated, has no length of fibre and makes a paper which soon turns brown and brittle under light since it retains all the intercellular matter which is removed in the other processes.

There are one or two special materials and papers which are worthy of note:

1. *Japanese vellum.*—This is a fine strong paper, made of Japanese shrubs, notably the Broussonetia; it has a creamy tint and smooth surface like vellum, and is much used for engravings. The surface is delicate and will not, for instance, survive the use of india-rubber.

    An imitation is made by treating thick ordinary paper with sulphuric acid so as to melt and coagulate the surface into a resemblance of that of Japanese vellum. It has no merits.

2. *China paper*, very thin and silky, used for proofs of woodcuts.

3. *Ramie*, one of the finest materials, normally only used for textiles and bank-notes. A certain amount of textile waste is used for paper.

4. *India paper*, very thin and strong, thoroughly made of rags and rendered opaque by judicious loading.[1] A small consignment was

---

[1] Heavy loading is to be deprecated. It gives a smooth surface and opacity, but at the cost of interference with the felting of the fibres, which is the essential strength of any paper.

brought from the East (in old parlance all further Asia was "the Indies") in 1842 and used by the Clarendon Press; in 1875 this was successfully imitated at the Wolvercote Mills, and is now familiar. Very popular for private use, and especially for pocket editions, being only one-third as thick as ordinary paper.

MANUFACTURE

Bad workmanship is given only to bad material; the best material gets the most expensive and careful treatment. In all the processes of paper-making the chief expense is time and the chief essential patience; the processes must be gradual and natural if the finished product is to be of high quality.

Whatever may be the basic raw materials of a paper, the first step is always the treatment, either by chemical or mechanical means, to change that material into its constituent fibres. The first processes to which rag material is subjected are the cutting, sorting and dusting. The strips are then thrown into a large vessel, in which they are boiled in water containing caustic soda or other alkaline solutions. The action of this is to loosen or dissolve any non-cellular matter, leaving behind the fibrous material. It will also partially remove dyes, depending upon their colour and fixity. Esparto grass and straw, after dusting and cleaning, are boiled under pressure with caustic soda. In the case of mechanical wood, the logs are brought into contact with a revolving

47

grindstone and the pulp so created is washed away by a stream of water. For the chemical wood pulps, the wood, after having been sliced into chips, is boiled in a digester with chemicals. The bisulphite process of chemical wood pulp manufacture will use sulphur dioxide with bisulphite of calcium or alternatively a mixture of calcium bisulphite and magnesium bisulphite. The alkaline process, which originally used caustic soda, now frequently uses sodium sulphate.

The pulps which result from these various processes next pass into yet other receptacles called *breakers*. The object of this part of the operation is to separate the fibres from each other in the pulp and the extent of the treatment will vary greatly from one material to another. The result is the creation of the *half-stuff*, as the pulp is called at this stage, which now passes into the *beaters*. Here mixtures will be made of various pulps, size will be added in the case of engine-sized papers, and filling materials will be added for loaded papers. This stage is also used for bleaching. Bleach is mixed with the stock, which is subsequently passed into further receptacles in which it is washed to rid it of the residuary bleach, a fertile source of deterioration if allowed to remain. Most important of all, however, is the fact that the paper will vary greatly depending on its treatment in the beater. The pulp will be passed between a beater roll, which is a drum fitted with protruding metal bars, and the bottom or "bed plate" of the beater. If the bars are blunt the fibres will be torn apart but, if sharp "tackle" is substituted for blunt, the fibres will be chopped short and a paper of featherweight or blotting-paper quality will result.

At this point machine- and hand-making diverge; hitherto they have only differed in the greater care and patience lavished on paper to be made by hand. The pulp, with the addition of any necessary colouring matter, is further mixed with water for machine-made paper, since it has to be poured into the mould. For hand-making a thicker consistency is kept.

In hand-making the mould is a shallow sieve, set in a large oblong wooden framework. Over the top of this frame fits another, called the deckle, rather like an empty picture-frame, the object of which is to restrict the area of the mould over which the pulp can flow. The edge of hand-made paper, known as the "deckle-edge", is the rough and wavy edge which uncut books have, and is due to some of the liquid pulp's seeping under the deckle frame. Although it may be considered that too much stress is laid by some kinds of book collectors upon having the complete deckle edge of a book untouched, and its artificial production in a machine-made paper is an absurd falsification, yet the presence of the deckle is evidence that the binder has not cut down the book's original margins. A careful distinction must be kept between a book which is "uncut" and one which is not "opened". There is a point in preserving it in the former state, but none in preserving it in the latter, in which it cannot be read.

The vat-man takes the mould, dips it into the vat

and lifts it up covered with a layer of semi-liquid pulp. He shakes the mould, as the water begins to drain through the mesh, and so causes the fibres to cross and interlace. It is a very delicate and subtle craft which nothing but the human hand can accomplish, and it is upon this that the strength of the paper chiefly depends.

The mould is of two types:

(1) The "laid" mould, making "laid" paper, which consists of a close mesh of fine wires, running lengthwise and crossed at intervals of about three-quarters of an inch by stouter wires. Till the nineteenth century nearly all paper was "laid".

(2) The "wove" mould is a very fine mesh, closely woven.

Paper made on a laid mould shows the lines of the wires whiter and more transparent than the rest when held up to the light. These markings in the paper are known as "laid marks"; the thicker ones, caused by the cross wires, are "chain-lines"; the thinner ones, caused by the lengthwise wires, are "wire-lines". The wove papers show similarly a faint network which gives a rather mottled appearance to the paper. This is because the soft wet pulp is thinner where it has rested on the wire or metal; the marks are not the structure of the fibre, which is to be seen in cloudy masses when a piece of paper is held up to the light.

There may also be seen a pattern or device in transparent lines. This is the "watermark", which is made by twisting or soldering wire into the mould.

It is of the greatest importance in collation, as will be explained in its place.

The water in the pulp, as it lies on the mould, drains away. When the sheet is turned out it is in a more or less solid form. It is gently pressed between sheets of felt and is then hung in a loft to dry. When dried, it is still what is called "water-leaf", i.e. it readily absorbs water. The next process is to give it a non-absorbent surface, on which printer's or writing ink will not run. For this it has to be "sized". Any unsized paper will act as blotting paper.

Size is animal gelatine, into which the leaf is now dipped, being said to be "tub-sized". If tub-sized papers lose their size by the action of damp or of bacilli, they can be dipped again and re-sized. Inferior paper is "engine-sized" in the beater with rosin and various acids, which have an injurious effect. The paper is then air-dried, smoothed, and pressed, and is given a glazing, which if moderate may actually add to its strength by compressing the fibres, but if excessive bruises and breaks them.

Paper-making by machinery is a lower level of the craft, but one which is nevertheless capable of producing a durable material. The machine process was invented just before 1800 by Nicolas-Louis Robert, an employé in the French publishing house of Didot, but first practised in England. The principle is that of an endless wire mesh on to which the pulp flows. As this mould passes along and the water falls through the mesh, the belt is shaken from side to side in an attempt to simulate the shake of the hand paper-maker. This is successful only up to a point, since it can shake from side to side but not backwards and forwards, while the vat-man can shake in both directions. The strength of hand-made paper is thus in two directions; that of machine-made paper in one only. To test whether paper is hand-made, tear off a piece and drop it into water. A hand-made paper will turn up, i.e. contract, in all directions. Machine-made paper will turn up two edges only, because its matting runs chiefly one way. A machine mould-made paper, on the other hand, can be produced with little difference between the strength of the two dimensions.

More water will be removed from the pulp by suction-boxes over which the mesh will pass and will also be squeezed out under rollers. In what always seems to be a surprisingly short time, the paper will be strong enough, although still very damp, to be transferred from the wire-mesh to pass between felting and surfacing rollers. A variety of surfaces can be achieved in papers according to the number and type of cylinders between which the paper passes. At length it will be wound on to reels and the manufacturing process can be regarded as virtually completed.

The watermark in machine-made paper is not made by the mould, but by a special roller called the "dandy", which revolves over the mould and impresses at every revolution upon the moving pulp the device which is in relief upon it. The watermark is of small value in collating books printed on machine-made paper.

It does not matter which way a hand-made sheet is folded in book-making, the folds will have equal strength. But machine-made paper must not be folded along the flow (i.e. the direction in which the pulp moves on the mould) or the fold will not cross the fibres, and will lack strength and in time will probably split. The direction in which the paper is cut, however, is perfectly arbitrary, since the sheet is endless and is not originally a limited oblong, as in hand-making, but is subsequently cut to the required size and shape. Paper-makers can be persuaded to cut the paper so that the folds cross the fibres.

Papers are regularly tested, microscopically for their composition, chemically for their resistance to light and heat, and mechanically by folding and pulling. But these are matters for professional experts; the ordinary person can soon learn to recognize a good, solid paper by sight and also by its sound when tapped with the finger.

The common sizes, in inches, of English book papers, in open sheet and folded in octavo, are:

	Broadside	8vo
Large Foolscap .	$17 \times 13\frac{1}{2}$	$6\frac{3}{4} \times 4\frac{1}{4}$
Crown . . .	20×15	$7\frac{1}{2} \times 5$
Large Post .	$21 \times 16\frac{1}{2}$	$8\frac{1}{4} \times 5\frac{1}{4}$
Demy . . .	$22\frac{1}{2} \times 17\frac{1}{2}$	$8\frac{3}{4} \times 5\frac{5}{8}$
Medium . .	23×18	$9 \times 5\frac{3}{4}$
Royal . . .	25×20	$10 \times 6\frac{1}{4}$
Large Royal .	27×20	$10 \times 6\frac{3}{4}$
Imperial . .	30×22	$11 \times 7\frac{1}{2}$

THE DURABILITY OF PAPER

In the early years of the nineteenth century the problem of the durability of paper began to be of some
concern. Papers made before 1800 were found to be
still in good condition, while many of those made in
the nineteenth century were showing signs of decay.
In 1829, John Murray expanded some notes which
he had contributed to the *Gentleman's Magazine* of
1823, and published them as *Practical Remarks on
Modern Paper*. He believed that the main causes of
decay were:

(*a*) damage to the fibres on the machine,
(*b*) mineral loading,
(*c*) alum, used in the sizing, which reacted with
any excess chloride of lime, used in the
bleaching, to form muriatic acid, and
(*d*) excessive bleaching which damaged the fibres.

The position was further complicated during the
period 1840–1860 by the introduction of new raw
materials, such as mechanical wood, chemical-wood
and esparto grass.

In 1898, a Special Committee of the Royal Society
of Arts issued a report entitled *The Deterioration of
Paper*. In it, they arranged paper fibres into four
main classes which, in order of permanence, were:

Class A. Cotton, flax, hemp.
Class B. Wood celluloses.
Class C. Esparto grass and straw celluloses.
Class D. Mechanical wood pulp.

Other important investigations were made and reports published in the early years of this present century, but the next significant one in this country was the report issued by a Committee of the Library Association in 1930 entitled *The Durability of Paper*. The Committee approved the classification of fibres in the Royal Society of Arts Report and agreed with their order of permanence. On two papers, both in common use at the time, the Committee made special comment.

(*a*) Featherweight paper. This is frequently of esparto, is loose and puffy in texture, and very light for its bulk; it is produced by chopping up the fibre and leaving it half felted and full of air, sometimes up to 75 per cent. as against some 25 per cent. in a sound paper. Its disadvantages are: (1) it lacks flexibility; (2) it is easily cut by binding thread, which involves guarding in rebinding; (3) it flakes, both when the leaves are cut open and on the press, when it may clog the type; (4) it occupies needless shelf-room. Its advantages (to the publisher) are: (1) air is cheaper than fibre; (2) it makes a book double its natural thickness and enables the publisher to charge double its natural price. Fortunately, it it less common than it was, but it has not disappeared entirely.

(*b*) "Art" paper. This is a paper, often of poor enough quality, coated (not loaded) by brushing on China clay, sulphate of barium, or sulphate of lime and alumina, the last-named for "satin-white" finish, and then polishing. The surface thus produced

reproduces sharply the excessively shallow relief of
the half-tone process, especially in fine screens. But a
material largely made of clay is obviously in danger
of coagulation if exposed to damp, while folding
cracks the coated surface; and the shiny surface is
very dazzling to the eye and should in any case not
be used for letterpress. The adhesive used to fix the
coating is to be chosen carefully; casein is insoluble
and is better than starch, and much better than
gelatine, which may set up decay. It is a paper which
is frequently used for half-tone plates. The Committee pointed out that equally good results could be
obtained by the use of well-etched half-tone blocks,
moderate pressure and good inking, and printing
on a smooth but not shiny paper.

Imitation Art paper is heavily loaded, not coated.

Finally, the Committee laid down specifications
for two main grades of durable paper.

> Grade 1, when "absolute" permanence was re-
> quired,
> Grade 2, when relative permanence was required
> and where a commercially competitive price
> was of importance.

The actual specifications of the recommended papers
were as follows:

> *Grade 1 (a).* All rag. Hand-made. Tub-sized.
> Only white, cream, or unbleached rags of best
> quality to be used. No mineral matter to be
> added in loading. Alum and iron salts to be

56

present in smallest possible quantity. Pulp to be well washed to free it from any bleaching residue.

Grade 1 (b). To be, in all respects, as in Grade 1 (a), but to be machine-made, and either tub- or engine-sized, or both tub- and engine-sized.

Grade 2. Properly prepared all-chemical-wood. Machine-made. Engine-sized. Pulp to be well washed to free it from bleaching residues. Ash content to be no more than 5 per cent. Alum and iron salts in smallest possible proportions. Rosin content not more than 1·5 to 2 per cent. Mineral matter not more than 5 to 6 per cent.

Although considerable research into paper has been conducted during the years since the Library Association's Report, nothing has transpired to invalidate its general findings. Such changes as might need to be made now would be mainly of emphasis rather than of fundamental principle. As far as the librarian is involved, it has to be remembered that he is concerned almost entirely with the way in which storage conditions affect the deterioration of papers. Although some knowledge of the materials and methods of manufacture of paper will be essential to him, his problem will be that of devising methods of eliminating the dangers of fire, damp and the impurities of the atmosphere.

READING LIST

LIST *A*

CHAMBERS' ENCYCLOPEDIA. Articles on "Paper", "Papyrus", "Parchment".

ENCYCLOPEDIA BRITANNICA. Articles on "Paper", "Paper manufacture", "Paper materials", "Papyrus", "Parchment".

LIBRARY ASSOCIATION. The durability of paper; report of the special committee set up by the Library Association. 1930.

LIST B.

BOWATER PAPERS. Issued irregularly by Bowater Corporation from 1950.

BRIQUET, C. M. Les filigranes, dictionnaire historique des marques du papier. 2nd ed. 4v. 1923.

BRITISH PAPER AND BOARD MAKERS' ASSOCIATION (INCORPORATED). Paper making: a general account of its history, processes and applications. 1949.

CHURCHILL, W. A. Watermarks in paper in Holland, England, France, etc., in the XVII and XVIII centuries and their intercommunications. 1935.

CLAPPERTON, R. H. Modern paper-making. 3rd ed. 1952.

HUNTER, Dard. Paper making; the history and technique of an ancient craft. 2nd ed. 1947.

KENYON, *Sir* F. G. Books and readers in ancient Greece and Rome. 2nd ed. 1951.

LABARRE, E. J. Dictionary and encyclopedia of paper and paper-making, with equivalents of the technical terms in French, German, Dutch, Italian, Spanish and Swedish. 2nd ed. 1952.

NORRIS, F. H. Paper and paper making. 1952.

PAPYRUS, PARCHMENT, VELLUM, PAPER

PAPER PUBLICATIONS SOCIETY. Monumenta chartæ
papyraceæ historiam illustrantia, or, collection of
works and documents illustrating the history of
paper. 1950—
Vol. 1. Watermarks *by* E. Heawood.
Vol. 2. The Briquet album.
Vol. 3. Zonghi's watermarks.

III

PRINTING AND BOOK-BUILDING

The process of book production or, as A. W. Pollard called it, "book-building", has been many times described, and in its elements is quite easy of comprehension. It must now be outlined because the bibliographer, in examining books, will constantly be faced with problems which can only be solved by reconstructing in the mind exactly what happened in the printer's office. As R. B. McKerrow said:

The numerous processes through which all books pass are perfectly simple, and very little trouble will suffice for the understanding of them. What is needed is that they shall be grasped so clearly as to be constantly present to the mind of the student as he handles a book, so that he sees this not only from the point of view of the reader interested in it as literature, but also from the points of view of those who composed, corrected, printed, folded, and bound it.

The first three of these processes are included in the generic term printing.

TYPE

When we speak of printing we generally mean book-printing, but if so we are using the term loosely. "Printing" covers the very ancient art of taking impressions from blocks of wood or metal on paper or on textiles; taking impressions from a block built of

60

movable letter-units or "types" is the invention of
Gutenberg (or perhaps another) in Western Europe
in the mid-fifteenth century, and is called "typography". The complete collection of "sorts" (a, b,
etc., being each a "sort") of any one design makes

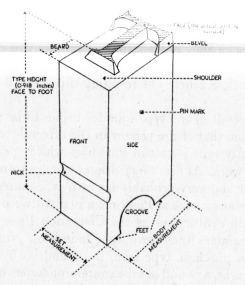

FIG. 1.—A TYPE.

up that "fount" (pronounced and sometimes spelt
"font"). The original artist's design for each is transferred to a tool or "punch" of hard metal on which it
is cut in relief. The punches are practically eternal,
and a fount of which the punches survive can always
be revived, as occurred when Whittingham and
Pickering had recourse, about 1840, to the old firm of

61

Caslon for their round founts of the early eighteenth century.

The punch is stamped with force into a block of soft metal, frequently copper, which thus becomes the "matrix", in which the face of the type is cast. The stem or shank of the type is cast in the mould which is placed in position over the matrix before the molten type-metal is poured in. The type-metal, which is an alloy of lead, tin and antimony, is cast in the form of the letter or other symbol and reproduces the punch in relief. The resulting slip of metal is the type.

The craft of the type-founder began to be separated from that of the printer in the fifteenth century and today type is cast in foundries which specialize in this work. At first every printer was his own type-founder and very probably his own type-cutter also. Great houses, such as Plantin's was at Antwerp in the sixteenth century, or as the Clarendon Press is to-day, maintain their own type-foundries. Normally printers purchase type from the foundries by fount and weight, a pound of type containing letters of each sort in a recognized proportion for any language.

The diagram above shows the shape and the names of the parts of a piece of type. Type is of a standard height, from foot to face, of 0·918 of an English inch, so that the faces, which stand up in relief and take the ink that is rolled over them, make an even surface and give a consistent impression on the paper.

Of the three great divisions of type-faces, gothic, roman, and italic, regarding which and their minor varieties more will be said later, the compositor will have two, roman and italic, at his hand. All founts are made in a variety of sizes. These used to be known by a number of picturesque traditional names, differing in different countries, and in any case not easy for any but a printer to keep in the memory. Moreover, as C. J. Jacobi, a printer of great experience, tells us, the old system "resulted in chaos, for as a rule no two founts of the same body made by different founders could be used together". In the last half-century or more, they have been largely superseded in this country by the point-system, which is of American origin. By this method, types are known by the number of "points" which they measure from back to front of a piece of type; this measurement is called the "body". A point is 0·013837 or approximately $\frac{1}{72}$ of an inch. It must be remembered that the type is not measured by its type-face but by its body. Thus, when it is now common for faces to be cast on larger bodies to save leading, an expression such as "an 11-point type on a 12-point body" is used. The American point-system, which was introduced in about 1870, was based on a similar system devised by Fournier le jeune in 1737 and improved shortly afterwards by François Didot. It is this Fournier-Didot point which is still largely used on the Continent. No exact equations can be drawn up between the present point sizes and the old English names of "Pearl", "Brevier", "Pica", "English", etc.

The "set" of a type is its width and is also measured in points, and certain founts are spoken of as having a "wide set" or a "narrow set", meaning that the letters are inclined to be wide or narrow in relation to their size. This is a matter of some importance when a type design is being chosen for any work, affecting, as it does, the amount of paper which will be necessary. Type is measured laterally and the extent of a piece of composition is reckoned in *ens*. An *en* is half the measurement of an *em* which is the square of the body-height of the type and therefore variable. Thus in a 10-point type, an em equals 10-point, or in an 18-point type an em equals 18-point. In modern printing parlance an em is frequently regarded as 12 point, since this is the type size in the most general use. Opinions vary as to whether the word "em" had any connection with the letter *m*. The early types, however, were cast solid (that is, the face-height equalled the body-height), as can be tested by laying a rule along the tops of the ascenders of a line of print and noting if the descenders of the line above touch it. Otherwise the type may be either leaded or cast on a large body and either is comparatively rare in the early period of printing. When the letter *m* is cast solid, then the piece of type would be practically square and the letter *n* would be about half the width of the letter *m*. Remembering this, it is difficult to believe that the words "em" and "en" originally meant anything but the letters.

COMPOSITION BY HAND

We will assume that the publisher and printer have

64

settled the "lay-out" of a new book, i.e. the type or types to be used, the number of lines to a page, whether leaded or solid, the length of the lines, and so forth, and that the author's copy has been handed to the compositor (or, as he is familiarly called in the trade, the "comp") to "set up" or "compose".

The compositor stands before his case with the copy in view. The case is a sloping cabinet of shallow pigeon-holes, each of which contains all the types of a single sort. The sorts are not arranged alphabetically but in order of frequency of use, as on the typewriter, and the quantity of each sort in any fount varies, of course, for the same reason. The case is also divided horizontally, the upper part being devoted to the majuscules, hence called technically "upper-case letters", and the lower to the minuscules, called "lower-case".[1] In very many later instances a pair of cases were used, set one above the other at slightly different angles.

In the compositor's left hand is his curiously-named "stick", a small shallow tray, capable of holding as many lines of type as are not uncomfortably heavy. The modern stick is provided with an adjustable end, which is screwed before work begins to the required length of line. In this the compositor places the types as he picks them out of the case, using (as the typist and pianist do) not his eye but the habit of his hand to find the pigeon-hole holding the right

---

[1] The term "Capitals" is strictly kept for the large decorative letters at the beginning of chapters ("Capita"); but printers speak of "caps" and "small caps".

sort. In order to produce the proper impression the type has to be set upside down and backwards, and printers acquire a peculiar facility in reading type in this position. In this setting the compositor is helped by the nicks on the front of the piece of type which will be uppermost when the type is correctly set in the stick.

After each word a space (or sort consisting of body and no face, which will therefore not reach the paper or make an impression) is inserted, and when the end of the line is reached these spaces (which are made in different breadths) are graduated so as, if possible, to end the line with the end of a word. This process is called "justification". In the earliest days of printing the line ends were often left uneven; this is one of the tests by which the frequent undated books of the early printers can be at least approximately dated, since having acquired the trick of justification they may naturally be assumed not to have relapsed. It is sometimes found in modern private presses, where it is a pure affectation.

The spacing is one of the tests of really good printing. The gaps between words should not be wide (as so often in cheap magazine work), nor should they be found one above another so as to give an effect of a crack (a "river") down the page. Too closely compressed, the type-page looks handsome but is not so legible. The machine processes of composition cannot quite equal the finest hand-setting in this, though in the hands of a good workman (who incidentally is best trained in hand-setting) they get

66

very near it. Ends of paragraphs are filled up by long spaces, called "quads". These often in proof—and alas, occasionally in the finished book—have jumped up and printed a solid black square. If it has been decided that the type is to be "leaded", the compositor places along the foot of his line (actually above it in the stick) a strip of base metal which, like spaces and quads, is of body-height, having no face, and is not intended to touch the paper. This serves to separate the lines of type. It is important in a book with a wide page that there should be a fairway for the eye to run back from the end of one line to the beginning of the next. The lead provides that fairway. Types are frequently specially cast on a larger body so that the effect of leading is obtained without the labour.

A type-page with very little spacing presents a more solid and decorative appearance than one which is widely spaced; and some printers have mistakenly abolished paragraph-breaks, indentations, and sentence-ending spaces, with the effect of practically preventing anyone from reading the book.

The first line set and leaded where necessary, others are added until the stick is full. The compositor then slides them off it on to a larger tray called a galley. Galleys are made in different sizes, but for book-work they normally hold about three octavo pages. Stickful follows stickful of type on the galley till the column of type fills it. The "matter" (as standing type is called) is then made fast and a proof taken or "pulled"[1] on a hand-press kept for the purpose; for machine-presses can only be economically used for the rapid printing of large numbers of copies, or "runs".

This first rough proof does not reach the author, but is read by the printer's reader; a second and cleaner proof goes to the author. "Readers" are a wonderful race of men, all but omniscient, who can correct specialist authors on their own subjects. If the reader's suggested corrections are sometimes gratuitous, it is very easy not to accept them; he has done his best for you in calling your attention to a possible error, and there is no cause for irritation.

All corrections should be made at this stage of galley or "slip" proof, as when once the matter is locked in the chase in pages corrections involve much more work. And any corrections that must be made should be made with a clear conception of the work which will be caused and an active conscience or at least consciousness of the bill for author's corrections. It is generally possible, for example, to insert words running to about the same number of ems as those deleted; otherwise the correction may disturb the type of eight or ten lines. Similarly, an insertion can be fitted in at the end of a paragraph without disturbing any of the standing type.

---

[1] The printer never uses the phrase "struck off", a transference from the mint which is sometimes inaccurately used by amateurs. A single impression from any portion of type is called "a pull".

MECHANICAL COMPOSITION

In recent times the labour of composition has been minimized, by the invention of machines for the purpose; the two chief of these are (in order of date) the linotype and the monotype.

The linotype is a single machine on which the operator, by striking the keyboard, resembling that of a typewriter, brings into position in the line the appropriate matrices. When the line is completed, the matrices are moved up to the mould in front of the orifice of a cauldron of molten type-metal. The whole line is then cast in a solid "slug", a peculiarity of the process to which it owes its name. The slugs are passed direct on to the galley, and proofed in the same way as hand-set matter.

The monotype method, the later to be invented, involves two machines. On the first the operator strikes the keyboard, and in so doing punches a series of holes in a spool of paper, resembling that used in the pianola. The spool finished, he marks it in pencil with the title of the book, etc., and the founts to be used, and passes it to the casting-room. Here it is affixed to the wonderful and intricate monotype casting-machine, which, like the linotype, has a cauldron attached. The operator selects, according to the instruction pencilled on the spool, the die-case of the appropriate fount. This die-case is a small square of steel in which are sunk matrices (usually brass) of all required sorts. The spool is fixed over an air-pressure bar, the blast from which, passing through the holes punched in the spool, and passing there only, sets the die-case in motion, bringing the appropriate matrix over the flow of molten type-metal. Single letters are thus cast, whence the more scholarly name of this process. They are extruded one by one on to the galley, and when the line is complete it is automatically moved up, and a fresh line begins to form beneath it.

It will be seen that both the linotype and monotype processes have certain marked advantages over hand-setting. First, and most obvious, is the saving in time, even in monotype, where two operators and two machines are involved. Against this must be set the initial cost of the elaborate apparatus, especially with monotype. Second is the complete elimination of the whole process of redistribution, since the type, when "broken up", is simply thrown into the melting-pot and cast afresh on the next occasion. As a result there can never occur (unless by damage to the die-case itself) battered or broken letters. Nor can "foul-case" occur, that is, the placing of a letter after use in the compartment in the case belonging to another sort. It is possible, though not a frequent occurrence, in linotype for a wrong matrix to get into the magazine and so produce recurrent wrong fount.

In monotype, too, the spool can easily be stored and stereotyping saved; but as the spool will not carry the corrections this advantage is limited to matter which is practically "clean". The original corrected proofs can, of course, be kept and used for the amendment of the text type. The advantages of being able to store a paper spool instead of heavy

70

type-metal plates are obvious, but the disadvantage of not having the formes ready for printing has to be borne in mind.

The chief difference between monotype and linotype is that implied by their names. Monotype-set matter, consisting as it does of single types, is naturally corrected by hand letter by letter. But in linotype the unit is the line, and the correction of a single letter means throwing out and re-setting the line in which it occurs.

During recent years both Monotype and Linotype Corporations have shown a great and scholarly interest in type-faces. For each of these machines there is now a very fine range of founts of good design which is being steadily increased.

It seems not unlikely that, in the near future, there may be developments in the field of photographic type-setting machines, such as the "Fotosetter". Should this be so, it will be a revolutionary change in mechanical methods of composition with considerable effect upon the printed book.

IMPOSITION

At this stage the matter which will make the first sheet (e.g. if the book to be printed be an octavo, pp. 1–16) is transferred from the galleys to a large metal-topped table called (from its older form) the "stone". The title-page and other preliminaries will, of course, be printed last and will make a separate section, unless the book is a plain reprint. The type is already divided into page lengths, and these are now divided into outer and inner "formes", in other words into the set which will be printed on the recto of the open sheet of paper, the same side as page 1, and those which will be printed on the verso, the same side as page 2. In the press the forme, and not the sheet, is the unit, as will be explained in due course.

The arrangement of the pages for different formats, so that they will fall in the right order and the right way up, is very strange to the eye of the layman, but is perfectly familiar to the printer. There is no need for the student to learn these schemes, since they can be readily referred to in a number of books on printing practice. In order to familiarize himself with the procedure, however, the student should fold sheets to each of the main formats, number the pages, and then spread the sheets open, when the various "lay-outs" will appear. It is important that he should remember the difference between the imposition of the type-pages themselves and the reversed order of those pages when the sheet is printed. Errors in imposition are perhaps the rarest on the printer's conscience, though in hurried work such have been known.

The pages are now provided with pagination, signatures, and headlines. In the earliest printed books none of these are found; like the capitals at the head of chapters they were left to be filled in by the hand of the rubrisher or owner, as they had been in the manuscript book.

Pagination.—Fairly early, however, there begins

to be printed at the head of each recto page, not a page number (pagination), but a leaf number (foliation); pagination is at least very rare till 1500 and not really common for another half-century. The printer took little interest in either, as it was intended only for the reader's convenience in reference, and early foliation and pagination abound in gaps, repetitions, and errors of all sorts.

Signatures.—From his (or more strictly from the binder's) point of view, the vital thing was, and is, the signaturing or guide to the binder. In the manuscript book the scribe would write in the bottom outer corner of the margin of the first recto of a quire the letter "a" and the figure "1", in the next "a 2", and so on till the middle of the quire and the sewing was reached. Beyond this he would continue for one recto, thus showing that nothing had dropped out, as could very easily occur unless the binder had lined the fold where the thread came with a strip of vellum to prevent it cutting the leaves. The remaining leaves formed integral parts of the signed leaves, and therefore when the book was unbound followed automatically in their proper places. It is therefore rare to find them also signed. The next quire would be lettered "b", with leaf-numbers as before; and so on. The binder, having obeyed the directions thus given him, normally cut the signatures off with his plough, though sometimes the whole or sufficient traces for our use remain. It never entered his mind, good man, accustomed to mediæval standards of workmanship, that a book once bound might need binding again.

73

The earliest printers followed the scribe in this, as in everything else, and left the signatures to be supplied in the traditional position in pen-and-ink.

The earliest printers may have been deterred from setting up types for letters and figures at a distance from the type-page, since the page was surrounded and held tight by "furniture" consisting of bars of wood and metal. About 1470, however, in several centres of Northern Italy experiments were made in stamping in type-set signatures by hand: they are found, not in the old position, but irregularly near the fore-edge and generally near the head. This rather ugly device was of short vogue, for in 1472 Johann Koelhoff of Cologne showed the way to all subsequent printers by setting up a last line to the pages which needed signing, consisting of the necessary letter and number and, for the rest, of a row of quads or other spaces which left it blank in printing. The invention spread and in a dozen years was general. The presence or absence of signatures is one of the several aids to ascribing dates to undated books of that period.

The signature alphabet, being frequently the Latin, consists not, like ours, of twenty-six letters, but of twenty-three, having no *w*, and reckoning *i* and *j*, *u* and *v*, as alternative forms of but two letters. When the first alphabet was exhausted the printer went on with upper-case if he had begun in lower, or by duplicating, triplicating, and multiplying to any number necessary the signature letters. Nowadays Arabic numerals are frequently used in place of letters. Volume numbers are sometimes found added in roman. It is also now usual to sign not every recto before the sewing but only the first page of each gathering.

When two or more books, uniform in style, are being printed simultaneously in the same office, and also (as would doubtless be usual) bound in the same shop, it is very helpful to distinguish by the signature, which can be read on the standing type in the forme as well as on the printed sheet, the book to which the forme or sheet belongs. For want of this the binder may mix the sheets of two books forming part of the same series, an annoying mistake but one which can be rectified. The printer can also print on two sides of the same sheet, formes belonging to two different books, and this is incurable but by reprinting the sheet. The present writer once found among the cheaper sort of books coming into the British Museum under the Copyright Act a strange case of this confusion of the formes, the printer having printed on one sheet formes from two books forming part of a series on games, one on bridge and one on lawn tennis, the pages alternating in a manner likely to cause the maximum of bewilderment to the student of either of those arts.

The difficulty had been recognized and provided against in the fifteenth century, when although the "publishers' series" did not exist under that name, certain Parisian presses specialized in books of Hours of the Virgin (the layman's prayer book) in general appearance exactly the same, but differing in various

parts according to the local "use".[1] To avoid the confusion which would inevitably have arisen it was the
practice of these printers to add to the signature an
abbreviated form of the name of the diocese of whose
use the book was, such as "Sar." for "secundum
usum Sarum", or "Par." for "secundum usum
ecclesie Parisiensis". Similarly, Wynkyn de Worde,
who printed quantities of small quarto books of verse,
employed the same device. Modern printers habitually practise it, and so save much trouble. It may be
pointed out that risk of these errors is not saved, if
some trouble in composition may be, by the more
recent device of using a small oblong block, called "a
back mark". This is printed in the margin, where the
outer fold of the first and last leaves of the sheet will
come, in such a position that when the sheets are
folded and piled for binding (or rather "casing") the
black oblongs follow each other in a slanting sequence
down the back of the book, thus showing at a glance
an omission or a duplication. Still less is error saved
by the total omission of signatures, a recent product
of the uninstructed desire for modernity.

Catchwords.

A catchword is the first word of a page printed at the
foot of the preceding page. In the manuscript these
were most commonly found only at the foot of the
last verso of a quire, and like the signatures were a

---

[1] The use prevalent over the larger, and particularly the southern, part
of England, and also in Scotland, was that of Salisbury or "Sarum", the
York use being confined to the North; Sarum books were largely produced in Paris and Rouen.

guide to the binder. Later they appeared at the foot of every verso, and sometimes of every page; but the catchword, which, when accompanied by signatures, served no useful purpose for the binder, died out in the nineteenth century. In their other use, as an aid to reading by giving the first word on the succeeding page, they have been given occasional life by certain printers and are common in modern typewriting practice.

Press Figures or Press Numbers.—Although experience should soon help to guard against any great possibility of error, it is important that signatures should not be confused with press numbers. These latter were small figures usually printed in the lower margin and are frequently found in eighteenth- and early nineteenth-century books. It is thought that each press or pressman was allocated a number and that this number would record the amount of work done by each and therefore assist in the computation of wages.

Headlines.—The first function of the headlines was, and still is, to guide the reader turning over the leaves in search of a particular section. But they have also that of helping a reader running through a "tract-volume" of pamphlets, and of identifying the volume a loose leaf or pair of leaves belongs to. For the former of these uses the headline must clearly be a shortened form of chapter or section heading, or even descriptive of the matter on the page or open pair of pages; for the latter it must be a shortened form of the book's title. A usual plan is to combine

77

the two, printing as the verso headline the book's title, as the recto the chapter or section heading; thus all purposes are equally served. A singular and entertaining example of analytical headlines is Thackeray's *The Rose and the Ring*, whose headlines form a complete running summary of the story in rhyming couplets, as for example:

Verso: MUCH I FEAR, KING VALOROSO,
Recto: THAT YOUR CONDUCT IS BUT SO SO.

The headline normally includes at the outer ends the pagination; but the pagination is also found in the middle of the foot of the page, an innovation in which there seems to be little advantage. Eccentricities of all sorts are found, of course, such as pagination numbers in words instead of figures. At least one book exists in which the pagination occupies the centre of the head, and the headline is a footline.[1]

Margins.—An important part of imposition is the proportion of the margins to the type-pages. It will be noticed that the type-page never lies in the centre of the page of paper. William Morris stated the reason for this rule, which is that what the eye sees when a book is opened is not the single page but the pair of pages. Allowance must be made for a little trimming by the binder, and for the optical illusion caused by the reader's thumb covering a part of the margin. The relative proportions which were suggested by the Library Association's Book Production Committee can be accepted as a good general guide.

[1] James L. Molloy: *Our Autumn Holiday on French Rivers*, n.d.

They were as follows: inner ("gutter") margin, 4; head, 5; fore-edge, 7; tail, 8¾. A. W. Pollard stated the rule in somewhat different terms: that "the breadth of the paper and height of the type-page should be identical".

The type required to print on one side of the sheet, made up into pages and duly provided with all the necessary headlines, signatures, pagination, etc., is then enclosed in an iron frame called a "chase". The spaces between, which will constitute the margins on the printed sheet, are filled in with furniture consisting of iron bars, wooden blocks, and wooden or metal wedges ("quoins"). Wood was used as being more elastic than metal, but nowadays is frequently replaced by metal furniture which can be expanded by means of a ratchet. Once the type is properly positioned it is "locked up" by hammering in the wedges or securing the furniture. The finished result is the "forme", which is the actual unit of printing laid on the bed of the press. Flat pieces of wood are then laid over it, and gently hammered, so that any pieces of type which have been raised by the pressure are knocked down level with the rest without the face being damaged. The whole can then be lifted bodily and either stood on its end in store or sent direct to the press.

PRESSWORK

The press in its simplest form, as it was used with little alteration for three centuries, may be seen in a number of sixteenth-century woodcuts, several of

79

which are reproduced in McKerrow's *Introduction to Bibliography*. That used by Froschover at Zurich in the middle of the century shows as clearly as any the essentials of the press as well as of the composing cases.

Existing presses of the old type can be seen in the Musée Plantin–Moretus at Antwerp, and an interesting modern copy of one is operating in University College, London.

The press resembles an old-fashioned linen-press, and the framework reaches from floor to ceiling, as befits a structure that has to work with so heavy a weight of metal. The screw is turned, and the impression made, by pulling a long handle. Under the screw is seen a flat, heavy board; this is the platen, which the action of the screw brings down upon the paper and type.

The forme is laid upon the bed of the press and is inked. In modern presswork the inking is carried out by a mechanically regulated flow of ink from a supply tank, the ink being carried over the forme by rollers. But in the hand-press of the fifteenth to the eighteenth centuries the ink was dabbed on by heavy "ink-balls", somewhat resembling the padded heads of gong-sticks, as may be seen in Fig. 2. In spite of this apparently primitive method, uneven inking was much rarer in those years than might be at first supposed.

The problem was to position the paper so that the platen could press it upon the inked forme and take the impression. A frame was necessary, and this is called the tympan (Greek τύμπανον, a drum); it may be seen on the left of Froschover's press, a double-hinged frame, from which a pressman is lifting a printed sheet, while his mate inks the forme for the next pull. The purpose of the outer half of the frame is not clear at sight. This is the "frisket", and its

FIG. 2.—THE HAND-PRESS (C. FROSCHOVER, ZURICH, 1548).

purpose is to double in over the tympan and so to come between the paper and the inked surface when the tympan and frisket are together turned down upon the forme. In this way the margins are protected from the ink. The frame of the frisket is fitted

81

with a sheet of stout paper or parchment, which is first of all brought down upon the type and inked, and out of which the inked type-page areas are cut, like windows, to admit the paper to the type just where it is wanted and nowhere else.

When the sheets have been printed on one side they are piled up ready to be "perfected", i.e., printed on the other side from the second forme, which will probably be done by another press working at the same time. Many modern machines can perform both operations, dealing with the two sides of the sheet in rapidly succeeding revolutions of the roller. Printing with more than one colour, or printing from two different surfaces such as relief and intaglio, on to the same sheet nearly always necessitates a separate impression. One of the most common secondary colours to be used in printing was red, and the fact that red printing was from the earliest times done by an independent impression (even though the problem was not complicated by the ink-roller) is clear from the fact that red and black often overlap, which would be impossible at a single impression.

But before the forme can be "put to bed", or, in other words, printed off, it is necessary to make sure that the face of the whole type surface is absolutely even, as otherwise those parts which are standing the least bit above the level will make too strong an impression on (and perhaps even into) the paper, while those below it will not be impressed strongly enough, and the result will be the familiar one of alternating patches of heavy black and of grey. This process is called "making ready", and completes the work begun by the hammering flat of the type-face. It should first be explained that the tympan is padded with layers of paper and textiles, in order to prevent the type from cutting through the paper. A first trial pull shows what parts of the forme are printing too heavily or too lightly. The workman takes sheets of paper to add to the padding of the tympan, and from this he cuts out patches corresponding to the heavy patches in the impression, while he pastes on extra pieces of paper corresponding to the light patches, thus correcting the inequalities by pressing the paper further down into the latter, and allowing it to be pressed not quite so far down into the former. It will readily be imagined that making-ready is the work of a highly skilled hand and eye, and that there is nothing mechanical about it. It is in fact the test of good printing, and the first process which the cheap printer cuts out. In modern rotary presses the make-ready sheet is fixed to the roller itself, while with blocks, such as half-tones, the paper is applied to the back of the block.

The modern hand-press, a modification in metal of that described above, is now used largely for pulling proofs. The actual "working-off" is more economically accomplished by the machine-press. The essential difference between the two is that, in the latter, the bed bearing the forme slides automatically in and out, while the sheet to be printed is not brought down upon it by the weight of a flat platen, but is pressed on to the printing surface by means of a roller.

The rotary press, which is now in such widespread use, is quite different in principle. There the forme is cast as a curved plate, either a stereotype or an electrotype, and fastened to the roller, with the result that the printing is done by the revolution of the forme itself.

The quality of the ink is also of importance, but really poor printer's ink is not so common as is thought. Printer's ink differs entirely from writing ink. The latter is a liquid made (at its best) from oak-gall and water; the former is a very viscous substance made from linseed-oil and lamp black. Some of the block-books which are contemporary with the first generation of typography are printed with liquid writing ink which has turned brown with age; but it seems to have been perceived at once by the pioneers of printing with movable types that black (and red) oil-based ink was the only suitable medium.

STEREOTYPING AND ELECTROTYPING

Stereotyping and electrotyping are both methods of converting the forme of movable letters into a solid block. The object is to avoid resetting of the type for later editions in which alterations are not required. It may be said to have been anticipated by the block-book, which achieved the same result without the use of type. But a nearer approach to the present practice was made by William Ged of Edinburgh (1690–1749); he experimented with soldering the foot of the type into a solid mass. The failure of his invention, which was defeated by the fear that it would throw printers out of work, was little loss, since it did not allow the original type to be distributed. Some forty years later than Ged's stereotyped edition of Sallust (1744), Joseph Hoffmann of Strasbourg made similar experiments, and was defeated by the same opposition; but Louis-Etienne Herhan and the firm of Didot at the same time were perfecting a system of setting up in punches (Herhan's method) or in moulds (Didot's), from which in either case, indirectly or directly, a printing surface could be cast. The defect of this was that it needed special composition in the first instance. The taking of a mould direct from ordinary composed type is the essence of stereotyping as practised today, and is the invention of Alexander Tilloch, partner of Andrew Foulis the younger, in 1782, and was perfected by Charles, 3rd Earl Stanhope, in 1805.

It is now not uncommon for the whole printing to be done from plates, the type being broken up as soon as the moulds have been made from it; and wood-blocks are rarely put into the press. A great advantage of the process is that the printing-face can be not only perpetuated but also multiplied, so that where a "long run" is in question the same forme can be printed at several presses simultaneously.

Stereotyping is the cheaper form of plate-making of the two and is widely used, especially in newspaper work. "Flong", or papier mâché mixed with a paste which renders it non-inflammable at a

85

high temperature, is mechanically pressed (formerly brushed) over the original printing-surface, and the moulds so made, which are light and yet lasting, can be stored till required, when type-metal casts are made from them and mounted "type-high" for printing. In electrotyping, copper is deposited by electrolysis on a wax mould taken from the face of the type, and is then backed up to bring it to type-height. In both cases, they are greatly used with modern high-speed rotary presses. The main drawback to printing from plates is that, once the moulds have been made, correction is difficult. Words or phrases which can be cut out and replaced by words or phrases occupying the same amount of space are comparatively simple, but such occasions are naturally rare. Otherwise, fresh type setting and complicated printing methods are involved. As can be readily appreciated such an event will frequently result in irregularities in pagination and signatures which must be watched. While the existence of plate printing has doubtless multiplied books and kept many valuable works from going out of print, it has also probably prevented many from being revised.

If the type has been distributed before the need for reprinting has become apparent there is now an alternative to the expense of fresh setting, an expense which would otherwise have to be met unless the first setting was by monotype, when the spool can be preserved. This alternative is to photograph the printed pages of any perfect and clean copy of the book, and to reproduce it, normally by some variety of photo-litho-offset. The photographic reprint, if well done, is difficult to distinguish from the type-printed original. Corrections must, of course, involve the re-setting of the pages affected.

In the middle of the nineteenth century unaltered reprints were made, especially in France, for cheap work, by the "anastatic" process. An inked offset of the type was made on metal plates, which were etched in relief. But the offset was rarely perfect, and the pages usually showed ugly and sometimes disastrous breaks and gaps. It is difficult to see why the process was ever introduced, since stereotyping did its work better, and was already in use.

EDITION, IMPRESSION, REPRINT, ISSUE, VARIANT, CANCEL, LARGE PAPER

These terms are very loosely used in common speech and writing, but it is absolutely necessary that bibliographers should use them exactly, if their descriptions of books are to be lucid and unambiguous. Into few parts of the bibliographical jungle have there been more determined efforts to throw light of recent years than this one. Terms, which should be capable of accurate definition, are still the subject of debate, and the following pages are no more than an introduction to a complicated subject.

1. *Edition*.—An edition of a book consists simply of all those copies which are printed from a single setting-up of the text. A "new edition" need not involve any revision of the text, though naturally any misprints observed will be corrected—and probably

87

some new ones made. In this way, the term will include all those copies printed from plates, even when this may extend over years. Some bibliographers will also urge that it must include copies printed from text set up again from a stored monotype spool. There is some difference in the use of the term in publishing and bookselling circles. In 1898 the Publishers' Association put forward the following definition, which was endorsed by the trade a second time in 1929. "An edition is an impression in which the matter has undergone *some* change, or for which the type has been reset."

2. *Impression*.—An impression is the term to cover all those copies which were printed at any one time. This is normally interpreted as meaning without the type having been removed from the press and, consequently, without any very great possibility of variation. In modern times, there will frequently be several impressions to an edition. In earlier times, impression and edition were usually synonymous because the type was broken down and redistributed when the forme came off the bed of the press. A new impression is one which is taken from the same standing type or plates as the original. This would also constitute a *reprint* or more fully in the latter case, a *reprint from plates*.

Pocket editions are produced by reprinting from plates on thinner and smaller paper. The resulting appearance is often so different that the inexperienced eye needs to see the two side by side to be convinced of their typographical identity.

88

The Publishers' Association defined impression as: "A number of copies printed at any one time. When a book is reprinted without change it shall be called a new impression to distinguish it from an edition."

3. *Issue.*—An issue similarly consists of all those copies of an edition which are put on the market at one time, if differentiated by some substituted, added, or subtracted matter from those copies of the same setting of the type which were put on the market at other times.

If a new title-page be printed, or an introduction or appendix be added to the unsold original sheets, which clearly establishes the copies with them as sold later than those without, they form a new issue or a re-issue.

4. *Variant.*—When the press was worked slowly and by hand, it was exceedingly easy and a common practice to stop it and to withdraw the forme for the correction of any error that had been observed on the pulls already made. There is no reason to believe that when the completed sheets were stacked for the binder any attempt was made to distinguish between the corrected and uncorrected pulls. Indeed, it was quite possible for a further correction to be made while the forme printing on the other side of the same sheet was in the press, and if in the work of perfecting (printing the second side) the printer chanced to start with the last printed copy, there would result sheets of which in some copies the outer forme is in uncorrected and the inner in corrected state, and in others exactly the other way round. Manifestly neither of

these could be called the earlier or the later issue, and the word issue, dear to booksellers, is therefore disallowed for these cases by bibliographers, who speak of them as variants.

A sensational example of the confusion between issue and variant, which cost the vendor of a book £1,500, was seen in the sale in 1926 of a copy of the first (1678) edition of Bunyan's *Pilgrim's Progress*, Part I. Of the six perfect copies known of this book apparently only three have a very small note of errata printed below the Finis on the last page of text. After the printer had printed off the formes containing the erring passages the author noticed the errors. It was too late to correct any copies of those formes; nor was it worth while to reprint a whole leaf for each as a cancel (*q.v.* below). But there was one chance left (as the errata slip was rarely if ever used then), and that was to utilize any blank space, which would otherwise be filled with quads and spaces, on the outer forme (that containing the last page) of the last sheet; and this he did. Of course he did not issue the copies with the last forme in this state separately from the others. The auctioneer's cataloguer did not notice the errata, and simply (and correctly) described the copy as of the first edition. The purchaser actually returned the book as misdescribed; and, more surprisingly still, the auctioneer accepted its return. It was resold as a "second issue", which it was not, and its owner had to take £1,500 less. Yet it represented Bunyan's intentional first text, and what more does the collector of first editions desire?

Variants are astonishingly numerous in books of the age of the hand-press, but it is not worth while to stop the power-driven machine-press for a correction; small corrections are therefore now reserved for an errata slip, while a large one would be dealt with by reprinting the sheet.

5. *Cancel.*—If an error were discovered when the forme had been printed off, and if it were of too great substance for uncorrected copies to go out into the world, the leaf could be reset and separately printed. The corrected copies of the leaf would then be bound in place of the peccant original, which would be cut out by the binder, a scissor-slit in the tail being the signal to him to do so.

Where the book would otherwise have a blank last leaf, and the last sheet had not been printed off when the cancel was decided on, it was obviously economical to set up the corrected version as part of the formes for that sheet, and to cut the leaf away afterwards. In fact, the reprinted leaf is sometimes found at the end, overlooked by the binder, and this is the bibliographer's delight, for thus he has both texts, and can record the reason for the cancel.

Reasons for cancels are often the most interesting and important elements in the history of a book. They involve conflicts of politicians, libels, and entertaining errors. Striking examples are given by McKerrow, and one or two are mentioned in the present writer's *Sources of English Literature*. The frequency of cancels, too, is surprising. Dr. R. W. Chapman has estimated that in the eighteenth century one book in three will be found to contain one. In modern books they are rare, except in title-pages reprinted for the sale of the book by another publisher than the one for whom it was printed. As observed above in the case of variants, if an error be found deserving correction more drastic than can be administered in an errata slip, the publisher will probably instruct the printer to reprint the entire sheet. But a remarkable case of a modern book which abounds in cancels, and in which no attempt has been made to fill in matter in place of that removed, so as to make the reprinted leaves uniform with the rest, is Neville Lytton's *The Press and the General Staff*, 1921. In this book it will be noticed as significant that the name of a well-known statesman is several times found in the immediate context of a cancel.

Both the original and the corrected leaves are indiscriminately called "cancels"; but it is more exact and preferable to call the former the *cancelled leaf* or the *cancellandum*, even when it should have been, but has not been, cancelled, and the latter the *cancelling leaf* or the *cancellans*.

In collation a cancel may be recognized by the appearance of the butt of the conjugate leaf, on to which the *cancellans* is pasted; the substitution may also throw out the regular sequence of watermarks.

6. *Large Paper*.—Special and more expensive copies are manufactured in various ways. The commonest is by printing on a larger and finer paper ("L.P." and "F.P." in catalogues). Occasionally copies of the products of private presses are printed

on vellum. William Morris revived the use of vellum at the Kelmscott Press, and the Ashendene Press and some others followed his example.

Early examples of large paper copies, as in the Elizabethan law books printed by Richard Tottell, were sometimes intended for the utilitarian purpose of private annotation. In the nineteenth century, and particularly towards its close, there arose a fashion for excessive margins, bulking out (more agreeably, it must be said, than by means of featherweight paper) small books into important looking tomes. One of these was once drastically described by a critic as "an epigram in one volume". Nor is the fashion purely modern. A century before the *Yellow Book*, Richard Brinsley Sheridan had satirized such books as having "a rivulet of text meandering through wide meadows of margin", while the same thing may have been in the mind of Callimachus when he enunciated the opinion that a big book is a big evil, μέγα βίβλιον μέγα κακόν. Callimachus was the Chief Librarian of the great library of Alexandria, and modern librarians, to whom also shelf-space is always a painful thought, will agree with him.

The fine paper copy is today more popular than the large paper, since, as a margin has an ideal relation of area to that of the printed page, there is only a trivial economy in cutting it down for the cheap copy, and no artistic gain, but rather loss, in enlarging it for the expensive copy. The modern French book, especially if illustrated by engravings, is usually issued in two forms, the fine copies containing the early impressions

93

of the engravings, sometimes in more than one state. Occasionally extra introductory matter is inserted in them, which brings them under the definition of a separate issue.

A peculiar form of variation between copies of one edition, made by the publisher in order to create a difference in sumptuousness, is the reimposition of the pages for another format and consequently a larger margin. Thus Pope's *Essay on Man* appeared, in an identical setting of the type, both in folio and in quarto for issue separately, 1734, and in the second volume of the *Works*, 1735.

Before the printer sees the "copy", the author and publisher will have the chance to make or mar a book by faulty "book-building"; and throughout, the production of the book is the work of all three in co-operation.

PARTS OF A BOOK

A book falls into certain parts, about each of which some comments are to be made:

A. Preliminaries

These are usually printed last, and on a separate sheet or sheets, except where no new prefatory matter is expected. They should be paged separately, in roman figures, if printed last; otherwise it is best to start the main arabic pagination with the preliminaries, and make no break. The pagination should in any case reckon from the first recto of the book, whether blank or not. Good make-up is important, and no tipped-in single leaves should be tolerated; the unit in sound book-building is the sewn "fold" of two leaves.

1. The *Half-title* or bastard title (French, *faux-titre*), which precedes the title-page, carries on the recto the book's short title. The verso may bear the printer's imprint. The half-title exists to keep the title-page clean, and at the same time to identify the book the first sheet belongs to, which a blank first leaf does not. This is the place for the series title, should the book form part of a series. In German books the series title and the book title usually and conveniently face each other.

2. The *Title-page*.—There are many examples of deceptively worded title-pages; one of the best instances gave rise to a story dear to H. B. Wheatley. A Midlothian stockfarmer saw in an Edinburgh bookshop a copy of Richard and Maria Edgeworth's *Essay on Irish Bulls* (1802), which is decorated at the head of the text with a wood-engraving of that animal. Having read it through with becoming gravity, he observed that Miss Edgeworth must be "a fule body, to write a book of bulls and no ane word of horned cattle in it a', forbye the bit beastie at the beginning".

Fancy titles must be allowed to human weakness, but should be explained by a sub-title.

The title-page should carry a clear and succinct statement of (*a*) the book's title and subject-matter, with or without the aid of sub-titles; (*b*) the author's name, and relevant facts as to his status in relation to the book's subject, e.g. his academic position and authorship of similar works; these must on no account be given the appearance of an advertisement; (*c*) the name of any translator, editor, introducer, or illustrator; (*d*) the edition number; (*e*) the imprint, giving the place, the publisher's name and (unless well known) address, in other words information as to whence copies can be procured, and, lastly, the date. Some publishers decorate the title-page with their device.

Undated books were common in the fifteenth century, because the manuscript had normally been so. They are common in the twentieth because some publishers, who have little contact with intelligent readers, believe that books will not sell unless they are, or at least are not confessedly not, fresh from the press. Some make the best of both worlds by hiding the date on the verso of the title-page or even on the foot of the last page of the text. In books from private presses there is a fashion for imitating the early book and printing the date in the colophon, but that, if an affectation, is at any rate honest.

Intelligent readers demand dates on books, and preferably in the traditional and conspicuous position at the foot of the title-page. They also demand a statement of the date of the first edition of the book itself, and of the present recension of it. It is vital to them to know whether the author wrote, or revised what he had written, before or after certain events or publications. In most branches of natural science, knowledge advances and theory changes with such rapidity that a book five years old or less is out of date and if undated is a fraud. It may be said at once that this type of book is not that which the publisher leaves undated in order to deceive.

The manuscript and the quite early printed book had no title-page; the text, with normally an incipit ("here begins"), began on the recto of the first or second leaf, and in the latter case the first leaf was blank. A very short "label" title, like our half-title, began about 1480 to be printed on the blank recto of the first leaf, though the actual first title-pages known, to a Bull of Pius II printed at Mainz in 1463 by Fust and Schoeffer, and to a sermon by Rolewinck printed by Arnold ther Hoernen at Cologne in 1470, are wordy. But the Parisian publishers from about 1485 filled the space below the short title with their device and name and address below; the printer's imprint was in the colophon, as in all other books of the period.

The title-page, itself a wrapper to the (often decorated) first page of text, began in the latter half of the sixteenth century to be preceded and protected in its turn by another leaf, which often bore merely the signature letter A on the recto. From the mid-seventeenth century the verso of the half-title was used for the imprimatur, and in the latter part of the century it became common to print the short title on the recto, resembling the early title-page; and this is the half-title of today.

There has arisen a practice of printing the half-title not on the first but on the second or even the third recto, in order to save any page with print from the paste where the end pages of the casing are pasted to the sheets. But this elaboration seems as needless as the provision of dust-jackets for the protection of casings which themselves exist in order to protect something else.

3. The *Statement of Editions* and impressions, which generally stands on the verso of the title-page. In American books this is the place for the date of copyright, which in that country it is a legal obligation to state. It is necessary to be ready for one deception here; where a book has been transferred from one publisher to another, the latter will sometimes, while setting out an apparently full table of editions, entirely ignore any not published by himself.

4. The *Imprimatur*, or licence for publication, granted by secular or ecclesiastical authority, carrying not only the name of the licenser, but also the date, which may not be that of the imprint. The imprimatur is now rarely found except in the form of the words "permissu superiorum" on works of Catholic priests. The imprimatur is to be distinguished from the privilege of copyright ("cum privilegio ad imprimendum solum") granted by the Crown to publishers in the first half of the sixteenth century in this country and then and later abroad, generally for a term of years.

5. The statement of the *number of copies printed* in the different forms, large paper, etc. Commoner in French books, as the "justification du tirage", than in English.

6. The *Dedication*.—This in English books of the

sixteenth and seventeenth centuries is often the only place where the author's name appears.

7. The *Preface*, useful for the author's after-thoughts, for first aid to reviewers, and for those acknowledgments to helpers which can so easily be overdone. Its old name was "To the Reader".

8. An *Introduction* by a writer other than the book's author.

9. The *Table of Contents*.—This should be analytical: in a short and well-arranged book a really well-drawn-up table of contents makes a brief index sufficient. In French books the Table is usually found at the end.

10. The *List of Illustrations*; it should cover the frontispiece, which should be called No. I, and should distinguish between plates and figures in the text, each series having a separate sequence of numbers, as in this book.

11. *Errata*.—Usually printed on a small slip of paper pasted in; it has a short life. It is better to utilize a blank half-page in the preliminaries, putting the sheet through the press again.

B. *The Body of the Book*

12. The *Text*, sometimes headed by a chapter entitled the Introduction. The text begins on a recto, about a third or more down the page, and is headed by a short title, called the "drop-down", which should be the same as the "running title" in the headlines. When this running title differs from that on the title-page, the latter is possibly a *cancellans*.

99

C. Subsidiaries

13. The *Notes*.—They can be massed at the end either of the work or of the chapters; if not voluminous there will be no great difficulty in printing them in the handiest place, at the foot, or still better, if not numerous, at the side of the page. In the fifteenth century an even more difficult arrangement than voluminous footnotes was successfully dealt with, text in a large type and in two columns being framed all round with commentary, also in two columns, printed in type exactly half the size of that of the text. Notes should anyhow be printed in a size of face at least two points smaller than that of the text type.

Footnote references made to other books and articles should, unless the reader is to be infuriated against the author, be given in a form full enough to enable the book to be readily found in a library catalogue. "See Smith", "See Meyer", are criminal notes, and even short of these it has been calculated that a careless annotator can waste scores of hours of a student's time over one book in this way. An exact page or chapter reference should be added.

14. *Bibliographies* and other *Appendices*.—It is not for the author of the present work to decry the practice, now very common, of appending bibliographies to books, nor does he, when they are real ones, whether exhaustive or select lists of books the author has drawn upon, and are compiled by the author and not by a hack.

15. *Index* or *Indexes*.—A high proportion of books

have their usefulness diminished through bad index-ing. There should be no need now to insist on the necessity in any book of information of an index adequate to its scope and purpose. Unfortunately many indexes are spoiled by having a mere string of page numbers following the indexing word. This is an uninformative practice and cannot be too vehem-ently denounced. Analytical indexes are of great use, giving some idea of the nature of the passage referred to. Sectionalized indexes, which have a long and honourable history, are now frequently a bone of contention. Their advantages are obvious, their sole disadvantage seems to be that the reader may not know to which index he should refer. There are, however, some notable examples available to the student of this kind of index and they should be studied with care.

16. The *Imprint* or *Colophon*, which may include the printer's device.

The colophon (Greek κολόφων, a summit or con-clusion) is occasional in MSS., where it gives the scribe's name and the date. In printed books it first appeared on the Psalter printed by Fust and Schoeffer in 1457, and gradually became common, but was driven out by the title-page imprint towards 1600. In its full form it has been revived and is in more general use in France than in England, where it is chiefly used by private presses. But the printer's imprint occurs either here or in the preliminaries in all books printed in the United Kingdom, as by law provided (2 & 3 Vict. c. 12. s. 2).

17. *Finis*, in a book in more than one volume, should be kept for the last volume, the others ending "End of Volume I" (etc.).

18. *Blank Leaves* forming part of the book are unnecessary at the end, as at the beginning. There should be stout end-papers provided by the binder.

19. The *Plates*, which are needed for engravings which cannot be printed with the text, should be printed in pairs on double leaves, or, if singly, on wide leaves, which will fold round the sewing. Tipping-in should be avoided wherever possible. "Tissues", which serve to protect the page and plate facing each other from set off while the ink is fresh, should be removed later. In no case should anything be printed on them. The plate-numbers and lettering, corresponding to those in the list in the preliminaries, should figure on the plate-leaves themselves, and so should an abbreviated title identifying the book they adorn; should they ever come away this will enable them to be replaced.

Plates and maps can be inserted facing the text they illustrate, or if numerous they can be massed at the end. The latter is probably the more business-like and the former the more attractive method. Maps and plans can also be issued folded in a pocket in the casing; but they are liable to be lost, and in libraries they will have to be bound in. The purpose of issuing plates loose is, of course, to enable the reader to compare them with any page of text. This end may be attained, and consistently with security, by printing (or mounting) the map on the edge of a leaf of the size of those in the book, so that when it is opened out it is all outside the book.

Plates and maps can of course be published in a separate portfolio. If this is done the text should be printed in a volume of the same size, however absurd it may seem. Otherwise the two will have to be placed on different shelves in the library. In a public library this will double the work of issuing the volumes to readers. In a private library it will probably result sooner or later, perhaps at a sale, in the divorce of the two, which will wander thenceforward separately through the world, imperfect, unhonoured, and useless.

20. Bibliographically, *end-papers* and *dust-jackets* are not truly parts of the book. They do not form a part of any of the sheets on which the book is printed and they can, without undue difficulty, be easily and permanently separated from the book. It is important that, in neither instance, should they contain any matter of importance which is not contained in the book itself. Dust-jackets, to which so much time and money is now devoted in current book-production, are purely advertising media and should be treated as such.

READING LIST

LIST A

CHAMBERS' ENCYCLOPEDIA. Articles on "Printing", "Printing ink", "Typography".

ENCYCLOPEDIA BRITANNICA. Articles on "Calligraphy", "Printing", "Printing type", "Typography".

LIST B

BIGGS, John R. An approach to type. 1949.

COWELL, W. S. *Ltd*. A handbook of printing types. 1947.

EDE, Charles *ed*. The art of the book. 1951.

JENNETT, Seán. The making of books. 1951.

McLEAN, Ruari. Modern book design. 1951.

MORISON, Stanley. The typographic arts. 1949.

NEWDIGATE, B. H. Art of the book. 1938.

SIMON, Oliver. An introduction to typography. 1945.

UNWIN, *Sir* Stanley. The truth about publishing. 5th ed. 1947.

WHETTON, Harry *ed*. Practical printing and binding. 1946.

Students should also study recent volumes of the *Penrose Annual*; examples of modern type-specimen books; and a file of the periodical *Signature*.

IV

LANDMARKS IN THE HISTORY OF PRINTING
AND PUBLISHING

THE INVENTION OF PRINTING

Printing from movable types was invented in China, preceding the European invention by four centuries. The employment of wood-blocks for printing in the Far East was even more in advance of its European use. In the absence of definite evidence of dependence of Western inventors upon Eastern models or reports it is not possible to say more than that there had always been overland trade routes, however slow and indirect, and connection therefore is not impossible.

Wood-block printing had been practised in Western Europe for textiles, playing cards, figures of saints, and so forth, for perhaps a century before the invention of typography. Surviving cuts, dated in the years round 1420, induced the belief that the "block-books", or books printed from woodcuts, were of the same date and that they were a stepping-stone to typography, but this is most probably not true. They exist in four forms: rudimentary "block-books", in which the cuts are (1) merely pasted or (2) directly stamped into spaces in MS. books; (3) books in which the woodcut text and figures are

printed on only one side of the leaf ("anopistho-
graphic") and in writing ink which has turned brown
with age; (4) books printed on both sides of the leaf
in printer's ink. The mass of block-books are datable
from 1460 to 1480 and no date earlier than 1460
can be certainly assigned to any example of this class
of printing. Moreover, typography took its rise
among workers in metal, and it is not likely that between them and the quite separate craft of workers in
wood there was much communication. The advantage of the block-book was that a book of which frequent unaltered editions were wanted (especially if it
were freely illustrated, like the scenes from the life of
Christ called the *Biblia Pauperum*), could be reproduced without the labour of fresh setting of type. It
is curious that block-printing was not perfected for
this purpose, which is that fulfilled by the modern
processes of stereotyping and electrotyping. In the
fifteenth century the output of block-books appears
to have been almost wholly German and Netherlandish, but in the early sixteenth France produced
at least one and Venice a few. All are books of
popular instruction, and the latest examples known
are of about 1517.

A woodcut text can always be distinguished from
one which is type-set by its variant, joined or over-
hanging letters, and other irregularities.

The frequent suggestion which sees in the Renaissance a source of inspiration for the introduction
of printing from movable type into Europe is largely
discounted. The motives of the inventors were

purely practical: to give the book-buying public what it wanted in greater quantity and at a lower price than before. There is not the slightest reason to suppose that they knew anything of the Renaissance in Italy. There are, indeed, reasonable refutations of any such theory. In the first place, they were inventors, but that did not make them prophets as well. The fall of Constantinople, which, if it did not create, certainly gave body to the Renaissance, occurred in May 1453: by this time the art of printing was in its preparatory stage and possibly even being practised. Secondly, attention should be paid to the books they first printed: Bibles, Church Service books, old standard theological treatises, Indulgences, tell their own tale.

The actual invention is still surrounded by obscurity, and has given rise to an immense, very technical, and too often highly controversial and prejudiced, body of writing.

In spite of the assertions of several eminent scholars in the later decades of the last century, it now seems highly improbable that typography sprang directly from xylography. Wood-workers and metal-workers were organized, and closely organized, in quite separate guilds, and had little contact.

The problem was to produce a printing surface which could be used again and again, and which could be built up without the labour of cutting out the letters every time. Towards this end there had long existed the art of casting "formae", or, as we say, "formes", slabs of metal with designs and lettering

in relief. The next stage would be to stamp
punches, a letter or line at a time, into clay or
founders' sand at first, but later, more probably,
using some soft metal like copper in which the depth
of the punch was easier to control. Into the mould so
formed molten metal could be poured, producing
the printing surface. The process, somewhat akin to
stereotyping, was, it is thought, called *jet en moule*;
we can call it metallography or cast-printing.

Clear allusions to printing by *jet en moule* are
found in the *mémoriaux* of Jean le Robert, Abbot of
Saint-Aubert at Cambrai, who in 1445 and 1451 recorded the purchase at Bruges and Arras of copies of
the Doctrinale "gette en molle". The Arras copies,
he complained, were very inaccurately printed, but
here is further evidence of the circulation of these
cast-printed books, and, what is more, two exact
dates. Some writers have identified the Abbot's pur-
chases with the "Costeriana", or typographically
produced Dutch books, to be mentioned later, of
which many fragments survive: but this seems less
likely.

As early as 1436, we know that Gutenberg himself
was at work at Strassburg on an invention, which,
however carefully he and his associates concealed its
nature, involved a press and must have had to do
with printing. Our knowledge is derived from the
records of a law-suit of 1439, which allege that
Gutenberg had been in partnership with a certain
Andres Dritzehen. It may well have been from
Strassburg that the knowledge of how to produce

cast-printed books spread. If so, it spread not only to the Netherlands and to Mainz but also to the South of France. From contracts and receipts for the money involved, we know that at Avignon between 1444 and 1446 a Bohemian goldsmith, named Procopius Waldfoghel, was engaged in an occupation (*ars scribendi artificialiter*) which sounds like printing. Waldfoghel, who, from his previous career, may well have met Gutenberg's Strassburg partner, worked in conjunction with one Girard Ferrose of Trèves. They possessed alphabets (including Hebrew letters) cut in steel and iron, as well as formes (*formas ad artem scribendi pertinentes*) of iron and tin. The letters, to judge by the hardness of the metals employed, must have been punches; the formes were probably cast blocks from which impressions could be taken, perhaps on to materials, or bindings or, possibly, paper. No fragment which is identifiable as printed from one of them survives.

One much-debated group of typographically printed books has been held, but with their primitive appearance as the sole proof, to precede the first achievements in Mainz.

In Holland, to judge by the type forms and the provenance of fragments, were produced a number of undated and very rudely printed editions, as already mentioned, of the famous Latin grammars of the Middle Ages, those of Donatus and Alexander Gallus (the Doctrinale). These appear to be earlier than the first datable Dutch incunabula, those printed at Utrecht in 1473 by Ketelaer and Leempt.

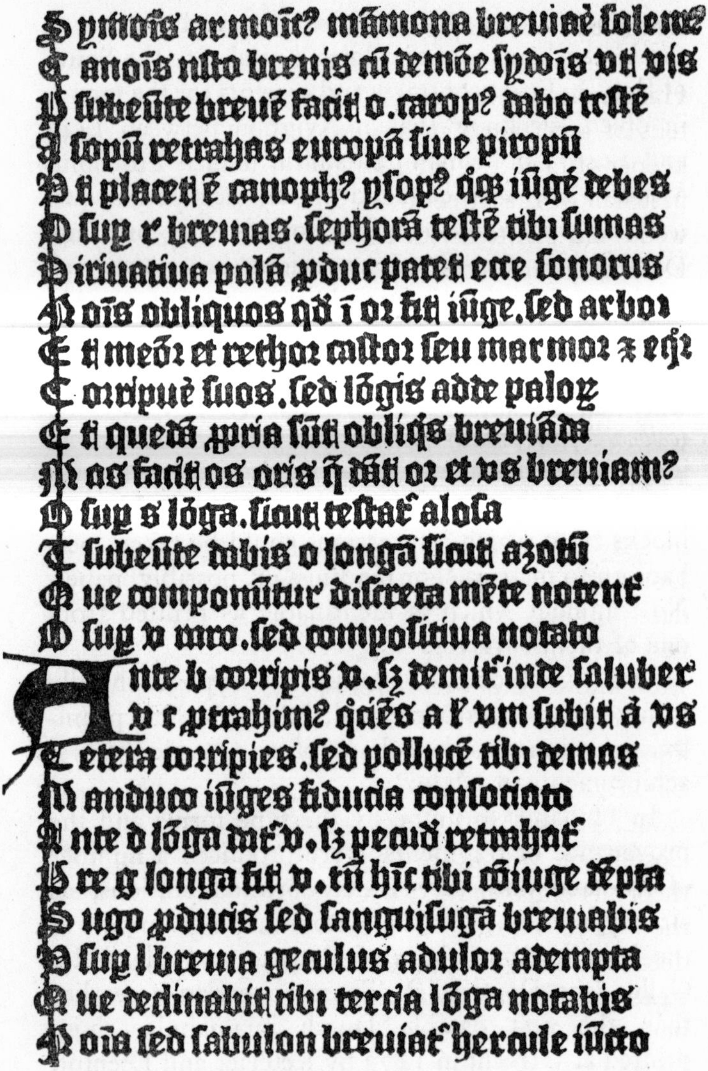
Synthosis ac moie? mãmona breuiarẽ solent
Canois nsto breuis cũ demõe sydois vel vis
P subeũte breuẽ facit o. carop? dabo testẽ
Esopũ retrahas europã siue piropũ
D t placet ẽ canoph? ysop? q̃s iũgẽ debes
O sup r breuias. sephorã testẽ tibi sumas
Diriuatiua palã pduc patet ecce sonorus
Nois obliquos qd ĩ or fit iũge. sed arbor
Et meõr et rethor castor seu marmor ⁊ eõr
Corripuẽ suos. sed lõgis adde palorẽ
Et queda ppria sunt obliqs breuiãda
Nas facit os oris q̃ dãt or et vs breuiam?
O sup s lõga. sicut testat alosa
T subeũte dabis o longã sicut azotũ
Que componũtur discreta mẽte notent
O sup v raro. sed compositiua notato
Ante b corripis v. sz demit inde saluber
Vt r ptrahũn? qñes a l vm subit ã vs
Cetera corripies. sed pollucẽ tibi demas
Manduco iũges fiducia consociato
Ante d lõga dat v. sz pecud retrahat
Vre g longa fit v. tñ hic tibi cõiuge depta
Sugo pducis sed sanguisugã breuiabis
O sup l breuia geculus adulor adempta
Que declinabit tibi tercia lõga notabis
Nois sed sabulon breuiat hercule iusto

FIG. 3.—"COSTERIANUM" (ALEXANDER GALLUS, "DOCTRINALE").

These editions may possibly be the productions of a real person concealed behind the legend retailed by Hadrianus Junius in his *Batavia* (1588). Junius tells of a certain Laurens Janszoon Coster, an innkeeper of Haarlem (such a person existed there in the first half of the fifteenth century), who cut letters in wood and printed with them. These Donatuses and Doctrinalia are accordingly known as Costeriana. An earlier and more important reference possibly to these books is a passage in the *Cologne Chronicle* (1499), quoting Ulric Zel, the first Cologne printer, who had presumably gone there from Mainz (he was described as a *clericus Morguntinensis*) in about 1464. Zel's testimony was to the effect that Mainz printing had come into being towards 1440, but had had a "Vurbyldung", or prefiguration, in some Donatuses printed in the Netherlands before that date. Junius's story that Coster's servant stole and fled with his types is hardly convincing to anyone who knows the weight of types and the rate of travelling in the fifteenth century. But Zel must have known Gutenberg, and the story in the *Cologne Chronicle* sounds likely enough, if we identify the Donatuses with the *gettes en molle*, and not with the Costeriana, which are probably later in date. This theory is enhanced if we allow the possibility (as in the "1468" Oxford imprint) of an error here of a decade and if we suppose that Zel gave 1450 and not 1440 as the date of Mainz printing. This would be a date which more nearly suits the surviving books and documents, and also covers the fact that Gutenberg was at Strassburg at least as late as 1442.

Whatever may be the uncertainties as to the place of the actual invention of movable type printing in Europe, it is certain that it was the printers in Mainz who made it capable of great things. In their hands the forme was for the first time built up of letters separately cast. The difficulty must have been to cast so small an object as a single type.

Gutenberg's invention or improvement of the art must be pieced together from a combination of legal documents and surviving pieces of printing. Amongst these latter special mention must be made of the so-called "Cracow fragments", the study of which has so fundamentally changed our knowledge of the early Mainz printers.

In 1455, Johann Fust, a goldsmith, sought by law to recover from Johann Gutenberg two loans of 800 guilders each which he had made him in 1450 and 1452. The purpose of the loans, on Gutenberg's statement, being for maintenance and all expenses while perfecting the art of printing. The security for the loans was the printing apparatus, which, on Gutenberg's default, would pass to Fust.

Before August 24, 1456, appeared the first substantial printed book, for on that date Henricus Cremer, Vicar of St. Stephen's at Mainz, finished rubricating a copy of a great folio Bible. This work is known as "the Mazarin Bible", from the library where it was first noticed or, more commonly now, as "the 42-line Bible" from the number of lines of text on a normal full page. The copy which Cremer rubricated is now in the Bibliothèque Nationale.

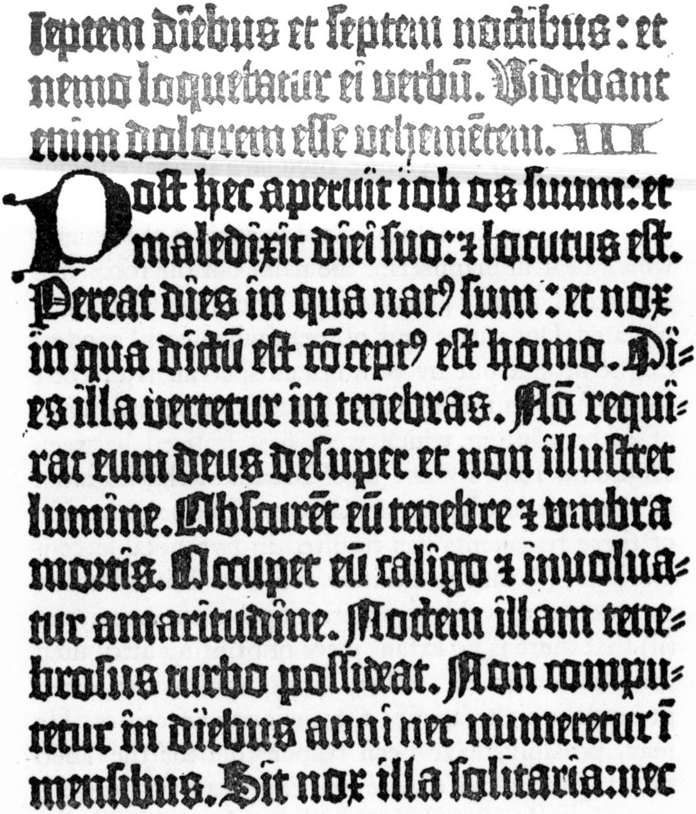

septem diebus et septem noctibus: et nemo loquebatur ei verbū. Videbant enim dolorem esse vehementem. III

Post hec aperuit iob os suum: et maledixit diei suo: z locutus est. Pereat dies in qua nat⁹ sum: et nox in qua dictū est rōceptꝰ est homo. Dies illa vertetur in tenebras. Nō requirat eum deus desuper et non illustret lumine. Obscurēt eū tenebre z vmbra mortis. Occupet eū caligo z inuoluatur amaritudine. Noctem illam tenebrosus turbo possideat. Non computetur in diebus anni nec numeretur ī mensibus. Sit nox illa solitaria: nec

FIG. 4.—PART OF A COLUMN OF THE 42-LINE BIBLE.

There is no doubt now that this book was produced by Gutenberg's former servant, Peter Schoeffer, now in the service of Fust. Fust and Schoeffer's names appear together in the following year in the first printed colophon, that to the fine Psalter of 1457, which is distinguished by its colour-printed capitals. Fust was no doubt only a financier (and a very trusting one, to have speculated in Gutenberg): Schoeffer must have been very young at the time, since he did not die till 1502.

Earlier than the 42-line Bible are several editions of an Indulgence issued to those who should make gifts of money to help in the war against the Turks, which bear in manuscript the names of the recipients and dates in 1454 and 1455. There are also some undated Donatuses and other small pieces, such as might be put out by printers as specimens of their work. Among these smaller pieces are the fragments of early printing which were first noticed between 1834 and 1858 by Dr. Josef Muczkowski, librarian of the Jagellon library in Cracow. The examination of these fragments has resulted in two notable conclusions; (i) that *no* positive evidence exists for any product of movable type printing before 1454, and (ii) that there is no extant piece of printing attributed to Gutenberg on either typographical or other grounds which satisfies the majority of critics. He may, possibly, have been responsible for the 1460 printing of Balbus *Catholicon*. This bears no printer's name but glorifies God and Mainz for the invention of printing. A part of the colophon translates, "printed at Mainz in 1460 with the help of the Most High . . . who oft-times reveals to the lowly that which he hides from the wise". It is often accepted that this refers to Gutenberg and the invention of printing and that it is language which suits the use by the inventor rather than by anyone else.

THE SPREAD OF PRINTING

The event which contributed largely to the spread of printing from Mainz was the sack of the city in October 1462. From this date onward German printers, including many who had connections with Mainz, were taking the art of printing throughout Germany and, subsequently, throughout Europe. Two German cities, however, had begun printing before 1462. In about 1460 Johann Mentelin printed the third Bible at Strassburg and that town became a centre of considerable importance. Many of the early books are uninteresting until the Renaissance produced there, towards the end of the century, some delightfully illustrated classics such as Terence. Mentelin was followed by his son-in-law and associate, Adolf Rusch, and between them they began to use types which showed some tendency towards Roman. At Bamberg Albrecht Pfister used the type of the 36-line Bible, the second of the two great early Bibles and believed to have been printed by Gutenberg, in order to produce a group of small illustrated books to which it was not suited. These popular works, in which Pfister specialized, begin to appear about 1461. Many of them had woodcut illustrations, an experiment which was not imitated for another decade. At Cologne Ulric Zel, already mentioned as the authority for the Netherlandish

"Vurbyldung" of Mainz printing, established himself in 1464, and founded the local speciality of printing theological quartos, mostly mere pamphlets. In Augsburg (from 1468), Nuremberg (from 1470), and Ulm (from 1472) there was much use of woodcut illustrations and decorative capitals, both no doubt originally intended to be the groundwork for colours applied by hand, but most pleasing when left in black and white. At Nuremberg, Anton Koberger (from 1472) developed an enormous business as both printer and publisher. Basel had, in the person of Amerbach, a scholar printer and friend of scholars, and in the next century became one of the great centres of learned printing.

In 1465 two Germans, both citizens of Mainz, Conrad Sweynheim and Arnold Pannartz, carried printing into Italy. An imaginative description of the journey of the two printers may be read in Charles Reade's *The Cloister and the Hearth*. They produced, at the Benedictine Abbey of Subiaco, in the hills above Tivoli, on their way to Rome, four books, of which an edition of Lactantius bears the earliest exact date (Fig. 5). It is printed in a gothic type which is at least half way on the road to Rome, and it is the first book containing Greek type.

Sweynheim and Pannertz established themselves at Rome in 1467 and started printing the *editiones principes* of classical authors from the manuscripts which scholars were discovering. But, like many of their followers, they overestimated the demand and fell into financial difficulties. Printing was introduced

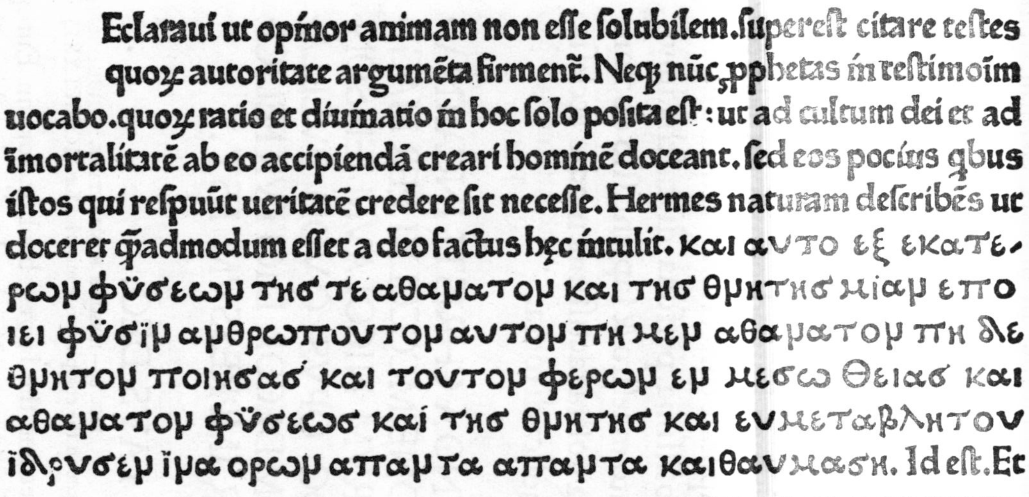

Eclaraui ut opinor animam non effe folubilem. fupereſt citare teſtes quoɽ autoritate argumēta firmēt. Neɋ nūc ɸpphetas in teſtimoim uocabo. quoɽ ratio et diuinatio in hoc folo poſita eſt: ut ad cultum dei ex ad immortalitarē ab eo accipiendā creari hominē doceant. fed eos potius ɋbus iſtos qui refpuiit ueritatē credere fit neceſſe. Hermes naturam deſcribēs ut doceret ɋadmodum effet a deo factus hec intulit. και αυτο εξ εκατε, ϼον φυϲεων τηϲ τε αθαματον και τηϲ θμητηϲ μιαμ εττο ιει φυϲ ῒμ αμθϼωποντουτον αυτομ πη μεϼ αθα ματομ πη δε θμητον ποιηϲαϲ και τουτον φεϼωμ εμ μεϲω θειαϲ και αθαματον φυϲεωϲ και τηϲ θμητηϲ και τηϲ θμητηϲ ευμετταϼλμτον ιδ,ονϲεϼ ῒμα οϼομ απταμ τα απταμ τα καιθαν ιλαϲη. ld eſt. Et

FIG. 5.—THE FIRST BOOK PRINTED IN ITALY, THE SECOND IN ROMAN TYPE, AND ONE OF THE EARLIEST TO CONTAIN GREEK TYPE.

"LACTANTIUS", SUBIACO, SWEYNHEIM AND PANNARTZ, 1465

into Venice in 1469, by another German, John of
Speier; but the chief figures in printing at Venice

io in alcuna coſſa haueſſe p ignorãtia
o per inaduertentia manchato traſfor⁄
mato:ouer incompoſitamente,pferto
ueramente rechiedo perdono ſempre
ſopponendoui ad ogni ſpirituale &
temporale correctione de qualunque
diuotiſſima perſona di zaſchaduno
perito maeſtro & ſapientiſſio doctore
de la uoſtra ſãctiſſima madre eccleſia
catholica di roma.

ANNO A CHRISTI INCARNA⁄
TIONE.MCCCCLXI.PER MAGI⁄
STRVM NICOLAVM IENSON
HOC OPVS QVOD PVELLA⁄
RVM DECOR DICITVR FELICI⁄
TER IMPRESSVM EST.

LAVS DEO.

FIG. 6.—JENSON'S ROMAN TYPE.
(The date in the colophon is a misprint for MCCCCLXXI.)

(which became the largest book factory in Europe)
were a Frenchman, Nicolas Jenson (working there

from 1470), formerly master of the mint at Tours, and famous for cutting a most beautiful roman type, which has had much influence on later founts (Fig. 6), and a native Italian, Aldo Manuzio, commonly called Aldus. He was the founder of the family and the press bearing his name, and also the inventor of the dolphin and anchor device which marks an "Aldine". After printing from 1495 onwards a number of Greek and Latin books, including a splendid Aristotle and the *Hypnerotomachia Poliphili* of Francesco Colonna (1499), with its wonderful woodcut pictures, Aldus began in 1501 (with a Virgil) to print the long series of pocket classics by which his name is best known. It was for this last series that he caused to be cut the first italic type.

The first generation in Italy saw many wandering printers, who printed a book here and a book there. In Florence from 1476 printing in Greek types was carried on, and between 1490 and 1510 Florentine presses produced a very large number of small quartos illustrated with charming woodcuts of a well-marked local style.

The first press in France was academic, and the first type accordingly was roman. In 1470, at the invitation of two professors of the Sorbonne, Heynlyn and Fichet, a press was set up in the Sorbonne itself by three German printers, Gering, Crantz, and Friburger. Three years later, Guillaume le Roy started printing romances and other popular books at Lyons. Later, the printing of vernacular books spread to Paris, where the most prolific printer for this market, Antoine Vérard, produced a series of romances of chivalry of which copies on vellum, decorated like manuscripts, but rather coarsely, were bought by the thrifty Henry VII and are now in the British Museum. The most distinctive feature of Paris books in the last two decades of the fifteenth century is the large device, with short title above and publisher's imprint below, which is constantly found on title-pages. The printer, who here began to be differentiated from the publisher, printed his imprint, as hitherto, in the colophon. Paris became (with Venice) the great centre for printing service books, and had almost a monopoly of Hours of the Virgin, and (notably for English bibliographers) of those of the use of Sarum; the most finely decorated Hours were those from the press of Philippe Pigouchet. The English market was also being served at the same time by the presses of Rouen.

Books for the English market were equally a work of the Antwerp press, especially that of Gerard Leeu. The date for the introduction of printing into the Low Countries depends upon the interpretation of "Costeriana", but the date usually accepted is 1473, when printing begins in Utrecht and Alost.

Doubt also surrounds the date of the earliest printing in Spain, but it is possibly as early as 1473. Throughout the fifteenth century, however, the output of the Spanish press remains small. The only certainty is that Spain, like so many other European countries, received printing at the hands of German craftsmen.

120

THE FIRST CENTURY OF ENGLISH PRINTING

One of the earliest books printed in French, and the earliest in English, were produced by William Caxton at Bruges; they were the *Quatre Dernières Choses* (1475) and Caxton's translation (1474) of the *Recueil des Histoires de Troye* (Fig. 7).

Of all the prototypographers we are naturally most interested in Caxton, and he was in fact a more striking figure than the men who introduced printing into Italy, France or Spain in that he was a public man, a man of letters, and an amateur.

Caxton had established himself in the Sanctuary of Westminster Abbey by the end of 1476, and began, as most printers did, by printing some small pieces while larger works were preparing. A copy of one of these, an indulgence printed for John Sant, Abbot of Abingdon, was identified in 1928 in the Public Record Office. It is filled up in pen and ink to Henry Langley and his wife Katherine, and is dated partly in print and partly in manuscript, December 13, 1476. Caxton's first substantial book printed in England and dated was the *Dictes or Sayengis of the Philosophres*, November 18, 1477, like the Troy book a translation from the French, though not by Caxton himself. Although it is possible that the *Dictes* may have been preceded by the undated translation of the romance of Jason, the lapse of time from Michaelmas 1476, when Caxton took his lease from the Abbey, shows how slow were the preliminaries in setting up a press in a country where none existed.

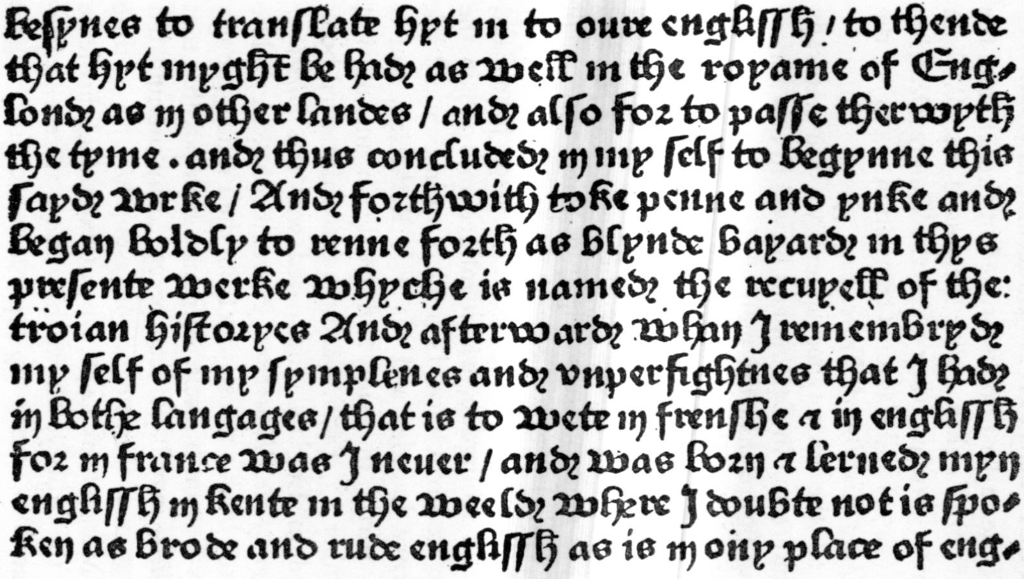
besynes to translate hyt in to oure englissh / to thende
that hyt myght be had as well in the royame of Eng-
lond as in other landes / and also for to passe therwyth
the tyme . and thus concluded in my self to begynne this
sayd werke / And forthwith toke penne and ynke and
began boldly to renne forth as blynde bayard in thys
presente werke whyche is named the recuyell of the
troian historyes And afterward whan I remembryd
my self of my symplenes and vnperfightnes that I had
in bothe langages / that is to wete in frensshe & in englissh
for in france was I neuer / and was born & lerned myn
englissh in kente in the weeld where I doubte not is spoken as brode and rude englissh as is in ony place of eng-

FIG. 7.—PART OF PAGE OF CAXTON'S PREFACE TO "RECUYELL OF THE HISTORIES OF TROYE".

(Printed in bastard letter.)

Caxton's output till 1491, when he died, consisted largely of romances, varied by devotional books, which were assured of a sale. As George Parker Winship pointed out, "his venture, even though it was intended primarily for his own purposes, did not cost him more than need be". The most famous works printed by him were Chaucer's *Canterbury Tales* (two editions, 1478 and [1484?], from different MSS.); Malory's *Morte d'Arthur*, 1485; Gower's *Confessio Amantis*, 1483; poems by John Lydgate; *Reynard the Fox*, 1481; *Aesop's Fables*, 1484; *The Golden Legend, or Lives of the Saints* [1483], and more than one English chronicle. The debt of English literature to Caxton is thus very great. What more he may have printed, of which no copy has come down to us, can only be guessed. A very high proportion of his books exists in single copies and fragments, since they were popular and, consequently, copies were worn out. It is hard to believe that he did not print the travels of Mandeville.

Caxton's press was carried on from his death till 1534 by his foreman, Wynkyn de Worde. Caxton's work is primitive and suggestive of the manuscript; much of de Worde's was frankly bad and suggestive of nothing but cheapness. The eight hundred or so pieces which he produced in his forty years of independent activity, do not really imply great productivity, since with rare exceptions they are hardly more than pamphlets, and a large number, such as the stock Latin grammars of the day, were printed over and over again. But those which survive are so

123

rare that many more must have been lost, and with them doubtless much attractive early Tudor verse.

Meanwhile, in 1478–1487, Theodoric Rood printed, at first in a Cologne type, a few academic books at Oxford, the first, S. Jerome (or rather Tyrannius Rufinus) on the Apostles' Creed, having the date misprinted MCCCCLXVIII for MCCCCLXXVIII and thereby appearing to give Oxford priority over Westminster in English printing. Classical and scholarly books, however, could be produced much more cheaply and accurately by the well-equipped presses of such towns as Lyons and Venice, and for a century and more classical printing was only sporadic in England. Oxford had two other short-lived presses (Scolar and Kyrforth) in 1517–1519, and Cambridge one (Siberch) in 1521–1522; but printing was only permanently established in the Universities in 1584 (Cambridge, T. Thomas) and 1585 (Oxford, J. Barnes). The Cambridge press was set up under the University's printing charter of 1534.

A law-press had been set up in London in Caxton's time; the printers were John Lettou (the Lithuanian) and his partner William Machlinia (of Mechlin or Malines), 1480–1491; they were succeeded by Richard Pynson, a Norman, who printed from 1490 till 1529 or 1530, and was a much better printer than de Worde, varying his style and achieving some dignity: he was appointed Royal Printer in 1508 and introduced roman type in 1509, a result of his closer connection with Continental printers.

In 1480–1486 the schoolmaster of the Abbey School at St. Albans printed a few books, and deserves mention here on account of the celebrity of one of them, "the Bokys of Haukyng and Huntyng, and also of Cootarmuris" [i.e. heraldry], 1486, generally called *The Book of St. Albans* and attributed to a certain unknown Dame Juliana Barnes or Berners; he got his type from Caxton.

Printing appeared sporadically in various English provincial towns in the first half of the sixteenth century, but nowhere for long or to very much effect; John Oswen, who printed at Ipswich in 1548 and at Worcester in 1549–1552, and was skilful enough to print the first Prayer Book of Edward VI, was the chief provincial printer. In London, Thomas Berthelet (1528–1554), who was also Royal binder, printed large quantities of the law Year Books; but the most distinguished work was done by Richard Grafton, who made free use of a very pretty italic, and Reynald Wolfe, who was Royal printer for Latin, Greek, and Hebrew, and introduced Greek printing into England in 1543, whereas to 1520 Siberch at Cambridge had had to have Richard Croke's *Introductiones in rudimenta Græca* printed abroad.

The first books printed in Scotland were a number of poetical pieces, surviving in one copy in the National Library of Scotland, which came in 1507 from the press of Walter Chepman and Andrew Myllar; the latter had in 1505 and 1506 editions of Garlandia, *Multorum verborum interpretatio* and the *Expositio sequentiarum Sarum*, printed for him at

125

Rouen, the Sarum book bearing the most decorative "rebus" device (Fig. 8) used in this island, except

FIG. 8.—DEVICE OF SCOTLAND'S FIRST PRINTER, 1506.

Grafton's tree or "graft" springing from a tun; it was, no doubt, cut by a Rouennese or Parisian artist. Scottish printing did not reach any great competence

126

till the latter half of the sixteenth century; it is worth noticing that (as a glance through the earlier pages of H. G. Aldis's list of Scottish books printed before 1700 will show) few reprints of English books came from Scottish presses.

LATER FOREIGN PRINTING

The sixteenth century on the Continent was the age of the scholar-printer-publisher. Josse Bade, of Aasche, better known as Iodocus Badius Ascensius (and his press as the "prelum Ascensianum", figured in woodcut devices), printed a number of scholarly works, perhaps without high technical distinction; but he was the father-in-law of two famous learned printers, Michel Vascosan and Robert Estienne, and through the latter connected with a third, Simon de Colines (Colinæus). This group of men completely converted French book-buyers from the mediæval to the Renaissance taste in printing, that is from the rich and heavy effects of gothic to the light effects of roman with woodcuts designed to match. Nor were they mere imitators of Italian models, though they were influenced by them both directly and through the designer, Geofroy Tory, whose *Champ Fleury*, 1529, studies the theory of proportion and beauty in lettering in the new manner, and who took from Aldus the idea of publishing cheap editions of Greek and Latin classics for students. François I was the active patron of good printing as of the other arts, and saved Robert Estienne, who leant to the Reformed Church, from

127

persecution till the King's death in 1547, after which
(in 1550) the Estiennes had to remove to Geneva.
François also promoted Greek and Latin printing
by his foundation in 1530 of the Collège de France
and its professorships. The Estiennes (Stephani, or
anglice Stephens) were themselves scholars, and
edited or wrote some of the most important works
they printed. Robert wrote the *Thesaurus linguæ
Latinæ*, 1532, and Henri the *Thesaurus Græcæ
linguæ*, 1572; but the latter's best-known work
today is the anecdotic *Apologie pour Herodote*. The
family device, introduced by Robert, is an olive-tree.

The only French city to vie with Paris was Lyons.
Early printing here had been vernacular. But trade-
routes connected Lyons, at the head of the navigable
Rhone, more closely with Basel and with the Mediterranean than with Paris. Basel had early had in
Johann von Amerbach (printed 1478–1512) a
printer who was a friend of the men of the new
learning, notably of Sebastian Brant, author of *The
Ship of Fools*, and Erasmus's friend and publisher,
Johann Froben or Frobenius (printed 1491–1527),
who had been in Amerbach's service, carried on the
tradition. Accordingly, we find Renaissance scholarship in such printers as Sebastian Gryphius (d. 1556),
who printed small texts in the Aldine style with his
griffin in place of the dolphin and anchor; Etienne
Dolet, who was hanged for heresy in 1546; and Jean
de Tournes. De Tournes was distinguished as a publisher by issuing the works of the Lyonnese literary
set, notably the poetess Louise Labé, and as a

printer by his use of magnificent arabesque title-borders and tail-pieces strongly suggestive of metal lantern-supports (*culs-de-lampes*).

In Italy the house of the Aldi, as the Manuzio family of Venice were called, carried on the business till the end of the sixteenth century, though with less originality than the founder had shown. The Giunti, who had begun at Venice in the fifteenth century, printed mainly at Florence in the earlier and middle sixteenth century, and the Florentine lily, their device, is the mark of sound work (as the Sessas' cat is of bad); they hardly rivalled in excellence of workmanship the Florentine ducal printer, Lorenzo Torrentino, but they were important for the quantity of solid work, as well as imitations of Aldines, which they turned out. With them should be studied Gabriel Giolito of Ferrara, who printed at Venice from 1539 to 1578, had bookshops at Naples, Bologna, and Ferrara, and specialized in decorated books.

Spanish printing, though it does not boast a figure like these, unless it be Coci of Saragossa, has a remarkably constant national quality which makes it interesting. Even when the types are roman the feeling is mediæval. A page of a Spanish book of the fifteenth or sixteenth century, especially if decorated, has a rich, sombre, and stately appearance which is unknown in the productions of other countries, but which is consonant with the other arts in Spain in that period. The greatest single achievement of a Spanish press is the polyglot Complutensian

E

Bible printed at Alcalá de Henares (Complutum) in 1514–1517 by Arnald Guillen de Brocar under the patronage of Cardinal Ximenez.

Almost the first really good printing done in the Low Countries was that of Christophe Plantin, a French bookbinder by origin, who settled at Antwerp and in 1555 commenced work as a printer and publisher. He obtained patents for printing for the Spanish authorities and produced many service books, but also many large and handsome illustrated works in the sciences; his most ambitious production was the polyglot Bible of 1572. Plantin's house was the resort of learned men, and continued to be a successful publishing office till the nineteenth century in the family of his son-in-law Moretus. It is now, as mentioned in an earlier chapter, a museum, full of the archives and material of the sixteenth-century printer, and a place of pilgrimage to the bibliographer.

A little later than Plantin there arose in Holland a family of printers and publishers who, with less learning but more business instinct, repeated the success of Aldus. These were the Elzevirs of Leyden (Lugdunum Batavorum), and later of Utrecht and Amsterdam also. Louis, the founder, began at Leyden in 1580, but the next two generations were the more famous, especially Bonaventure. They were excellent men of business and produced handy books, both texts of the classics and books of reference, such as those on the different countries, entitled *Respublica* so-and-so. They employed scholars to edit the books,

130

but without contributing much, if anything, to scholarship. Nor are Elzevirs pretty or easy to read. Their vogue in their own time may possibly be accounted for by the amount of time which courtiers had to spend waiting in ante-rooms, which could be beguiled by reading pocket volumes in the window-embrasures. They are frequently referred to in general books on book-collecting but they are not now so highly prized as formerly.

In its long-term effect, one of the main events of the seventeenth century must be the establishment of a permanent press in North America. The earliest press to be set up anywhere on the American continent had been that of Juan Pablos in Mexico City in 1539. Juan Cromberger, a leading printer of Seville, had been commissioned by the Spanish Archbishop in Mexico to print a catechism in the Nahuatl dialect. Work began in Seville but, in order to complete it satisfactorily, Cromberger decided to establish a press among the people for whom the book was designed. Accordingly, he despatched Pablos to accomplish this and from 1539 till 1560 a number of works issued from this press. Although printing spread widely throughout Spanish America, it was a century later, in North America, where the art developed the most.

Stephen Day, a locksmith of Cambridge, England, arrived at Boston, Massachusetts, in September 1638. In that same month, an earlier pilgrim, John Harvard, had died, leaving his books, about 300 in number, to the College at Newtown. The College took Harvard's name and Newtown was renamed Cambridge. It was there that, in 1639, Stephen Day set up his press and issued his first works, the *Freeman's Oath* and an *Almanack*. No copies of these are extant and a 1640 printing of *The Whole Book of Psalmes faithfully Translated into English Metre*, known as "The Bay Psalm Book", is the first book of which any copies are known. Some years later, two printers who followed Day at Cambridge, Samuel Green and Marmaduke Johnson, printed the translation of the Bible into the Indian language by John Eliot the missionary. The New Testament was issued in 1661 and the whole work, when the Old Testament had been completed, in 1663. For some time to come most of the book trade in North America was carried on by English printers and booksellers, but gradually, and especially after the colonies had declared their independence, it became less firmly attached to the place of its origins. The work of such noted printers and individualists as Benjamin Franklin and Isaiah Thomas did much to establish a purely American tradition in printing and publishing. After the death of Thomas in 1831, the nineteenth century became a period of settling down, and of the growth of large-scale commercial publishing enterprises. Out of this, as in Europe, came the private and fine presses, and the modern American type designers who have contributed so much to the art of the book in our time.

ENGLISH PRINTING FROM 1550

At the end of the reign of Philip and Mary, in 1557, the Company of Stationers of London, a body which had existed since the beginning of the fifteenth century, was incorporated by Royal Charter. In order to concentrate printing under the eye of authority, the Company's members were given the monopoly of printing. The Stationers' Company kept a register of copies and generally controlled the trade. Hence came into existence that foundation-stone of English bibliography, the Register of the Stationers' Company, now available in print from its inception to 1708. As a documentary source of knowledge in the history of books, it is only rivalled by the records of the Guild of Parisian Bookbinders.

In the seventeenth century the Company was harassed by continual edicts limiting the number of printers and type-founders. By a Star Chamber decree of 1637 the number was restricted to 20. After the Commonwealth period the Act of 1662 re-imposed this limit; but in the following year L'Estrange estimated the number of master printers at work in London at 60. Nor, in spite of Milton's *Areopagitica*, was the press any more free during the power of the Parliament men than during that of Laud before or of Sir Roger L'Estrange after. The restriction of printing to London, with all other censorship, apart from that of the common law, lapsed in 1695, and from this period date the earliest permanent provincial presses other than those in the Universities.

England in the sixteenth and seventeenth centuries could boast no figures like Plantin. But largely by the aid of the great antiquary and Church historian Archbishop Matthew Parker, John Day, the printer who printed for Parker as well as on his own account, did work which is not only important on account of the books printed, but is technically accomplished. He cut the first fount of Anglo-Saxon type in about 1566. Otherwise there is little to be proud of in English book-production till the eighteenth century. The small Elizabethan books often have pretty "lace-borders" built up of type-flowers round title-pages generally ruined by variegated types; and Richard Tottell's black-letter octavo law-books have an air, partly contributed by the excellent and large paper on which they are printed; made for him, it bears his mark, the hand and star. The small Jacobean book, too, when not spoilt by engraved frontispiece and title-page, has an amateurish charm consisting of good proportion in the pages, which are often framed in wide-set double rules enclosing marginal notes. William Dugard (1606–1662), the Royalist head master of Merchant Taylors' School, was better than the poor standard of his time. He was imprisoned for printing in 1650 Salmasius's *Defensio regia pro Carolo primo*.

This was the period of the earliest publishers who were not also printers; one of the first, if not the first, was Humphrey Moseley, who throughout the

Commonwealth and earlier Restoration period issued romances and play-books in quantity. More celebrated publishers succeeded him in the persons of Jacob Tonson (1656?–1736), publisher to Dryden and many other men of letters, of Bernard Lintot (1675–1736), who published for Pope, Gay, and Steele; and of the notorious Edmund Curll (publ. 1706–1747), who, while deserving most of the ill-repute he has, was also a very intelligent publisher. In the next generation Scotland had a very distinguished publishing house in that of the brothers Robert and Andrew Foulis of Glasgow, 1741–1776, which was noted for its scholarly and textually accurate editions of the classics. The publisher begins now for the first time to be an important figure in literature, and we have fortunately in the letters and remains of Swift, Pope, and other writers a mine of knowledge of the trade; but nowhere more so, nor more curious, than in the *Life* of John Dunton, himself a bookseller. From this period date some old surviving firms, such as Messrs. Longmans. But a capital date in the English book-trade is 1672, when John Fell, Dean of Christ Church, was largely responsible for the purchase by The Oxford University Press of the whole range of types and matrices which are usually known by his name. From this beginning developed the great University Press, later called the Clarendon from its acquisition of the copyright of Clarendon's history of the Civil War, out of the profits of which the printing house was built.

From the early sixteenth century increasingly

publishers had shared the cost and the copies of publications, each normally having his name and address printed on the title-pages of his copies. De Worde and Pynson occasionally did this, while another notable early example is the 1542 Chaucer. At the end of the seventeenth century publishers exchanged parts of editions after publication, and in these cases only the first publisher's name will appear on any copy. About 1730 there grew up a regular system of taking shares in a new book; and now all the shareholding publishers' names would appear on all copies. By the end of the century, possibly because publishers were more highly capitalized, the practice was disappearing, and is now dead.

The size of book-papers increases after the Restoration and all the formats therefore naturally differ in general appearance from their earlier counterparts. An Elizabethan octavo is a very small book; one of 1750–1800 is about twice its size. Late in the eighteenth century, there arose (especially among lady readers) a taste for very small books, which were made up in twelves or twenty-fours, and issued in two or more volumes. A return of this fashion might be an agreeable change at the present day.

The early nineteenth century was in many ways the golden age of English publishing and printing, though not of type-design. The country's wealth was greatly increased, and the romantic revival had brought with it a love of the picturesque and an interest in antiquities, producing together not only such futilities as artificial ruins, but also many splendid and useful publications, and notably county histories.

A remarkable English publishing and printing combination of the nineteenth century deserves mention here. This is the alliance of William Pickering, the publisher, with Charles Whittingham the younger, which commenced in 1828. Pickering started early in life as a bookseller, and in 1820 began with Horace his well-known series of "diamond" classics, which it must be confessed are more curious than beautiful, but which served to attract attention to their publisher. Pickering was the first publisher to issue books in cloth casings, with the paper labels which preceded gold-stamped title-blocks.

In 1828 he commissioned work from a young printer, Charles Whittingham the younger, of the Chiswick Press in Tooks Court. This press had been started in 1789 and in 1810 transferred to Chiswick. Whittingham started alone, and adopted the well-known device, based on that of Aldus, of the dolphin and anchor with the legend *"Aldi discipulus Anglus"*. Between them Pickering and Whittingham enormously raised the level of English printing, especially in printing liturgical and semi-antiquarian books, in which fields they owed much to the patronage of Oxford Movement scholars. But the Chiswick Press did all sorts of work well, as it continues to do.

The important influence exercised on English printing by Pickering and Whittingham's revival of Caslon's old-face roman fount will be touched on

137

later, as will the movement in fine printing in this and other countries headed by William Morris, and some important figures in Continental printing.

A feature of the century was the rise of publishing societies. The Royal Society had issued its Philosophical Transactions since 1665 and the Society of Antiquaries the *Archæologia* since 1770; but a crop of antiquarian literary societies came into being, notably the Roxburghe Club (1812), founded by T. F. Dibdin to celebrate the sensational sale of the Duke of Roxburghe's library, and the Bannatyne Club (1823), founded by David Laing and others for printing early Scottish poetry. These were followed by the foundations of that remarkably dynamic scholar Frederick James Furnivall, of which the Early English Text (1864), Chaucer (1867) and New Shakspere (1874) Societies are the chief. These were not quite like the academies of the Continent, which were mostly creations of the seventeenth and eighteenth centuries; they were, and are, a device to secure subscriptions for antiquarian reprints or specialist studies which might not seem a good speculation to the ordinary publisher. They are really only a variety of the publication by open subscription, which, largely owing to Johnson's onslaught on Lord Chesterfield (1755), had taken the place of the earlier system of private patronage.

The present century has seen a remarkable development of publishing, and one which has flourished peculiarly in England, in the various publishers' series. At its best this plan is a very worthy one, making available, and usually at a modest selling price, important books in a uniform publishing style. Following the well-deserved success of some of the earliest examples, such as the *Golden Treasury* series, published by Messrs. Macmillan from 1881, came other now well established favourites such as Dent's *Everyman's Library* and the Oxford University Press's *World's Classics*. No one could doubt the great and beneficial effect of such series on the reading tastes of today. But at the other end of the scale, the success of these series has led other publishers to use it merely as a device for selling books, since the reputation of the successful books in a series is believed to sell other titles which, if separately published, would not succeed. This may be true, and some of these hangers-on have no doubt been books which deserved to be published. But, at the same time, it has produced a vast progeny of worthless books, manufactured at the behest of their publisher and serving no end except to provide him with a "line" with which to compete with other publishers.

Another present-day phenomenon, which cannot be viewed with satisfaction, is the plethora of book clubs of various kinds. These are now legion and their committee-chosen wares are distributed with regularity among a quiescent clientele. As an idea originally to encourage more serious reading in certain sections of the public there may have been some merit in the scheme; but, as they are viewed today, few of the clubs would seem to have any real merit.

A far more successful attempt at encouraging the

wise use of books and an appreciation of them as works of art has been seen in the work of the National Book League. This organization is now an established part of the English book scene and its influence is growing steadily. It can certainly be regarded as one of the formative movements of the present day.

Finally, among the important achievements of the last quarter century must be reckoned the great and deserved success of the Penguin books in all their manifold forms. From the earliest days of printing onwards there has been a continual search for the legible, portable and cheap book. Traditionally, the British reading public is supposed to distrust the paper-backed book. With an impressive range of titles to their credit, many of them specially written for one or other of the series, Penguin Books appear to have overcome this prejudice and have made great writings available in literally enormous quantity. The careful attention which has been devoted to problems of typography and lay-out has ensured a remarkably high standard of production throughout the series.

Type-Faces

1. *Gothic*

Every large district had, in the age of manuscript, its peculiar style of hand, and these fell into the broad classes of cursive, rapid book-hand, and formal book-hand.

The business of the printer was to provide something closely resembling the manuscript book; accordingly, his founts of type reproduce the book-hands of the locality. Generically, these local styles are called *gothic*, or in the descriptive English phrase, "black letter", as opposed to roman or "white letter". It is now usual to divide the early gothic founts into four main classes. First is one representing the formal, pointed, upright scripts reserved for Bibles and service books for choir desks. This category includes the most formal of all the Gothic founts and is called *textura* by the Germans and *lettre de forme* by the French. Second is a smaller and more cursive type used for other Latin books. It retained very marked Gothic qualities but was considerably less formal than *textura*. This second class was known as *fere-humanistica* or *gotico-antiqua* by the Germans and *lettre de somme* by the French. Still less formal, was the third class of *rotunda* types which is largely an Italian style of gothic and shows a much more open quality. Lastly, most cursive of all, used chiefly for books printed in the vernacular, was the *lettre bâtarde* or, in the German, *bastarda*. In Germany there was developed out of *bastarda*, which is cursive, the *fraktur*, a pointed cursive of an unexampled ugliness, which in the sixteenth century ousted the other styles and reigned supreme till the nineteenth century. An extreme case of the length to which the flourish could go in German *fraktur* is seen in the books lavishly printed by Schönsperger at Nuremberg in and about 1517 under the patronage

141

of the Emperor Maximilian II, notably Melchior Pfintzing's *Theuerdank*. It is said that technically such printing was very difficult. One might go further, and, like Dr. Johnson, wish that it had been impossible.

In France and the Southern Netherlands, a local variety of bastard so called (*lettre bâtarde*) was used in the fifteenth century, especially for French vernacular and secular literature. This is the style of Caxton's first founts, both those he used with Colard Mansion at Bruges and his earliest Westminster founts, though the latter were of a more fantastic and pointed kind. The characteristic of true bastard (to use a paradoxical phrase) is that the letters are narrow and slope somewhat as in italic, and that there are more descenders, such as the *f*, ending in a point. The whole effect is strikingly cursive.

Except in Germany, where it has persisted into this present century, gothic was driven out by roman in the course of the first century of printing. In Italy, it was from the beginning excluded from the service of the new learning, though it was used for legal and medical books. Its native form was a rather narrow *rotunda*, except in Naples, where Spanish influence was strong and the typical book of the finer kind showed a rich and stately combination of heavy gothic text and solid black border decorations or woodcut illustrations. In France, gothic was driven out in the third and fourth decades of the sixteenth century by the roman types and

142

correspondingly light decorations of Tory and his pupils and followers. In Spain, in the Netherlands, and in England it lasted longer. Early English black letter had the heaviness and illegibility, without being redeemed by beauty, and it was most unfortunate that Caxton's later types were used and imitated for the next century. It was chiefly for the printing of law books that the use of gothic was retained in England and for the English text when it had to be differentiated from Latin. For these purposes it can frequently be found well into the seventeenth century. After that time it has been largely out of favour and even William Morris failed to restore it to fashion. Although his Troy type was a very fine simplified fount, and there is no doubt that two pages of gothic type, owing to its thick lines, and especially when combined with solid woodcut decorations, are a very handsome spectacle. Unfortunately, to the modern unaccustomed eye, it is not very legible. Nevertheless, it must be pointed out that much of the modern popular antipathy to the Kelmscott Press gothic books, is due to their having been seen mainly through reduced facsimiles rather than in original.

2. *Roman*

Italian humanists in the half-century which preceded the introduction of printing into Italy had been using for classical texts a small book-hand based on the beautiful "caroline minuscule", the hand taught

143

under Alcuin's influence in the schools of Charlemagne. This hand was afterwards called in Italy and France *lettera rotonda*, *lettre ronde*, or round letter, and elsewhere *antiqua*; it is the type we know, and use almost to the exclusion of all others, as *roman*. To the minuscules so designed were added majuscules based on the inscriptions of ancient Rome, and from first to last the finest roman upper-case has always been that which smacked most of its origin.

A humanistic type first appeared in Italy when Sweynheim and Pannartz printed the Lactantius at Subiaco in a type which was rather more roman than *fere-humanistica*. Following soon after this Adolf Rusch used at Strassburg a purer roman and before his recent identification he was known as "The R-Printer" from the distinctive upper-case 'R' which he used in that fount. Germany also produced, among her comparatively few roman types, one of the very finest in that used by Lienhart Holle at Ulm in 1482 to print his magnificent edition of Ptolemy's *Geographia*.

Sweynheim and Pannartz went on in 1467 from Subiaco to Rome, where they used a purely roman fount; but a better design was produced at Venice in 1470 by Nicolas Jenson, a Frenchman, who had been master of the Mint at Tours. This type has often been called the most beautiful ever cut and has been the inspiration of many later roman founts of importance, including William Morris's Golden type, Bruce Rogers's Centaur type and the American

144

Type Founders' Cloister type. Even so, it has probably been less influential than that of Aldus, especially in the improved form in which he employed it for Colonna's *Hypnerotomachia Poliphili* of 1499, a book which deserves to be as celebrated for its type as it is for its woodcuts, and not less for the harmony of the two.

Aldus's roman (and also his italic) was imitated in France about 1530 by Claude Garamond, a pupil of Geofroy Tory, who had studied in Italy. Tory was one of the greatest of all printing craftsmen in the sixteenth century, and in his attractively written book *Champ Fleury* (1529) had made a study of the design of roman letters. The types of Garamond, used by the royal printers of France, together with those of Robert Granjon, both of which were used by the great Antwerp printer Christophe Plantin, dominated type-design in Europe for a couple of centuries.

The most attractive achievements of French printing in the later sixteenth century, the small books printed by Jean de Tournes at Lyons, owe perhaps less to type-design than to his lovely arabesque ornaments, already mentioned. The Wars of Religion threw a blight over French printing, though not so badly as did the Thirty Years War in the next century over German. Louis XIV founded in 1640 the Imprimerie Royale, and made Sebastien Cramoisy the first director. In 1692 Philippe Grandjean cut for it an immensely influential type, the *romain du roi*, in which the movement

145

of the succeeding century towards lightness and the
effect of engraving, which culminates in Bulmer,
Bodoni, and Didot, is already to be seen. But it was
Simon Pierre Fournier, called le jeune, best known
by his *Manuel Typographique* of 1764–[1768] and
by being the first author of the Continental point-
system of measuring types, who designed types with
shading and decoration, adapting them to the engraved vignettes by Eisen, Moreau le jeune, and
others, which characterized the dainty little French
livres à gravures of the eighteenth century.

Roman type had appeared in England in the
hands of Pynson in 1509; it was used for Latin at
first, but by the end of the century it had pretty well
ousted black letter. Except for John Day, few English type-founders deserve praise. In 1672 Dr. John
Fell, anxious to present the University of Oxford
with a printing outfit, had to send emissaries to
Holland, and they, with infinite difficulty, purchased
matrices from Dutch founders. The Fell types are
still in use at the Clarendon Press, and are well
known.

In 1722 William Caslon the First cut for William
Bowyer his very pleasant round roman, resembling
the old Dutch, and not the new French royal model,
and this soon came into general use, only falling out
at the end of the century, to be revived forty years
later as what we call "old-face".

In 1757 appeared the quarto Virgil printed by
John Baskerville of Birmingham, formerly engraver
and writing-master, with types, cut by himself, of

greater lightness and regularity than had before been seen in any English fount. In the following year he was appointed printer to the University of Cambridge, an office which he held for ten years, printing notably a very fine Bible in 1763. His printing was appreciated in France, where it was in the movement set on foot by Grandjean with his *romain du roi* towards a light and engraved appearance of the printed page. After his death Baskerville's types were bought by Beaumarchais together with his stocks of paper and the secret of hot-pressing, and used for printing two editions of Voltaire.

Types of the latter half of the eighteenth century became narrower and lighter, notably in the hair-strokes; serifs lost the air of the pen's first touch on the paper, and were square; the shading and stress of letters was vertical rather than oblique; and types were either cast on bodies much larger than their faces or were extravagantly leaded. This is what we call the "modern face". The first was cut by Didot in 1784; John Bell's (1788) was the first English and the first here not to include the "ſ". The extremes were reached in England by William Bulmer (1757–1830) and Thomas Bensley (died 1833), and abroad by the Didots and Bodoni. Although several of the most important designers of modern-face began work in the eighteenth century, their most violent examples, accentuated by a fattening of the thick strokes, were not cut until well into the nineteenth century. Bulmer, in fact, used old-faced types in the earlier part of his career. The modern-faced

147

style is thought by some to have been influenced by Pine's Horace, 1733, of which the whole, text and all, is engraved. The condensed or narrow style was by now accepted on the Continent, not only in France but in Holland, and notably in the Enschedé foundry at Haarlem. But the great glory of modern face, the "classical" style, was Giambattista Bodoni of Parma. Mr. Updike, in *Printing Types*, speaks of his "great chilly masterpieces"; but they do undoubtedly sort well with the other crafts of the Empire period.

Modern face reigned supreme till towards 1850, when, almost simultaneously in England and in France, there began a revolt against it and a return to the round letter. Charles Whittingham had been in the habit of getting gothic type from the Caslon foundry (which still existed and still exists) for printing for Pickering; and from at least 1840 he got from the same source small quantities of "old-face", the round early eighteenth-century roman cut by William Caslon the First. The first whole book observed as printed in old-face by Whittingham is Herbert's *Temple*, 1844.

In France it fell out rather differently. Louis Perrin of Lyons, being commissioned to print de Boissieu's *Inscriptions antiques de Lyon* (1846–1854), declared that the available Didot types were only fit for printing railway timetables, and by studying the inscriptions which were the matter of the book, designed the beautiful round roman well known to most readers of French literature from its use in the

148

series of classics printed in it for MM. Lemerre. Old-face has not had the success in France that it has in England, and narrow founts are still common. But the present century has seen many experiments in French printing, as in all other civilized countries, and there is now plenty of choice of good, as well as of old-fashioned or excessively new-fashioned, founts.

The revival in England at the end of the century was immediately inspired by the first Arts and Crafts Exhibition of 1888, and by the lecture given at it by Mr. (later Sir) Emery Walker. It probably owed something also, even if less directly, to the Caxton celebrations of 1877. In 1891 William Morris, with Emery Walker's assistance, set up the Kelmscott Press at Hammersmith. In the next seven years, in fact till Morris's death, they printed a noble series of books, in which Morris's genius for design found play. His Chaucer is possibly the most splendid book ever printed in England. Morris hated the Renaissance, and after his first type (the "Golden"), which was based on Jenson's roman, he went back to German gothic, which gave a richer effect, especially when enclosed in his elaborately designed woodcut borders. The Kelmscott Gothic was a simplified *fere-humanistica*, the simplest form of gothic to start with, in two sizes, called respectively after the books they were cut for, the "Troy" and "Chaucer" types.

Morris was the first to enunciate clearly the vital truth, acted on instinctively by good printers, that the æsthetic unit in a book is not the page but the pair of pages. His books are mostly too rich and

149

heavy in appearance for comfortable reading, and his influence was more really valuable than his own achievement. All subsequent fine printing sprang largely from his inspiration and the high standards of modern commercial press work owes a very great deal to the private and fine press movement.

The Kelmscott wood-blocks were deposited in the British Museum, not to be used for a hundred years. The types are in the custody of the Cambridge University Press.

When the Kelmscott Press came to an end, Emery Walker started again with T. J. Cobden-Sanderson, better known perhaps as a binder, at the Doves Press, Hammersmith. There, from 1898 to 1916, they printed a long series of famous books, mostly small, but culminating in a magnificent Bible, in a style which was the antithesis of Morris's. The Doves type was a roman, based on Jenson's, but lighter and purer than Morris's Golden; the very perfect inking heightened the effect. A straight-tailed "y", a too-conspicuous feature of it, may be useful for recognition. At the close of the press's activity Cobden-Sanderson threw the types into the River Thames.

Of the very many and varied private and fine presses which have sprung up in this country since the time of Morris, passing mention can be made of two only. The Ashendene Press, under the guidance of St. John Hornby, printed a number of large works such as the Spenser and Malory, and a number of small ones such as the *Fioretti* of St. Francis.

After an early use of Caslon and Fell types, this press used a more gothic modification of the semi-gothic roman with which at Subiaco in 1465 Sweynheim and Pannartz brought printing into Italy. Later, use was made of a fine roman based on the Ulm Ptolemy of 1482. The finest achievement of the Ashendene Press, the Dante of 1909, frequently joins the Kelmscott Chaucer and the Doves Bible to constitute the "three ideal books of modern typography".

The Gregynog Press, established in 1922 by the Misses G. E. and M. S. Davies near Newtown, Montgomeryshire, produced a remarkable series of books during the eighteen years of its life. The best works of this press showed a delightful harmony of type, illustration, decoration and binding and the cessation of the press in 1940 may well have marked the end of the important private press movement in Great Britain.

Since the end of the nineteenth century private and fine presses have done equally important work in America, France, Germany, Holland, and Italy. Much that has been influential in modern type-design has grown out of the work of these presses. So marked has been the spread of good type-design that some of the greatest of the modern designers, men like Eric Gill, Frederick Goudy, Stanley Morison, Bruce Rogers, Jan Van Krimpen, have seen their designs enjoying wide and deserved popularity. Moreover, because of the interest taken in modern type-designs by the mechanical composing machine corporations, good designs are now readily available and there is no excuse for the retention of ugly, illegible, and unsuitable types.

3. *Italic*

Italic type, unlike gothic or roman, is definitely the creation of a single printer, Aldus of Venice, who designed it for a pocket series of classics, beginning with a Virgil in 1501, though a few words of italic appeared in a book of his in 1500.

The type was cut for him by Francesco da Bologna from one of the countless specimens of the scholarly cursive of the fifteenth century in Italy, and was first called "Chancery" (*cancelleresca*) or "Aldine". The statement, often repeated, that it was based on Petrarch's handwriting, is due to an egregiously careless misreading of Aldus's statement that his text of Petrarch's *Cose Volgari*, 1501, is "tolto con sommissima diligenza dallo scritto di mano medesima dal Poeta", in other words, that it was based on a holograph manuscript of the author.

At first Aldus's italic had no upper-case of its own, therein imitating the manuscripts on which it was based. To most modern eyes, though there are professed exceptions, the addition of its own upper-case, which came soon, was a great improvement on the small roman capitals used at first.

It has been stated that Aldus introduced italic because he could not print such small books in roman. This is ridiculous, but Aldus began his series with Virgil, and what is true is that italic is a narrow (or, as printers say, a condensed) type, and that an equally narrow roman (in which a hexameter would not overrun a line) would be intolerable, and a smaller fount would be needed. The result can be seen in the small Elzevir classics, which, though neat, are far less legible than the Aldines. There is, in fact, no more truth in another statement, often made, that italic is less legible than roman. Legibility amounts to little more than the habit of the eye, when types are equally free from flourishes and other distracting features.

Aldus's small classics and his type were immediately copied, especially at Lyons, though he did his best to protect his rights. A notably original italic type was cut, however, in 1524 by Ludovico Arrighi, of the Papal chancery, the effect of manuscript being very prettily preserved. Three years later Arrighi considerably modified his design. From these two, Aldus and Arrighi, descend all italic founts. Italic type was first introduced into England by Wynkyn de Worde in 1528 and in the earliest days of its use here it was Arrighi's earlier type which proved popular. It was, however, through Garamond's modified copies, taking elements from both, that Europe got the italic tradition. Garamond and Granjon, the chief type-cutters of the day, sold types to most printers, and not least to Plantin. From the seventeenth century on, italics have always been designed in relation to the romans with which they were to be associated; before that they had been independent.

153

In the sixteenth century italic had been used for whole books of verse, and especially Latin verse. By degrees the use of italic diminished except for its modern usage, which is chiefly as a differentiation type.

4. *Greek*

The earliest books to contain Greek type are both dated 1465. One is the Cicero, *De officiis*, printed by Fust and Schoeffer at Mainz, the other is the Subiaco Lactantius; in the former it is indecipherable, what was intended to be οτι μονον το καλον αγαθον appearing as an unintelligible phrase, since type-cutter and compositor alike knew no Greek; and for some time after this most printers preferred to leave blanks for Greek words to be filled in by hand. The Subiaco type and its successors (all Italian) were book-hands, broad and upright, intended to go with roman, and are called græco-roman. The best of the very early ones is that of Joannes Philippus de Lignamine, Rome, 1470, which shares the lapidary quality of its owner's roman, and which would not have been neglected by modern type-cutters had more of it been in existence; the letters are bold and square and ascenders and descenders occur very sparsely.

At Venice Nicolas Jenson cut in 1471 a Greek fount of the same family character as the Subiaco, but much better; in fact, it is worthy of his famous roman, and was in its way almost as influential in the modern revival of type-cutting.

The earliest continuous Greek texts printed were edited by teachers of Greek, and the types in which they were printed were no doubt designed by them, for they are more cursive and more genuinely Greek of the style of the day, having in particular narrow and ugly Byzantine upper-case. The first book entirely printed in Greek is the Ἐπιτομή, or Greek grammar, of Constantine Lascaris, Milan, 1476, and this was followed by some of the great classics. Theocritus (Milan, [c. 1480]); Homer (Florence, 1488); Aristotle (Venice, 1495); and Aristophanes (Venice, 1498) appeared before the end of the fifteenth century, side by side with the *editiones principes* of the Latin classics. The last two of these were printed in Venice by Aldus, in a style of type which was to its predecessors very much what his italic of a few years later was to roman. He gave the regular slope to the strokes which survives into our own time and the style may well be called "græco-italic".

But while Aldus's italic was a boon, his Greek proved to be a curse, and the more so in that it dominated Greek types for four centuries. While printers had, for practical reasons of simplifying composition, in fifty years gone far to clear ligatures and contractions out of the roman case, Aldus enormously multiplied them in the Greek case, thus adding simultaneously to the cost of printing and the difficulty of reading. Even the fine lay-out of such books as his Aristophanes cannot conceal the ugliness of the types themselves, closely modelled on script though they be, with all the pen's running

155

flourishes. Proctor went so far as to call Aldus "a man of phenomenal bad taste for his time".

One famous exception to the vogue of the Aldine Greek there was, and that was the stately round græco-roman of the New Testament (1514) of the Complutensian polyglot Bible printed for Archbishop Ximenes by Arnald de Brocar at Alcalá de Henares (Complutum), which was based on Jenson's Greek of 1471. It had no successors for nearly four hundred years and the rest of the world preferred Aldus's græco-italic to the græco-roman. The finest græco-italics of the heavily contracted kind were the *grecs du roi* cut in 1543–1544 by Garamond with the aid of a Cretan scribe named Angelos Vergetios. The founts were cut to the order of François I, as part of his scheme for printing the Greek classics in the Royal Library. The former year, 1543, saw the first book printed in Greek type in England, a Chrysostom edited by Sir John Cheke and printed by Reynald Wolfe.

In his *Greek Printing Types* Dr. Victor Schólderer wrote, "Such beauty as the contemporary Greek penmanship which he [Aldus] was imitating possessed consisted wholly in the abundance and freedom of its ligatures and contractions, and to reproduce these in the exceptionally unsuitable medium of type was not really a business proposition". But it was not until the mid-eighteenth century that this was thoroughly realized and there are several great landmarks which mark this period of change; the simple Greek printing of the brothers Foulis at Glasgow,

156

notably their famous Homer of 1756–1758, in which Robert Foulis persuaded the designer, Alexander Wilson, to omit contracted sorts; the large text Greek of Bodoni, as shown in the Longus of 1786, into which he introduced the peculiar qualities of the extreme modern face roman; and the Porsons of the Cambridge University Press, which are the plain but very clear græco-italics on which so many scholars in England were brought up.

In 1895 the stirring of the waters by Morris produced an experiment in a græco-roman cut for Macmillans by Selwyn Image. This was fat-faced and painful to the eye, probably in deference to Morris's admiration of gothic. It deserves the credit of being a first experiment on the right lines, though it had been preceded both in France and England by some upright types which were in essence Porson pushed up out of the slant. Soon after this Robert Proctor designed the "Otter", a modification of the Complutensian fount, and an *Oresteia* and *Odyssey* were printed in it. They are splendid books but Proctor's Otter type was not well adapted for reduction to a size suitable for normal texts. This adaptability has been found in the New Hellenic, designed in 1927 for the Hellenic Society by Dr. Scholderer of the British Museum, and based on a Venetian græco-roman of the 1490's. This Greek type is one which is available in varying sizes on monotype.

No single thing has done more to spread an appreciation of good type-designs at this present time than the influence of the modern mechanical composing machines. Many of the outstanding modern designs have been based on some of the great founts of the past, and in several instances they have been developed by the private and fine presses. Simplicity and clarity are the fundamental requirements of a good book type and no amount of delicacy or flow of line will make up for the irritation of having to pause and look longer at a word. Modern mechanical methods have also increased the availability to a general printer of some highly specialized categories of type, such as Hebrew or Oriental founts. Good examples of these are now as readily available as the more prominent roman, italic or Greek founts, and the standard of general printing has consequently risen considerably. Any student must, of necessity, acquaint himself with some of the best modern examples through the medium of type-specimen books and the printed works themselves.

READING LIST

LIST A

> CHAMBERS' ENCYCLOPEDIA. Articles on "Book", "Book trade", "Library", "Publishing".
> ENCYCLOPEDIA BRITANNICA. Articles on "Books", "Bookselling", "Libraries", "Publishing".

LIST B

> ALDIS, H. G. The printed book. 2nd ed. 1947.
> BENNETT, H. S. English books and readers, 1475 to 1557. 1952.

BOUCHOT, H. Le livre. 1890.

BRITISH MUSEUM. Guide to the exhibition in the King's Library. 1939.

BUTLER, Pierce. The origin of printing in Europe. 1940.

CLARK, J. W. Care of books. 1902.

DUFF, E. Gordon. Early printed books. 1893.

HARRISON, F. A book about books. 1943.

JOHNSON, A. F. Type designs, their history and development. 1934.

McMURTRIE, D. The book. 3rd ed. 1943.

MORISON, Stanley. Four centuries of fine printing. 2nd ed. 1949.

MUMBY, Frank. Publishing and bookselling. New ed. 1949.

POLLARD, Alfred W. Fine books. 1912.

REED, Talbot Baines. A history of the old English letter foundries. New ed. rev. and enl. by A. F. Johnson. 1952.

SIEBERT, Frederick S. Freedom of the press in England, 1476–1776. 1952.

STREETER, B. H. The chained library. 1931.

THOMPSON, J. W. Ancient libraries. 1940.

THOMPSON, J. W. The medieval library. 1939.

UPDIKE, D. B. Printing types: their history, forms and use. 2nd ed. 1937.

WINSHIP, G. P. From Gutenberg to Plantin. 1926.

WROTH, L. C. *ed.* A history of the printed book; being the third number of *The Dolphin*. 1938.

V

ILLUSTRATION

Decoration of the Manuscript

From the very earliest times books have been decorated or elucidated, as we say "illustrated", by drawings and paintings, or other reproductions; and it is necessary for the bibliographer to know something of the history and technique of the various processes, first that he may recognize them when found, and secondly that he may be able to select when necessary the most suitable process for the production of facsimiles. For the first of these ends, no theoretical training is worth anything by comparison with study of examples in books and in print galleries.

The written book was always decorated by paintings and drawings, but the earliest processes of engraving, by which drawings can be multiplied, are very little older than typography. Egyptian papyri of the Book of the Dead, dating from *c.* 1550 B.C., were already brilliantly illustrated in colours; and such ancient Greek MSS. as herbals were illustrated with drawings.

In the early centuries of our era classical texts were decorated with pictures, which were not necessary as the illustrations of herbals were; there survive illustrations to Homer and Virgil of the third and fourth centuries A.D.

But, in the period that followed, the great development of illumination, the regular form of book decoration in the middle ages, and one of the chief channels of art for nearly a thousand years, was fostered by two influences in the Eastern Empire—first, the sumptuous taste of Byzantine society, and secondly, the spread of Pergamene vellum, which provides a more solid and opaque ground than papyrus for gold and colours. Three types of decoration ensue: (1) rubrication, or in old English, "rubrishing", the plain painting of capital letters [1] in red and blue; (2) illumination, the painting of the letters in gold and silver, in the earlier period applied liquid, but after the thirteenth century burnished leaf; the silver has nearly always oxidized black, but the gold keeps its colour; and (3), combined with the other two, miniature painting of scenes, sometimes purely decorative, but frequently appropriate to the matter of the book. These three processes were generally the work of different hands.

The Byzantine art passed West through Italy and met the Celtic at the court of Charlemagne, producing the Carolingian style. Apart from the remarkable Anglo-Saxon school of outline drawing of the tenth and eleventh centuries, this was the basis of the style of Western Europe till the thirteenth century, when national styles began to be generally divergent. At the same time books became smaller, and certain features became stereotyped, in the next two centuries.

[1] *Capital* means not what the printer calls "upper-case", but the large initials of chapters, for which the scribe and early printer left spaces.

The border decorations, which were designed to flow out from a capital, were at first delightfully fresh and restrained, showing plenty of margin; they often ended in grotesque monsters, hares hunting men, and so forth. Gradually the fashion settled on smaller books, passing in the fifteenth century from the Psalter to the Hours of the Virgin, as it had earlier passed from Bibles and Apocalypses to the Psalter. The marginal illumination became more mechanical, until the margins were filled with a solid framework, and little vellum was visible. At the same time in the French and Flemish schools the enclosed miniature reached the highest point of beauty and delicacy, but also became common. Books of Hours of the later fifteenth and earlier sixteenth centuries, the produce of the stationers' shops, abound, and these are generally of small merit.

Illuminations and miniatures are not only worthy of study for their own sake as monuments of mediæval art; they enable us to fix the date and country of origin of manuscripts, which very rarely contain that information in their colophons.

The advent of printing killed illumination, though not at once. There are copies of books from the earliest Mainz presses which are elaborately illuminated; and in Italy the art, strongly coloured by the Renaissance, survived in printed books and MSS. into the sixteenth century. The best combination of the printer's and illuminator's arts is to be found in North Italian books of about 1470–1475, which often have the opening page of text exquisitely decorated with an illuminated capital set in a border of white vine-tendrils on a background of colours.

But it is not in human nature to go on applying costly decoration to a cheap article, and the normal decoration found in early printed books consists of rubricated capitals in red and blue, with more or less decoration. Printed decorative capitals, cut in metal, were tried by Fust and Schoeffer at Mainz as early as 1457, but were not successful; and it was only some twenty years later that the woodcut capital was introduced in the presses of South Germany and in the next twenty years gradually took the place of rubrication.

It is now time to turn to the production of printed illustrations.

Technically, these may be divided into three classes:

(1) *Relief*. In this group the printing is done from a raised surface as with normal letter-press printing. In most cases it is the design which is left standing while the background is cut away. The reverse of this is true in the case of wood-engraving which, in spite of its name, is a relief process. Particular care must be taken to understand this. The great advantage of relief illustration processes is that they can be set up and printed at the same time as normal type and plates can be taken from them.

The most important relief processes are woodcuts, wood-engravings, half-tones and line-blocks.

(2) *Intaglio*. Here the design is incised in the block or plate, which is then cleaned, inked and wiped.

163

Thus the engraved lines of the design alone retain the ink and the impression is made by strong pressure so that the paper is forced into the incisions.

All intaglio engravings will normally show a "plate-line"; the paper which is pressed by the plate is smooth and sunk, while beyond the edge of the plate it keeps its natural surface; the resulting line dividing these two areas is the plate-line. When the plate-line is absent it will be for one of three reasons. (i) The leaf has been cut down by the binder. When this is so the engraving is reckoned imperfect, as there may be lettering, or even part of the design, cut away. (ii) The plate was as large or larger than the sheet. This is common in small steel engravings of the early nineteenth century, which seem to have been regularly engraved together on a single plate as large as the open sheet, so that when cut for issue the leaves show no plate-line at all. (iii) The illustration was printed by the offset method.

The strong pressure needed for printing all intaglio plates makes it impossible to print at the same time with type-set text. They are sometimes printed on a page bearing letterpress, but by a second impression: and normally they appear alone on inserted plate-leaves; this is a fatal defect, and no metal-engraving ever appears to be an integral part of the book as woodcut does.

The action of the press flattens the edges of the incisions in the soft copper, and the finer lines gradually grow faint, so that a late impression is much less valued than an early one.

The designer's name, when it appears, is generally given at the foot on the left, followed by the word "del" (*delineavit*—drew) or "pinx" (*pinxit*—painted), and the engraver's on the right, followed by "sculp" (*sculpsit*—engraved, literally carved, the Latin for an engraving being *sculptura*); abbreviations which are said to have been mistaken by the beginner for surnames of singular frequency. The right way to express it in description is: Plates by So-and-So (the Engraver) after So-and-So (the Artist), e.g. by Blake after Lawrence.

The chief intaglio methods of illustration are, line-engraving, drypoint, etching, stipple, mezzotint, aquatint, and photogravure.

(3) *Planograph.* The design is neither raised nor incised but is on a flat surface. Printing is accomplished because certain areas will accept ink while others will reject it.

The chief planographic processes are lithography, including photo-lithography, and collotype.

WOODCUT AND WOOD-ENGRAVING

In a woodcut the drawing is made on or transferred to a smooth block of wood, planed along the grain, and the cutter with a knife cuts away everything which is to be left white. Being in relief just as a page of type is in relief, the two can easily be printed together. Moreover, if the strength of line of each is chosen so as to harmonize with the other, a pair of pages of text and woodcut makes an entirely harmonious whole, and this is accordingly the style of

165

illustration preferred by most lovers of beautiful books. Woodcut and line-engraving on copper were both in existence in Germany at the invention of printing. The technical advantage of woodcut over engraving, in not needing a separate printing, no doubt caused it to be the more popular of the two.

Woodcut-printing (xylography) was employed as early as the twelfth century for the decoration of stuffs; but it was only with the spread of paper in the later fourteenth century that it is found used for separate pictures. Examples of these, which are believed to have been sold or given to pilgrims at shrines, are found bearing lettering cut, like the picture, in the wood; one of the Virgin at Brussels bears the date 1418, one of St. Christopher in the John Rylands Library, 1423, while one at Paris has been assigned to 1408.

Late in the fifteenth century, and particularly at Paris, soft metal was used instead of wood, often punched with holes (criblé) to relieve the black mass; metalcuts do not have so sharp-edged an effect as woodcuts, and they never, of course, show wormholes or cracks, which often help the bibliographer to arrange in their true order undated editions of books illustrated with woodcuts.

The first use of woodcuts in printed books was made by Albrecht Pfister of Bamberg in 1460–1462; but they were not used again until a decade later, when they flourished in the South German towns. Early German woodcut uses a bold strong line and is very vigorous, if often crude. In Italy, where the art was later to be introduced, it is more graceful; the famous *Hypnerotomachia Poliphili* of 1499 at Venice is perhaps the highest point reached: but the school of Florentine cutters of 1490–1510 produced much charming work, using, as well as line, black silhouette lightened by white-line engraving.

In the sixteenth century woodcut gradually sank before the rise of line-engraving, which superseded it in the seventeenth and eighteenth centuries, leaving it to the jobbing printers for ballads and the like. Towards the end of the eighteenth century, however, woodcut met with a revival in the form of wood-engraving, first in France, and then notably in England, at the hands of Thomas Bewick (1753–1828), whose *Select Fables*, 1784, *General History of Quadrupeds*, 1790, and *History of British Birds*, 1797–1804, brought wood out of deep disrepute into favour again.

Wood-engraving differs from woodcut in that a harder wood is used, generally box, and the design is cut into the surface with a graver, not a knife, working against the grain on the end of the plank. As a result, although the block is still a relief block, it is the background and not the line which takes the ink. In the words of the British Museum's *Guide to the Processes and Schools of Engraving*, the design "prints white". There is nothing to prevent the use of black-line and white-line together on one block.

Wood-engraving flourished during the nineteenth century in England following its great use by Bewick and some beautiful work was done after many of the best artists. Later in the century wood was used in an attempt to produce tone rather than line and it achieved a result something like a photograph but not so good. When photographic blocks became cheaper, they killed the art. At the very end of the century, William Morris in his Kelmscott Press books, went back for decoration as well as typographical inspiration to the fifteenth century in Germany. He used woodcuts for illustrations, borders and capital letters with bold black line which harmonized with his types. During this present century the concentration has been mainly on wood-engraving and in no other field of book illustration and decoration has so high a level been reached and maintained. Thanks mainly to the inspiration and encouragement of the private and fine press movement, there is now a body of first-class wood-engravers whose work can be found in the ordinary commercial press book. Few things have done more to raise the standard of modern book production than the excellent work of the wood-engravers.

The actual woodcut is not often used in printing; both in order to save it from accident and to enable simultaneous printing to be done at more than one press electrotypes are made, which give a facsimile.

Another development on the same lines is lino-cut, in which, as the name implies, the block is surfaced with linoleum. It does not differ in principle from woodcut, but is coarser and not widely used in book illustration.

Line-engraving is executed on a plate of polished
168

metal, generally copper. The engraver pushes the graver or burin, which cuts the line, into the soft copper, throwing up a burr or furrow-ridge of copper. This is scraped away, and the plate is inked and then wiped, the ink remaining only in the lines, whence it is transferred to paper by very strong pressure, as the paper must be forced into the incisions to take up the ink.

Few illustrations engraved on copper are found in the fifteenth century. At Bruges and Florence, where engravers were at work, they appear as early as 1476 or 1477, and in 1481 the same Florentine press, that of Nicolaus Laurentii, produced the Dante with cuts once thought to be (and which possibly are) after designs by Botticelli. At Cologne an isolated Kalendar (L. Beham's) of [1476?] has copper-cut astronomical tables; and a series of service books of Würzburg and Eichstätt of 1479 and the next decade printed by the Reysers seems to owe its engraved illustrations to episcopal patronage. For map-making the process was eminently suited, as giving a finer line; and it is used for the purpose in the Rome Ptolemy in 1478 (planned by Sweynheim in 1474) and the Bologna edition of 1482, in which year the splendid edition of Ulm was produced with woodcuts.

Practically wherever the process appeared in book-illustration it preceded woodcut and was superseded by it, no doubt on account of the technical difficulty of combining the printings of incised and relief surfaces. Laurentii's Dante of 1481 is evidence that it was a pioneer process. Only nineteen of the many

169

illustrations planned are known; of these only three are pulled on the leaf itself, the rest being pulled on slips and pasted in.

A very remarkable line-engraving in an early book is that of an author, possibly Caxton, presenting his book to Margaret, Duchess of Burgundy, Caxton's patroness, which is found in one copy only (the Chatsworth-Huntington) of the *Recuyell of the Histories of Troye*, 1475;[1] but it is doubtful whether this can be considered as an integral part of the book. If it were, it would be the earliest engraved book-illustration. It may, however, have been added to this one copy.

Line-engraving became common in books towards the middle of the sixteenth century, particularly to reproduce fine topographical drawings, maps, etc., of which many were being produced. Woodcut, even in such choice books as the Ulm Ptolemy of 1482, was by comparison coarse. In England copper drove wood out of all but popular use in the seventeenth century, and it was very much used for frontispiece title-borders and portraits, of which Droeshout's portrait of Shakespeare in the First Folio of 1623 is one of the most famous and one of the worst. Engravers developed the use of shading and "crosshatching" to give tone, which was not only laborious but was also never really beautiful. It was namely the deficiencies of this process for tonal reproduction which prepared the way for the triumph of mezzotint

[1] Reproduced as the frontispiece of Seymour de Ricci's *Census of Caxtons* (Bibl. Soc. 1909), *q.v.*, pp. 4-5.

as a tone-process. Line-engraving (or "copper-plate") was also used for the copybooks of the writing-masters, such as Cocker, for which, by its delicacy and the slow and careful movement of the hand imposed by the process on the engraver, it was admirably suited. Otherwise, in spite of Faithorne, it fell on evil days, till it was revived on steel in the early nineteenth century. There is some use of copper engraving today but it is almost entirely limited to occasional fine book productions.

Steel Engraving.—The softness of copper, which prevented very many successful impressions being taken, was against the use of coppercut for large editions. A more resisting material was found early in the nineteenth century by English engravers in steel, on which they engraved the countless illustrations of the works of Campbell, Rogers, and others, and the *Keepsakes* of the time, after or in imitation of the mezzotints in Turner's *Liber Studiorum*. The extreme hardness of steel enabled them to outdo the delicacy of the line in copper, and the work is often microscopic; in fact it is a line process attempting tone. At its best it has great beauty, and it will always be associated with the Romantic movement in this country. By the middle of the nineteenth century it was dead, and it has not been revived.

Drypoint.—The engraver draws freehand on the copper with a pencil of steel, which throws up a great deal of burr to the side of the line. This burr is not removed but is carefully preserved. When the plate is inked and wiped (with very great care), the ink is

171

retained by the burr as well as in the engraved line itself. The result is an incomparably soft and deep line. But it takes very few impressions to flatten it down and destroy the beauty, and in consequence only a very few books, produced in small editions, are illustrated with drypoints.

Etching.—In the processes of this class the lines are incised, not by a tool, but by acid. The copper plate is protected by a "ground" of a transparent waxy composition, and at the back and sides by varnish. The etcher smokes the grounded face over a taper to make it opaque, and then draws the design on it with a blunt "needle", removing the ground but not cutting the copper. The plate is then placed in a bath of etching acid, which bites the copper where the needle has exposed it. If only one uniform length of biting were given, the etching would show only one thickness of line and would bear some resemblance to a line-engraving. It has been used in this manner by a number of very fine etchers. When the etcher requires greater variety of line, he removes the plate from the bath when the lightest lines have been deeply enough bitten, and "stops them out" by varnishing them over. He then replaces the plates to give the rest a re-biting, and so on by stages till he has his lines in every required strength from feathery touches to black patches where the lines have fused. The process is thus one of immense range and power.

Etching can be distinguished from line-engraving by the irregular (or, in etcher's phrase, "juicy") edges of the line, since the acid does not bite evenly, and also (though not so certainly) by the yellow impression of the film of ink which is often deliberately left on the plate. Also, being freehand, it gives more the effect of sketching.[1] In this and in the irregular line it is still more like drypoint; and the two processes are often used together; so that careful examination is necessary, if there be any doubt.

Blake used etching to produce a relief printing surface, biting away the background; this has been applied, as we shall see, to photographic block-making.

The new popularity of sketching in the latter half of the eighteenth century produced varieties of etching to reproduce the crayon and pencil line. The next three to be mentioned were the leading methods and they were frequently used in combination with each other and with normal line etching.

Soft-Ground Etching.—Here the etcher covers his plate with a soft granulated ground and draws on paper laid over it. The pressure of the needle makes the waxy ground on the lines adhere to the paper, which lifts it when raised, but does not leave the lines clean, a certain amount of ground remaining. The acid bites irregularly round these grains, and the line that results is composed of flecks, like that left by crayon or lead pencil on rough drawing paper.

Crayon Etching.—Much the same effect is produced by drawing with a toothed roulette instead of a needle. The ground is pierced in points and the

[1] The word "etching" is sometimes used as if synonymous with "sketching", but the use is illiterate. "Etch" = "eat", and without acid there is no etching.

printed line is accordingly made of dots, which can be distinguished from those of soft-ground etching by their regularity.

Stipple.—The ground (or the copper itself) is pierced with roulettes and multiple-pointed tools, and the resulting print, etched or engraved, shows a close mass of dots, which imitate soft pencil shading or light wash very well.

The early cutters had sometimes got a half-tone by punching the wood or metal block; and in the desire for tone the seventeenth-century engravers "flicked" the surface of the plate with the graver. Stipple, discreetly used in conjunction with other processes, is more delicate than these; but it lacks the strength to stand alone, as will be seen in the plates of Bartolozzi.

Mezzotint.—Late in the seventeenth century engravers were given a more powerful medium for reproduction of continuous tones than stipple (which was not used till much later), and that was mezzotint. Invented in Germany about 1642 by Ludwig van Siegen and brought to England by Prince Rupert of the Rhine, it was given its first perfection of method by Abraham Blooteling (d. 1690).

The process in its fully developed form differs from all others in that the mezzotinter works from black to white. He roughens the entire plate with a curved serrated tool called the "rocker" (from the similarity to that of a cradle), throwing up a burr in all directions; so that if inked, wiped, and printed from, it will give a more or less uniform black mass.

174

At this stage the mezzotinter *may* provide himself with a lightly etched outline, and of course any line he may want he can engrave or etch in afterwards; but the essential part of the process is entirely line-less. In the parts to be all but as deep as the absolute black, the burr is very slightly scraped down; in the next lighter parts a little more, so as to hold less ink, and so on to the high lights, which are not only scraped but burnished, so that, when wiped, they can hold no ink at all and are left white in printing. In other parts of the plate the work of the rocker can often be seen.

Mezzotint for fine illustration, especially for portrait frontispieces, drove out line-engraving in England, where it became so naturalized as to be called by the French *la manière anglaise*; but for cheaper work line-engraving, for all its laboriousness, continued to be used. At the end of the eighteenth and beginning of the nineteenth century the richness of mezzotint made it popular for topographical illustrations of ruins, etc.; no other process could give in the same way the gleam of sky and water, just as in reproducing oil portraits it excelled in rendering the gloss on armour, hair, and velvet and satin dresses. Mezzotint degenerated and fell into disfavour in the nineteenth century, but has been revived to a limited extent in this present century and has shown that it can still produce extremely good work.

Aquatint.——While mezzotint had established itself for the reproduction of oils, it gave rather too rich and sombre an effect for wash and water-colour drawings, which were very popular in the second half of the eighteenth century. Jean Baptiste Le Prince invented about 1768, and Paul Sandby imported in 1774, the aquatint process, by which the work of the rocker is accomplished less laboriously by acid, and at the same time the plate is nowhere roughened so as to print so continuously black as in mezzotint. The plate is grounded with powdered resin, which is fixed (i.e. half-melted and so caused to adhere) by heat. In the bath the acid bites (as in soft-ground etching) round the grains of the ground, and the printed surface accordingly shows a network of white dots where the ground has protected the plate, surrounded with black. As in other forms of etching, the plate is stopped out and re-bitten until all the required gradations of tone, from light to dark, have been obtained; and as in mezzotint, a guiding outline can be etched in at first, and any lines required afterwards.

Aquatint was enormously popular for books of picturesque travel, and indeed every other sort of illustrated book, until about 1830, when it gave way to lithography. Great publishers of aquatint books, such as Rudolf Ackermann, kept colourists at work tinting the plates. Like mezzotint, aquatint is, after a period of practical extinction, being again successfully practised, especially in some of its more modern forms such as "sugar aquatints".

Lithography differs from all other processes in that the plate is neither carved out in relief nor incised; the design is drawn out and printed from the flat sur-

176

face of the stone or metal. This apparent impossibility is achieved by means of the mutual antipathy of grease and water. On a polished stone surface the lithographer draws the design with a specially prepared greasy chalk pencil, or makes the solution and lays it on with a brush. Water is then rolled over it, and is absorbed everywhere, except where the grease in the chalk line rejects it. Printing ink is then rolled on, and is rejected by the wet spaces, but accepted by the greasy chalk, since it also contains oil. As a result only the design is reproduced upon the paper. Stone is more absorbent; but zinc can also be used for commoner work, such as music printing and the reproduction of typewriting. Instead of drawing or painting directly on to the stone, use is also frequently made of lithographic transfer paper. By this method, the artist draws, with his usual greasy medium, on to specially prepared paper. The grease in his design is then transferred on to the stone by simple pressure and the stone worked up in the normal manner.

Lithography was invented by Aloys Senefelder in 1798, and was immediately used with success. The exact facsimile of the pencil line, in which no engraver stands between the public and the artist, who could multiply his drawings without having to learn to engrave, was enough to account for this. Practised by such artists as Daumier and Whistler, it has never gone out of use, though it suffered an eclipse in the latter part of the nineteenth century for book illustration.

The ink of a lithograph is generally browner or "greyer" than ordinary printer's ink: and the line has not so sharp an edge as an engraved line; these two points (apart from the absence of a plate-line) will generally distinguish the process.

PHOTOGRAPHIC ILLUSTRATION

With the exception of lithography, none of the hand processes described above was, however beautiful, entirely satisfactory either to the artist or to the man of science responsible for an illustration. For each of these people wants, above all, an absolutely exact facsimile, faithful to the least touch of the artist's design and the least detail of the plan or object reproduced. But the design had to be rendered by the hand of the engraver, and while some engravers were meticulously careful, others were not. Even the careful ones were human and frequently were artists in their own right, incapable of divesting themselves of their personality. When, therefore, photography was added to the illustrator's resources, it was not an unmixed evil. All facsimile work was thenceforward on a firmer basis, although in nearly all photographic processes the merely mechanical work produces unsatisfactory results. The block or plate is generally fine-etched or otherwise worked over by a skilled engraver's hand.

It will be found that, just as each hand-process specially represents one variety of hand-design (e.g. line-engraving representing pen-and-ink drawing

178

and aquatint water-colour), so each photographic process represents one or more of these pairs, and is specially adapted for reproducing them. It is important to be able to select the best available process for any facsimiles for which we may be responsible.

Most of the photographic processes which have been evolved depend upon the fact that certain chemicals are hardened by light. A transparency of the subject (negative in all cases except that of photogravure) is exposed to light over a sensitized plate. The light, passing through the white lines or areas of the transparency, hardens the sensitive emulsion. Where no light passes through the black areas the emulsion remains unhardened and soluble, and will be washed away. This will leave the design of the original in hardened emulsion on the surface of the plate. This, in brief, is the general principle behind the photographic processes. The actual adaptation of this principle to each process and the treatment of the plate will be seen as each process is regarded in more detail.

Most of the modern photographic processes can, in one way or another, be adapted for use on high-speed rotary presses. Curved plates are placed on the press and printed either direct on to the web of paper or indirectly by *offset* process. This latter method is now widespread and has the great advantage of increasing the variety of papers on which the text or illustrations will print. In offset printing, a rubber or composition surfaced roller is interposed between the plate and the paper. The plate will print on to the offset roller and the roller on to the paper. In normal printing practice, the final print impression is the reverse of what is on the plate; in offset printing, the printed version will be identical with the plate. Since the rubber or composition surface possesses greater resiliency than the original block or plate, coarser surfaced papers can thus take an accurate impression of the original.

Zincography, commonly called "zinco" or "line-block," is a relief etching on metal. It will be remembered that Blake was a fore-runner in this field when he produced etchings in relief instead of intaglio. Other examples of this use can be found between the time of Blake and the advent of photography.

A photographic negative is exposed to light over the sensitized surface of a sheet of zinc. The image is thus transferred to the zinc in hardened emulsion. The unhardened emulsion is then washed away in water. The remaining design is dusted over with powdered rosin which forms an acid resist and the plate is then etched. The background is eaten away leaving the design in relief. The plate is then mounted type-high and is ready for printing.

Zincography is admirable for reproducing pure line and solid silhouette and is greatly used in printing facsimiles of woodcuts, title-pages, other type-pages and pen-and-ink drawings. Of itself, it cannot reproduce tone but attempts are made to give an appearance of tone by the use of Ben Day media or Bourges tints. These methods can produce fine line patterns over parts of the plate and so create an illusion of tone.

Half-tone is the common photographic stipple-print, and is most easily recognized in its crudest form in any newspaper.

The original photograph or drawing is photographed through a half-tone screen. This screen consists of two glass plates which are etched with fine diagonal lines. The lines are then filled in with black pigment and the plates are cemented together, the diagonal lines crossing each other, and so producing a multitude of tiny diamonds of clear glass. Half-tone screens are measured by the number of black lines to the inch. The coarsest screens have about 45 lines to the inch while the finest have 200 or even more on certain occasions.

Photographing the original through this screen breaks the image up into a multitude of dots of varying size. The dots which correspond to the dark areas of the original will be large, and those corresponding to the light areas will be small. This negative is then printed on to the surface of a sensitized copper plate. The dots are thus transferred to the copper as hardened emulsion, and when the plate is etched, as in zincography, these hard spots will be left in relief. When inked and printed they will reproduce the tonal qualities of the original.

The spots are so minute that the etching can only be of the lightest and the resulting relief of the shallowest, so shallow indeed that the copper-plate has to be held slanting to the light before the design appears to the eye. Consequently only the coarsest screens are suitable to paper of ordinary surface, and for fine work a smooth surface is necessary. To meet the need, clay-coated "art paper" was introduced, and the use of this is the fatal defect of half-tone. It is, however, possible to use a substantial paper in which the mineral is a loading and not a coating, and the surface is produced by calendering. Also, with the development of offset printing, owing to the surface of the offset roller being able to reach all the surface, a rougher paper may be used for coarser-screened plates.

For special qualities of work varieties of screens can be used in which the lines were engraved in other than diagonal directions. These include such things as "one-way" screens; "curved one-way" screens; "linen" screens; "Erwin" screens.

Photogravure.—This fine process is too expensive for any but the best work, or for "runs" amounting to tens of thousands of copies, for which in illustrated magazines it is much used, especially printed by offset. Technically, it is a photographic aquatint, but the general effect is darker than that of aquatint and closely resembles mezzotint which it reproduces perfectly. Like mezzotint it is admirably adapted to the reproduction of oil-paintings or anything which relies for its effect on good, rich tonal qualities. Its range, however, is very wide and, especially in magazine work, frequently reproduces text as well as illustrations.

As this is the only photographic intaglio method,

a transparent *positive* will be used and not a negative as in the other photo-mechanical methods. This positive is then printed on to a sensitized sheet of paper known as the "carbon" sheet. This sheet is then laid over a prepared copper sheet or cylinder and the design is etched through the gelatine, which is the main substance of the carbon sheet. Originally, the copper plate was "prepared" by grounding it with powdered bitumen, round which the acid would bite, as in an aquatint. Now a ruled screen of very fine lines is applied photographically in order to achieve the same effect. Etched pits of varying depth on the plate will hold varying amounts of ink and thus achieve varying tones when printed.

For modern commercial work, lithography exists today mainly as *photo-litho-offset*. It is widely used for the production of unaltered reprints of books.

Instead of the design being drawn on to a stone, it is transferred photographically on to a sheet of zinc or aluminium. The design is then worked up, inked and printed. The use of offset in connection with modern lithographic work is very general.

For facsimiles in which tone as well as line is to be shown, such as facsimiles in elaborate catalogues of pages of printed books or manuscripts in which the tone of the original paper is to appear, illuminations, or bindings, there is no finer process than *Collotype*. The plate is of thick plate-glass, and is covered, as in other processes, with sensitized gelatine; this dries into a network of fine wrinkles which is called the grain, and the delicacy of which regulates the amount of ink held when the plate is dampened and inked. Collotypes normally show a pale lithographic background, darker than the paper, to the plate-edge, but this can be cleaned out. The setting of the gelatine depends on a warm dry atmosphere in the shop, and there are fewer firms able to produce good collotypes than other types of illustration. It is, without doubt, the finest of all reproduction methods, but it is also an expensive one. It has the great advantage for scientific facsimile that no retouching is required as in the other methods.

It is of paramount importance that students should study examples of each of these methods for themselves. There is no substitute at all for this. They must, however, be warned about one thing. It is quite common to find a book described by its publisher as being "illustrated with aquatints (or mezzotints, etc.) by ——". They are correct in that the artist did execute aquatints, but they have usually been reproduced in the book by another means, frequently photogravure. Thus, although certain qualities of the original illustration will show through the reproduction, it has to be remembered that the viewer is in fact seeing photogravure and not aquatint.

Coloured Illustration

It is found that printing in more than one colour was the object of early experiment, since the finer manuscript book had been richly decorated in colours, and even the commoner book normally had rubrisher's capitals in red and blue. There is, however, the technical difficulty that, unless the forme is very meticulously inked with the different inks, the sheet has to go through the press twice or more, once for each colour. That this is so can often be seen in practice, as with the combination of type and engraving, in the overlapping of one colour upon another, which could not occur at a single impression.

At first rubrics were left blank, but soon began to be printed. Decorative colour, however, was not used early with much success or often. There is no doubt that the outline woodcuts in early books were meant to be hand-coloured, as they in fact often were.

Fust and Schoeffer, Gutenberg's successors at Mainz, used in the Psalter of 1457 and in later books metal-cut initials, imitating the decorative work of the rubrisher, and printed them in two colours (making with the black text three), the capital in red and the flourishes in blue. But their use was only occasional, and no other firm imitated them. In 1487 Erhard Ratdolt returned from Venice to Augsburg, at the Bishop's invitation, to print service books for the Diocese, and in these and others he used woodcut devices of a bishop and the arms of the diocese, printed in three or four colours.

The method used in the later instances of these cases was that by *multiple blocks* (sometimes called the "lithographic"). The black part of the picture, whether a mere outline or including mass, is cut alone, ignoring all else, on one block and printed

185

first as the "key"; then one (say) for the red, and so on. Each is inked with its appropriate pigment, which can be rolled or (in early days) dabbed on without the special care needed to keep it clear from the other colours at the meeting-lines of the masses. It is in securing exact "register", or superposition on the key, at each printing that this process requires care. If a block be printed out of register the whole mass will be out of place and the fact can easily be seen. In modern times coloured lithographs and wood-engravings have been largely produced by means of multiple stones or blocks. Examples familiar in England are the children's books illustrated by Randolph Caldecott, Kate Greenaway, and Walter Crane; those of Roger Boutet de Monvel afford a later parallel in France.

By the "multiple-block" method, each colour must lie in a separate mass or masses of even tone; the appearance of greater depth can be secured by black shading on the key block, but in no other way, and designs to be reproduced by this method must be specially coloured for the purpose in flat masses. A simple mixture of colours can be obtained by superposition in printing (chromo-lithography), and it is possible to blend the tints and make them fade into each other as in nature or ordinary painting, by dabbing the various coloured inks delicately on to the plate with a "dolly" (Fr. *poupée*). But this requires the presence at the press of an artist, preferably of the original artist himself, to refresh the plate after every few impressions, and it is obvious that any process which can be applied by a roller with reasonable care and skill must be much cheaper. It is consequently found that though true colour-prints were produced in some quantity in the great period of experiment in engraving, that is, in the latter part of the eighteenth century, and, when good, are much prized by connoisseurs, books were rather infrequently illustrated in so expensive a manner. The normal method of putting books with coloured illustrations on the market was for the publisher to employ professional colourists to colour the engravings by hand in a limited number of copies. Some of the most notable examples of this are to be found in the aquatint books of Rudolf Ackermann. Hand-colouring was largely applied to separately published engravings also, and these are to be distinguished from true colour-prints. The most careful colourist cannot prevent his brush from wandering slightly over the edge of the field, and this cannot happen in colour-printing by either of the methods described above. A small amount of hand-colour work has continued to be produced in this century, but only in rather special circumstances.

Three-colour.—The difficulty of reproducing the natural gradations of colours in nature and consequently in painting has been up to a point overcome by the "three-colour process", by which the colours of the original are split up in photography into the three primary colours, and then recombined in printing into their original combinations.

The primaries are yellow, red, and blue. A negative

187

is made by photographing the original through a light filter which allows only the yellow rays to pass on to the plate; then one for the red and finally a negative for the blue. From each of these negatives (or positives in the case of photogravure) a block or plate is made for each colour according to the illustration process being employed. Each plate is then inked with its appropriate colour ink and printed in succession, one being most carefully superimposed on the previous printing. It will be apparent that much of the success of this depends upon the care taken to ensure the most faultless register of the printings. If there is any error an untidy edge of one colour will be seen and the whole impression will be blurred. If, however, the colours used are good, there is absolute register and very careful press work, then excellent results can be obtained. But these are not easily or cheaply obtained. A carelessly printed colour plate is a most miserable spectacle.

In what is termed a three-colour printing there is usually a fourth plate printed. This is a black plate, used to give density to some of the colour areas and frequently to add line. Extra plates are often added in order to reproduce any especially important colours or to secure greater delicacy. It is not unusual to meet up to seven-colour processes, but it has to be remembered that, with each extra printing, the dangers of bad register increase.

In printing, the colours should not lie one over another in too solid a mass, or there will be obliteration instead of mixture. In colour half-tones, it is

188

usual to shift the position of the screen between each of the exposures so that dots which combine to produce a colour (e.g. yellow and blue for green) are not exactly superimposed. If the eye picks up a yellow dot not completely covered by a blue dot it will gain a truer impression of green than if the blue dot entirely covers the yellow. In photogravure, this problem is met by the more fluid inks employed, which are inclined to mix under the speed and pressure of printing.

READING LIST

LIST A

CHAMBERS' ENCYCLOPEDIA. Articles on—
"Illumination of manuscripts",
"Illustration of books", and the articles under the name of each individual process.

ENCYCLOPEDIA BRITANNICA. Articles on—
"Illuminated manuscripts",
"Illustration", and the articles under the name of each individual process.

LIST B

BLAND, David. The illustration of books. 1951.

BRITISH MUSEUM. A guide to the processes and schools of engraving. 4th ed. 1952.

CURWEN, Harold. Processes of graphic reproduction in printing. 2nd ed. 1947.

HIND, A. M. An introduction to a history of woodcut, with a detailed survey of work done in the 15th century. 2v. 1935.

JAMES, Philip. English book illustration, 1800–1900. 1947.

POLLARD, Alfred W. Early illustrated books. 3rd ed. 1926.

WHETTON, Harry *ed*. Practical printing and binding. 1946.

VI

BINDING

A. The Craft: Materials and Methods

Contemporary bindings of old books are now, so far as possible, retained, even when re-backing, or complete re-binding, is necessary, and most bibliographers are aware of the great mass of important knowledge which has been destroyed by careless re-binding. Not only do fly-leaves often bear owners' notes of value; the binding itself may be dated, and so help to date the book. An extraordinary example may be found in Gordon Duff's *Early Printed Books* (pp. 9–10). Writing of the earliest block-books, he says:

The copies of the *Biblia Pauperum*, *Apocalypse*, and *Ars Moriendi*, which belonged to Mr. Horn, were in their original binding, and it was stamped with a date. The books were separated and the binding destroyed. Mr. Horn asserted from memory that the first three figures of the date were certainly 142, and the last probably an 8. Mr. Conway very justly points out that the resemblance of a 5 of that date to our 2 was very strong, and that Mr. Horn's memory may have deceived him.

Thus a fact (if it were one) of great importance in the history of the book was lost for ever.

In the market, books now command higher prices

if in their original state or "mint condition"; but except for exhibition and in the case of collectors' books it is hardly practicable in a library to keep a book in its pristine condition, and anyhow libraries do not normally sell, and so need not consider the market.

Wherever strength requires it, it is better to bind, and the shelves of worthless broken bindings in all great libraries are a warning of the necessity to a librarian of a knowledge of the best materials and methods as well as the correct conditions for storage and preservation. Broken bindings can be rebacked, and the old covers saved.

The binder divides the processes of his craft into two series, "forwarding" and "finishing". Forwarding includes everything necessary to make a secure unit of book and cover; finishing, the last touches, such as lettering, decorating, etc.

The first task is to pull the volume to pieces, collate the book, and if possible rectify any faults, such as supplying a missing section if the book is in print or common, rearranging misplaced sections or folds, resizing, washing (if absolutely required), and mending. All damaged folds should be "guarded", i.e. strips of strong, thin, and flexible material, such as bank-note paper or linen, should be laid over them, so as to hold the threads, which would otherwise cut the paper. Original end papers which bear any notes or marks of ownership, and book plates should, naturally, be carefully preserved. When end-papers have been provided and added to the sections, the whole pile is pressed ready for sewing. The end-papers, with or without leather, or better still, linen, joints, should be sewn through as well as the sections.

The sewing is the essence of the whole craft; of

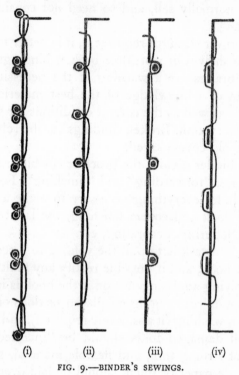

(i)   (ii)   (iii)   (iv)

FIG. 9.—BINDER'S SEWINGS.

that alone it is true that if it fails, all fails, and the book falls to pieces. It consists of (*a*) threads running perpendicularly up and passing through the fold in the middle of each quire or section (in its oldest and simplest form; now the same thread runs throughout

192

PLATE I.—A TUDOR STAMPED BINDING

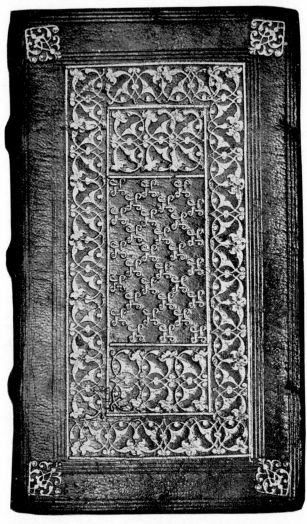

PLATE II.—ITALIAN GOLD-TOOLED BINDING, *c.* 1514

the book), to hold the pairs of leaves in each section together; and (*b*) cords or tapes, round or through which the threads are passed, to hold the sections together, running across the back (or "spine") of the book.

The material of thread and tapes must be, for good work, the best unbleached linen, and the cords, if preferred, must be best hempen sewing cord. There should be four to six tapes or cords, depending on the size of the book, and to these may be added two, at the very head and tail. They should be long, so as to lie a full third across the covers. The thread is carried through the fold of the first section and round the tapes (Fig. 9 (iv)) or cords (Fig. 9 (ii)) from head to tail, then across to the next section by means of a "kettle stitch", and up to its head. So it continues up and down across the entire back of the book. This is called "flexible all-along" sewing; it can only be done by hand and is the right method for single books where the aim is preservation. But where a short life of many issues is all that is needed, and where the paper is of poor quality, sound machine methods suffice well enough. In mediæval practice, when books were frequently heavier than now and greater strength was required, double cords were used and the sewing thread went between and round them (Fig. 9 (i)).

It will be seen from this how sewing achieves its double purpose of securing the conjugate leaves within each section to each other and also, by sewing the sections to the tapes or cords, fastens each section

G

to its neighbours. Various modifications of this sewing practice have been adopted from time to time, many of them very undesirable ones.

1. *Slitting Head and Tail.*—Certain "all along" machines did this in passing the thread from one section to the next, and it is obvious that the slits in the folds did not stop at the head and tail. These machines are now obsolete.

2. *Sewing Two Sheets On.*—In other words, halving the elaboration of the sewing and by so doing reducing the strength. The advantage is that full sewing ("one sheet on") may swell out uncomfortably the backs of books composed of many thin sections. Mr. Douglas Cockerell says that "two sheets on" with reasonably strong thread is better than "all along" with thin thread.

3. *Sawing In.*—This senseless practice consists in sawing trenches across the backs of the sections for the cords to lie in, thus avoiding ridges and allowing an undivided back (Fig. 9 (iii)). Even were this end worth taking trouble for, it can be just as well achieved by using tapes instead of cords. But the summit of mental confusion is found when, after sawing in, ridges are artificially made in the back as decoration.

4. *Stabbing.*—Sewing not in the folds but by piercing the pile of sections from front to back. Stabbing is very cheap and quick, but the leaves will not open to the back, will not lie open, and will tear at the sewings if one tries to make them. Eighteenth-century pamphlets were generally issued stabbed,

194

and the holes, often far out from the folds, can still be seen. The method is now practically confined to stapling (see below), except in very ephemeral matter.

5. *Overcasting.*—A more respectable form of stabbing, by which the folds are sewn together beyond, and enclosing, the ordinary sewing. It is used for the first and last sections of heavy books, and often throughout for newspapers, as being cheaper than the preferable device of guarding the folds.

6. *Stapling.*—Stabbing with wire clips or staples, either from the sides, or, less objectionably, in the place of the sewing through the folds. In the former method, the evils of stabbing are intensified by the use of metal, which tears the paper; even in the latter, the metal ultimately rusts and burns holes in it. Advertisements of rustless staples may be provisionally disbelieved.

7. *Tipping-in.*—Pasting the edge of a single leaf to the next leaf. Normally used for inserting plates but also sometimes for errata slips and single leaves of text, which ought incidentally never to exist, a "fold" (as the binder terms a pair of leaves) being the bindable unit. Where plates are printed on single leaves which are not wide enough to take the sewing, a fold can be made by laying to their edges flexible guards which will go round the fold of the nearest pair. Plates can also be guarded in this way in pairs.

8. *"Perfect" Library Bindings.*—Fifty years ago a method of binding cheap books was in force, in which the folds were cut off and the edges of the

leaves stood in rubber solution. The life of the binding was as long as the life of the rubber, which was a few months. After that period, the "book" became a collection of loose leaves. Slightly longer life was obtained by using flexible glue and securing on to a back-strip of linen mesh, the method used for some telephone directories. The method has now been resurrected, with a great burst of publicity, using a plastic adhesive instead of rubber. It is claimed that this will be much more lasting and will give great strength. The supporters of this method are enthusiastic in its praise; it has weathered its early tests well, and the result of its greatest test, that of time, will be awaited with interest.

9. *Spiral-backs.*—This method of binding has been widely adopted for books which are required to open absolutely flat, especially maps. Spirals of metal and the ubiquitous plastic have been used. While there are certain advantages in the methods, the life of such bindings is not usually long and their ugliness is excessive.

The complete book is sewn into a compact whole before the covers are attached. Their union is effected by the tapes or cords running across the backs of the sections and firmly held in place by the sewing. The slips are frayed out so as not to cause ridges on the side of the book, and are laced through the boards, in which holes are punched. For the best binding black board made from old rope is used; the old use of wooden boards has been revived for large and valuable books. It will be seen that, given good materials, the union between book and cover should be practically eternal. For modern casings, varieties of mill-board and straw-board are employed, which, at their best, are very satisfactory and, at their worst, can be regarded as merely temporary.

The edges of the leaves should now be cut with the plough, but not more than is necessary to tidy them. Old or valuable books should be left "uncut". While the worship of the rough deckle edge may be absurd, nothing is more hideous than merciless cutting down or cropping.[1]

The leather covering is then stretched over the boards and should be firmly pasted down to the backs of the sections (which have been rounded out, since, if left flat, the fore-edges will in time bulge), making a tight or flexible back. The first step in examining a binding is to open the book and see whether one can see down between the back of the binding and the back of the book. If one can, it is a hollow back, and strength has been needlessly lost, excessive strain being thrown on the joints, instead of being distributed over the whole spine. Hollow back is, in fact, the hall-mark of the shoddy binder, and is the rule with the shops that bind books for prizes.

Instead of a head-band, which used to be decorative silk work firmly attached to the top line of sewing on the spine of the book but is now usually merely

[1] "Uncut" must be distinguished from "unopened". The former term relates to the binder and his shears, the latter to the reader and his paper-knife.

stuck on to the top of the leaves at the spine, the leather at the head may be turned in over a strong cord. This will save it from breaking when the volume is taken off the shelf in the improper way by pulling it at the head.

It will be well, before dealing with leathers and other covering materials and the "finishing" applied to them, to distinguish here between true binding, as described above; the cheaper but still sound modification of it known as library binding; and the publisher's casing, often miscalled binding.

In essentials, *library binding* is the same as "extra", or luxurious binding. By both, permanence under hard wear is secured. But certain concessions to cheapness which only affect the appearance can be made. (1) The sewing can be done by machinery, if there are enough books being bound at one time to justify it. (2) Tapes may be used and laid with glue between split boards, i.e. two mill-boards, a thick and a thin, instead of cords being laced through the one stout black board. But the tape must not be cut short. (3) Flaws in the surface or irregularities of dye on the skins may be accepted; they do no harm. (4) Mr. Douglas Cockerell states that by using a French joint much thicker leather than usual can be used, with corresponding gain in strength. But the practice of paring leathers to secure flexibility in the joints, a very bad practice, is on the decrease, and thick leathers are more in favour. The French joint consists in leaving about $\frac{1}{8}$ inch between the edge of the cover-board and the back, which gives the leather

198

space in which to bend when the book is opened. (5) Substitutes for leather, as described below, can be employed, either for the whole cover, or as "half-bindings" for the sides only; in the latter method the corners, being most liable to wear, are often made of the leather used for the back.

Publishers' casing differs from binding in that it is manufactured as a whole independently and then lightly attached by paste to the book it is to cover. The slips of tape are short, and up the back is laid a strip of some linen mesh or mull. Both slips and strip can plainly be seen inside any cased book, since they are not inserted between split boards as in binding, but merely covered over by the end paper, which is pasted down over the inner face of the cover and the back edge of the outer section.

The practice of issuing books cased is general in the English-speaking countries, but is much less common throughout the rest of Europe. If reasonably sound, casing will keep a book in good order for a long time, so long as it is subjected to no more than normal private use. But for anything more than that it is no substitute for true binding. Indeed, it has certain active disadvantages. (1) When a cased book has to be bound, a second set of sewing piercings have to be made in the folds, as in re-binding; new books which will have to be bound should when possible be procured from the publishers in sheets, unsewn. (2) The casing adds to the cost, and thus the price, of each copy of the book, and this is an element in the high cost of English books. It is difficult to obtain any wide measure of agreement as to the possible decrease in selling price if English books were to be published in paper covers instead of publishers' casing. But the other old argument, that the English book buyer would not tolerate any serious work being issued in paper, is now null and void. The phenomenal rise and success of the Penguin books has proved that cheapness and compactness are matters of prime importance to the serious reader. And some learned societies are issuing their publications alternatively in their traditional cloth or linen and in paper covers. (3) Binding is far less used, and consequently is regarded as an expensive luxury—and becomes one. Many people seem to be unaware that it is possible to bind a book.

Reinforced publishers' library binding consists of muslin-lined end-papers with a cloth joint sewn in, inserted into the normal casing.

COVERING MATERIALS

The covers which are stretched over the boards were not always part of the earliest bindings. Their function was to protect the cords and sewings at the back or spine, a part as vital in a book as in a man. In the fifteenth century books were still often only half-covered, and had the wooden boards bare.

The materials for the covers consisted until very recently exclusively of skin, nor has any textile of equal flexibility, toughness, and durability yet been found to take its place. Many fantastic hides have been used, such as shagreen, snake-skin, fish-skin, and human skin. In the Middle Ages in England deer-skin was largely used, nor is the reason for its entire disuse apparent. At the present day five animals yield the leathers which bookbinders use; they are the pig, calf, goat, sheep, and seal.

(1) *Pigskin* is very strong, thick, and durable, but is rather stiff and should have a French joint, as it should not be pared. This is excellent for very large heavy books. Pig should not be dyed, as the strength of the skin may be damaged; in its native colour it takes a very pleasant "cheesy" tone. Very largely used by German binders of the fifteenth and sixteenth centuries, after about 1520 it was generally spoiled in appearance, though not in durability, by "tawing" with alum and salt. Pig does not show gold tooling up well. It can be easily recognized by the bristle-holes, which appear in triads.

(2) *Calf*, once very widely used, has fallen into disfavour. Early in the eighteenth century English binders took to a lighter-tanned brown calf, from younger animals, which they shaved thin at the joints and often patterned with panel-stencils and powderings of green vitriol, producing elegant effects, but losing strength. Few English calf-bound books between 1750 and the present day have not their joints either broken outright or at least (as the French put it) fatigued, and the sins of English calf have unjustly brought all English binding into condemnation abroad. Young calf has a perfectly smooth surface, without grain, and gives a pleasant polish, which was the reason for its popularity. It is used for school

prizes and other base uses in the worthless form known as "tree-calf", in which acid is poured over the leather in such a way that it takes stains some-what resembling the growth of a tree. Seventeenth-century and earlier dark calf is thick and has gener-ally survived in fair state. Some of this is from the hides of yearling calves, that of very young beasts having been used for making vellum. Modern cow-hide (seen in American and other law reports) is quite worthless. So usually is the form of calf known as russia, a soft-surfaced, scented leather, dyed a light chocolate colour and tanned (it is said) with willow and the bark of the white birch. Russia was popular in England in the early nineteenth century, and has almost universally yielded to red decay, but that used by Roger Payne is generally still sound.

(3) *Goat*, otherwise generically called *morocco*, from the country whence it entered Europe in the six-teenth and seventeenth centuries, is, properly pre-pared, perhaps the most generally trustworthy and suitable of all leathers for library use. It has a strongly marked network grain which can be modified by stretching in one direction into "straight grain" (a series of parallel ridges) or in two directions into "pin-head". Morocco, in its better varieties, is fre-quently "crushed". The leather is dampened and then subjected to great pressure between polished metal plates. This has the effect of minimizing the grain of the leather and giving a pleasantly smooth appearance which is ideal for tooling.

The finest morocco is crushed levant, and no

leather except vellum so well shows up gold-tooling; it is costly and is reserved for valuable books. For large and heavy books there is no leather better than niger morocco, which is thick and immensely strong. Its self-colour is a light fawn, but it is generally seen in the dye given it by the native makers, a kind of yellowish terra-cotta which is very pleasing to the eye. Native-tanned (perhaps by sumach) and native-dyed niger is still nearly always free from the dele-terious acids which have ruined so much leather. Some good binders import niger undyed and dye it themselves. A strong and serviceable morocco with-out quite the beauty of either levant or niger is cape goat. Some nigers, and indeed some other moroccos as well, are made from sheep-skin, but these are inferior to the goat-skin moroccos.

Sheep-skin is also met with in one other connec-tion with morocco, although not a very worthy con-nection. The grain of morocco unfortunately lends itself to deceptions. Moulds can be taken of it, since it is hard, and soft leathers such as sheep given the grain by pressure in these moulds. The fraud can always be detected both by testing the hardness of the surface with the finger-nail, and also by the price. The public indeed are far more to blame than the manufacturers for the existence on the market of sheep dressed as morocco, since it is their demand for an expensive article at an impossibly low price, or rather their acceptance of an imitation of an expen-sive article at the price of a cheap one, which creates this foolish and noxious trade.

"Persian morocco" has none of the sound qualities of real morocco and should never be used; it is derived from Indian goat and sheep and is badly tanned.

(4) *Sheep*, if whole, is good enough for binding books for which, either by reason of the use anticipated for them or of the paper on which they are printed, only a short life is required. It should not be used for the permanent preservation of books. In its split state, as "skiver" (having a pleasant soft suède-like surface) it is somewhat less durable than stout paper. "Basil" and "roan" denote various tannings, the latter by sumach.

Sheep has a rippling grain which is generally recognizable, and, as already observed, a soft loose texture.

Reddish-brown sheep was much used in England in the seventeenth and eighteenth centuries for account books, school-books and other cheap books, and is often in very fair preservation.

(5) *Seal* is the hide, not of the fur-bearing but of the Greenland seal, and is very strong. Unfortunately it is not cheap, the demand not making a moderate price possible. Seal has two great virtues. (*a*) The hide, as it has to protect a warm-blooded creature from the cold sea water, is full of oil, and this gives it a long-enduring life and flexibility. It does appear that the oil may stain the end-papers and neighbouring books on the shelf; but the present writer has a seal-bound volume which in twenty-five years has done neither of these things, nor has it shown the

least fatigue. (*b*) Since the seal's hide is equally exposed all over to the water, he has, unlike the land-animals, no sheltered or tender spots, and the hide is therefore good and strong throughout. There is a slight glister (no doubt a sign of oil) on the surface of seal, which otherwise has some resemblance to smooth morocco.

(6) *Vellum* is calf-skin, dressed with alum and polished. It has a beautiful, creamy-white surface and repays gold-tooling as no other background does; also it is very easy to clean. It practically never cracks at the joint, but unfortunately it is not very flexible, and will not give a tight flexible back. Damp causes it to "cockle" badly, and in extremes of light and heat it can sometimes become brittle. Nor is vellum cheap. Vellum leaves from large service books were often used in the sixteenth century for binding books. In Italy vellum (or more often parchment) long remained a much used material, as may be seen on any Italian secondhand bookstall. Both vellum and parchment when prepared for binding have their surface intact; when prepared for writing it is scraped off.

(7) *Parchment* is a similar product, but not so strong, being made of sheep, and recognizable by the grain, which is absent in vellum.

Apart from leathers, there is now a wide variety of covering materials suitable to modern needs. Of them, the group of textiles is probably the most important. First are cotton and linen cloths and cotton and linen buckrams. Although these have not the combined strength and flexibility of leather at its best, it is certain that a good fabric is better than a bad leather. In their lower ranges, they are relatively cheap, pleasant to the eye, and suitable for short term use. The best of the group, linen buckram, is by far the strongest and best, and makes an excellent binding material. It also has one great advantage over leather in not needing attention if it is to be stored for any lengthy period.

A number of patent preparations have come on to the market in recent years, many of them making very great claims for themselves. Some appear to be highly compressed paper, a material which has not inconsiderable strength and can be decorated in a variety of ways. Much progress has also been made with dyes, so that it is now possible to have a variety of colours which can be regarded as reasonably fast.

Plastics have entered this field also. Occasionally it has been as a wholly plastic cover, occasionally as a plastic impregnated cloth. Their main virtue seems to be that they can be wiped with a damp cloth to remove dirt. It may be that, for certain types of book, this can be regarded as a necessary attribute. As a general rule, however, it would appear simpler and more efficient to hope that people may learn to read without soiling.

FINISHING

The volume, duly covered, now remains to be lettered with its author's name, title, and date, and perhaps also to be decorated. The lettering must be legible, and the best medium for this is gold leaf, impressed with heated metal through a dressing of white of egg; but the decoration may be without colouring, or, as it is called, "blind". On modern book cloths a variety of colours are used for lettering on the spine but, on the whole, they have not the permanence of gold when well applied. The cord-ridges on the spine, if present, will be found to create admirable panels which for centuries provided the chief basis for the decoration of the spine. Today, when the ridges are very rarely present, lettering on the spine is still found, for the most part, in its traditional position. The great exception to this, and an extremely irritating one, is when, on a thin book, the lettering has to run either up or down the spine. Practice varies as to which of these directions should be adopted; both are confusing and most of all when found alternating on neighbouring volumes.

Very ornate decoration may make use of inlay of different-coloured leathers, enamel, and so forth; but a certain simplicity and, above all, avoidance of mass of gold, is more consonant with good taste. For beauty of the highest order nothing is needed but fine lines, elegantly disposed, of gold on the background of plain leather. The cover-design may be made in a single piece, or "stamp", and impressed, as is regularly done on publishers' casings. Blind-stamps, either one or two to the cover, were common on bindings in certain parts of Western Europe at the end of the fifteenth and early in the sixteenth centuries. But the greatest triumphs of the binder-designer have been achieved by the more normal process of "tooling", i.e. the repetition of small designs in relief called tools, which are impressed into the leather exactly as the letters of the title are.

REPAIRS

Books whose covers are broken or cracking need not be entirely re-bound. They can be re-backed, a strip of leather of the same colour being substituted for the original back (which can be laid down over it) wide enough to be firmly glued down on to the covers, which are thus held in place. New leather on the boards can be laid in as doublures and the original leather replaced over it.

Torn leaves can, and should, be mended and very bad confluences of worm-holes filled by pasting good paper into the defects. If the whole of the paper is weakened by damp it can be strengthened by resizing, i.e. dipping in gelatine size; the book must be "pulled", i.e. taken to pieces, first. Washing is not recommended; it is not easy to be sure of having removed all deleterious chemicals, and at the best the type on a washed page has a faint and ghostly appearance. But some cleaning can be accomplished, and if it is to be, it must precede resizing, which will fix the dirt. Books which are to have the heaviest use, or which are frail and valuable, can be protected by laying over both sides of each leaf a strip of the finest silk or linen mesh or Japanese tissue, which does not at all interfere with the legibility of the text. This is

PLATE III.—"LE GASCON" BINDING, *c.* 1640

PLATE IV.—SCOTTISH BINDING, *c.* 1720

PLATE V.—"JANSENIST" BINDING FOR LONGEPIERRE, c. 1700

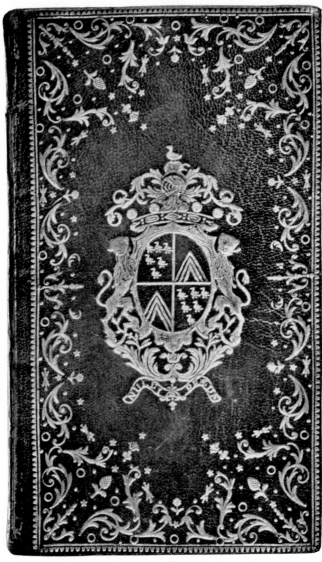

PLATE VI.—EIGHTEENTH-CENTURY FRENCH DENTELLE BINDING,
BY DEROME

practised in the British Museum, the Vatican, and other great libraries.

Fragments of papyrus, which are infinitely fragile, are usually laid between sheets of glass held together at the edges by *passe-partout*, although other methods of treating these delicate pieces have now been tried.

DECAY AND PRESERVATION OF LEATHER

If calf bindings of the last century and a half have for the most part failed to survive intact, this is because binders, in order to get a delicate surface, used the skins of animals slaughtered too young. But other leathers of the last half-century, and notably moroccos, have lamentably decayed. In 1900 the Society of Arts appointed a Committee to investigate the subject, and their report appeared in 1905. They found that decay had become common since about 1830, and markedly since 1860. They were able to show that the various forms of catechol tannin set up, under the action of light, the red powdery decay so noticeable in modern leathers, but that sumach is free from this objection. Gas fumes (this was soon after the days of naked gas-jets) were proved to be highly injurious, as containing sulphuric and sulphurous acid, and sulphuric acid was equally condemned when used in dyeing. Light and heat were also discovered to be harmful.

Later research, some of it abroad, but much in this country, especially by Mr. R. Faraday Innes, showed that the acid which is always found in rotted leathers may not have been due to the manufacturer, on whom the Society of Arts Committee laid all the blame, but to subsequent infiltration from the atmosphere. It was also found that old and durable leathers contained sulphuric acid, but that their acidity was controlled by certain other chemicals in the leather. The result was that decay was found to be of two main kinds. (1) Chemical decay due to the leather rotting by the action of sulphuric acid which was formed in the leather due to absorption of sulphur dioxide from the atmosphere. (2) Mechanical decay, which will be accelerated when chemical decay has already set in, due to the rubbing and pulling which the leather will receive in use. These disadvantages can be countered to some degree. Chemical decay can be guarded against by the use of 7 per cent. aqueous solution of potassium lactate; mechanical decay by the use of a good leather dressing. Of these latter, the best is that devised in the British Museum Laboratory and made by Messrs. Baird and Tatlock (London) Ltd. and known as "British Museum Leather Dressing".

The after-preservation of leather bindings consists otherwise mainly in their protection from atmospheric extremes, heat, light, damp, and drought. Books need much the same conditions which human beings need for health, one of them being fresh air. If dirt in the air makes glazed cases necessary, let holes be bored in the front or sides of the cases at top and bottom; and let the shelves not touch the back of the case, which in its turn should not touch an outer, or perhaps any, wall. Mere thieves can be countered by a sightly diaper of brass wires in place of glass in the case-doors.

HISTORICAL STYLES OF DECORATED BINDING

It is a general human instinct, comparable with Nature's *horror vacui*, that impels men to decorate any accessible blank surface; and few blank surfaces demand decoration more loudly than do the flat covers of books.

The outer sides of the ivory diptycha or folding tablets used by the Romans, from which the codex was evolved, were sometimes carved; and the idea was carried further by the use of metals, enamels, and inset jewels on the covers of the finest manuscripts of the Gospels and other sacred texts which were treasured in the richer monastic churches. This type of binding persisted throughout the Middle Ages, but the earlier examples, dating from the seventh to the ninth centuries, are more impressive than the later; such is the eighth-century Gospel book from Lindau, formerly in the Ashburnham collection and now in the Pierpont Morgan Library at New York, or the simpler one which bears an inscription stating that it was given by Theodelinda, Queen of the Lombards (d. A.D. 625), to her newly founded Cathedral of Monza, where the covers (without the book) are preserved. In later centuries the tendency to over-elaboration, to high relief, and to the insetting of large jewels, degraded the art. It must be remembered in their favour, however, that such projecting covers, however inconvenient now when books stand upon shelves, were not so when the books (and especially gorgeous examples like those mentioned) were kept lying on altars or in treasure-chests and aumbries.

Leather covers, laid over wooden boards, were also decorated in early times, in the West as well as in Near Eastern countries such as Egypt. There were two chief methods, incision with sharp tools, and stamping with blunt tools. The former method, though common in the Middle Ages, has only rarely survived into later times, except where inlay work in coloured leathers is in question. Famous and beautiful specimens are the Gospels of St. Cuthbert at Stonyhurst College (about A.D. 700), in which the pattern is heightened by *repoussé* work, and the simpler but even more exquisite ninth-century Gospel book of Fulda, in which a supremely satisfying effect is produced by triple fillets and diagonals producing four triangles in each of which is placed a three-pointed curved figure, roughly suggestive of a bird on the wing, the whole design being doubtless symbolic of the Trinity. Incised bindings, like their predecessors, also became over-elaborate, especially in Germany, where there was a tendency to depict elaborate scenes: the background was often well differentiated by being darkened by punching all over.

Tooled binding, which until the Renaissance was in Western countries always executed "in blind", i.e. without gold or colour, is also first known in the school of Fulda in the eighth century. At and soon after the Conquest there were flourishing binderies in the monasteries of Durham and York, and in Hyde Abbey, Winchester. The most noted surviving example of the last covers the Winchester Domesday Book, which is in the possession of the Society of Antiquaries. The variety of tools used at Durham in the bindings of the twelfth and thirteenth centuries, and the decorative sense in their disposition, are remarkable. There are palmettes, roundels containing fantastic beasts, square and triangular designs, and especially dotted strips which when set together suggest rope-work, and we find already the great variety of pattern obtained by combining simple elements which is the pleasure of tooled binding.

Unornamented bindings of the age of manuscript are often of vellum, stained to a red which must have been very gay; though the exteriors are now always faded to pink, the doublures, protected from light, show the original tint; in vellum-wrappered volumes the binding cords are carried through strips of horn or leather laid over the spine. Another plain style, which preceded and survived the invention of printing by no long period, was that of "half"-covering (more exactly about a quarter covering) the boards with the leather back. A common English material for plain binding was soft rough deerskin; the cover sometimes hangs loose for a considerable length below the foot of the book, and forms a "chemise". On small breviaries, intended to be carried about and hence named "portiforia", the chemise was at the head; the top edge was worked together into a knob which could be attached to the priest's girdle.

The larger volumes of the fifteenth century were provided with metal corner and centre bosses, intended to protect the leather from rubbing on the desk; also chains stapled to the lower cover, and a brass frame with transparent talc or horn slip for the title on the upper cover; these metal excrescences have often been removed as making the books bad neighbours on the shelves.

The field is generally divided into panels by fillets, and sometimes by diagonals into lozenges, which are also imitated in flamboyant style by curved tools. In the spaces is dotted a "semis" (sowing) of small tools, including ribbons bearing names of saints, which may indicate provenance, or more rarely those of places or men, which certainly do so. Rectangular spaces are also filled by parallel roll-stamps; these are produced by rolling along the desired line a cylindrical tool cut in relief or engraved in intaglio so as to repeat its designs in rotation. Roll-stamps were very popular in Germany and the Netherlands, and to some extent also in France and England. They are used in combination with large panel stamps, which they frame, representing saints (or later the Reformers) or royal and other coats of arms, the Tudor rose being a favourite device on English bindings till 1550. These large pieces, forming panels which are the major part of the design, are called stamps in distinction from the small tools.

Printers and publishers, from the very early days of printing, if they were in a large way of business, maintained their own binderies; and Caxton seems

214

not only to have done so, but to have brought with him from Bruges the Netherlandish style. No great number of bindings from his workshop has survived, owing to the misguided fashion which prevailed in the late eighteenth and early nineteenth centuries of having old books re-bound; but enough are known to enable the tools to be identified. Thick boards bevelled at the edges and lozenge spaces starred with small tools were characteristic of his shop. The large panel stamp superseded tools in the next generation.

Meanwhile, an entirely different style, heightened by the use of gold, was approaching. Gold tooling was introduced into Europe probably through Spain, but its use was mainly developed in Italy. Here a number of excellent craftsmen, some of them Oriental leather-workers, were at work in Venice, the natural meeting-ground of West and East. The binders worked in the traditional Eastern manner, with arabesques and gilding and cut-out (*ajouré*) leather over a coloured background. A simpler style, more natural to the West, which flourished in Italy and was combined with gold, is a variety of bent strips, which when placed together produce the effect of rope or knot-work and are strongly suggestive of some of the blind tooled bindings made at Durham three centuries earlier. Another characteristic of Venetian and Florentine binding of the first quarter of the sixteenth century is the fillet-roll built up of a restrained arabesque flowing in a series of circles; this and an elaboration of the rope can be seen in the Florentine binding on Plate II. By the mid-sixteenth

century typical Italian binding had abandoned elaboration for a simple arrangement of fillets giving a plain
border, sometimes with a little arabesque added, and
an equally plain centre panel, bearing the title of the
book and sometimes the name of the owner; the
leather was often morocco, a new importation into
Europe. We find this style imitated (in calf) on books
bound for Henry VIII, Edward VI, and Elizabeth I.

Just as German printers had gone abroad carrying
their new art with them, so now Italian binders
crossed the Alps and worked for collectors in France
and Central Europe. The most notable and perhaps
the earliest of these patrons was Matthias Corvinus,
King of Hungary from 1458 to 1490, the rare sur-
vivors of whose splendid collection confer even more
distinction upon any library possessing one than do
those from Grolier's. Some of the earliest gold-tool-
ings are on books from the "Bibliotheca Corvina",
which may be recognized by the King's rebus, a crow
(*corvus*).

An Italian style of the early sixteenth century, of
which fine examples are known, consists of a fairly
plainly tooled panel enclosing a sunk central cartouche impressed with a large cameo stamp. Thus
the British Museum possesses a Florentine binding
(not before 1514) which shows in the cartouche a
cameo portrait of Julius Cæsar; the stamp itself (of
course in intaglio) survives. A notable collector who
had bindings of this type was Pier Luigi Farnese,
whose books bear a stamp of Apollo driving a chariot
with the motto *ΟΡΘΩΣ ΚΑΙ ΜΗ ΛΟΞΙΩΣ* (straight

216

and not crookedly); these are generically called "Canevari" bindings, having till recently been supposed to have been made for Demetrio Canevari, physician to Pope Urban VII. The earliest bindings made for the famous Jean Grolier were in a variety of this style, the centre plaque being heightened with enamel.

Grolier (1479–1565) held the office of Treasurer of the French armies in Italy from 1510 to 1529, when he returned at the Peace of Cambrai, becoming Chancellor of France in 1545. He had, therefore, excellent opportunities; but there can be little doubt that the style named after him, since it first appeared in the books bound for him, was due to his taste. This, the true Grolier style, superseded the bindings with central plaquettes, and depends for its effect on light and graceful geometrical "strapwork", i.e. interlaced double fillets. Late in his career Grolier's binder employed colour, painting the straps, or else substituted the arabesques, hitherto used only as subordinate decoration. Grolier immortalized his name by having impressed on the covers of his books (after those in the earliest style, in which he merely wrote his name) the inscription IO. GROLIERII ET AMICORVM, and also often PORTIO MEA DOMINE SIT IN TERRA VIVENTIVM. The words of the former were no idle sentiment, for Grolier made his library, containing many of the best books of his day, and notably those from the press of Aldus, accessible to scholars, for whom no public libraries were then available. He was imitated in this by another Italianate Frenchman,

Thomas Mahieu, Secretary to Queen Catherine de Medici, whose books are inscribed THO. MAIOLI ET AMICORVM, whence his name was till recently taken to be Tommaso Maioli; and by some other less well known collectors.

Side by side with the influence of Grolier's workmen on French, and so on northern binding design, went that of Geofroy Tory, letter-cutter and publisher, who used the arabesque style, working into it a broken pot, a device which is said to commemorate the loss of his young daughter. The binders of François I and Henri II show the same influences and were probably (particularly the former's) Italians. François I marked his books with a crowned F; Henri II and his mistress Diane de Poitiers had their books adorned not only with Grolieresque strapwork and other decoration, but also with the interlaced H and D and crescent moons, symbolic of the name Diana, which are found so freely used at Fontainebleau and Chantilly.

The Grolieresque style was imitated with more or less success in other countries, but generally in a rather provincial fashion, notably by Thomas Wotton, who also adopted Grolier's form of ownership inscription; Wotton preferred Grolier's heavier style with coloured strapwork. The Grolieresque was directly or indirectly the ancestor of almost all ornate binding for two centuries, and Grolier laid the foundation of that supremacy of French binders which lasted almost uninterrupted for two centuries, and occasioned Ernest Thoinan's proud boast (only

218

false in using the present tense): "La reliure est un art tout français". It branched down in two lines of descent. The first was the Lyonnese style showing either exaggerated painted or enamelled strapwork, heavily and mechanically tooled, or else large sunk centre and corner stamps with arabesques in relief on a background of gold, and the free space thickly covered with a semis. This, one of the ugliest of known styles of binding, was the destruction of the art in some countries, and especially in Central Europe. The opportunity of so large an expanse of gold was too great a temptation. In a simple form small Lyonnese stamps are found on late Elizabethan books, but luckily the richer book-buyers here never took to the style; the finer Elizabethan bindings are mostly of the simple Italian type, with gilt fillet and panel, with a coat of arms or crest, or else the book's title in the centre. Their Jacobean and Caroline successors adopted and adapted the other style descending from Grolier, which remains to be mentioned.

This was the "fanfare" (flourish), long but unfoundedly associated with the names of Nicolas and Clovis Eve, the former of whom bound for Henri III. Bindings *à la fanfare* (the phrase is Nodier's) were richly covered, in defiance of an edict of Henri III forbidding costly decoration on books, with sprays of bay, worked into geometrical strapwork. As usual, it is most beautiful when most restrained, and when the leather has a chance to show, as in the examples bearing only the corner fleurons and the wreath surrounding the central cartouche for arms or book title; too often the rest of the field is filled with a semis. Nicolas Eve used the latter style, but not the more elaborate. "Fanfare" rapidly degenerated into wretchedly mechanical patterns, which look as though they were impressed with a single stamp on to the cover.

After the early sixteenth century we begin frequently to find decoration on the spines of books, a proof, incidentally, that books were now no longer kept lying on their sides, but upright on shelves; the appearance of titles on the spines and the disappearance of titles written on the fore-edge, which came later, are equally significant, as showing that books began to be placed with spine instead of fore-edge outwards.

Well into the seventeenth century the fanfare style was modified, possibly by a mysterious "Le Gascon", more probably by Florimond Badier. The strapwork is retained, and the enclosed spaces differentiated by inlaying leather of different colours; the sprays are lighter, not only in themselves but because impressed by pointillé tools, i.e. tools with a dotted surface.

The close relations between England and France immediately before and after the Civil War and Commonwealth produced in England a development of the fanfare and Le Gascon styles which is, perhaps, at its best the most delightful of any, at least for small books, and which reigned for nearly a century. This is a style which is frequently, even if somewhat unfortunately, named after Charles II's stationer and binder Samuel Mearne. It is not known whether

Samuel Mearne ever bound books himself; perhaps he merely contracted for binding. No one man could possibly have accomplished one-tenth of the work attributed to Mearne, a distinction which he shares with Chippendale and other eponymous founders of craft styles. The fine series in red Turkey morocco which he supplied to the Royal Library, for which we have the bills, show uniformly only a plain fillet with centre and corner fleurons of Charles II's monogram, crossed Cs, crowned and flanked with palm wreaths. But Charles Mearne, Samuel's son, did sign (with "C. M. fecit") at least one binding in the style known by his father's name, so that there is perhaps not so much occasion for scepticism as has been sometimes assumed. "Mearne", or as they may be better named, "Restoration" bindings, derive some of their charm from inlay of red in black, but more from the infinitely varied combinations of a comparatively few types of tool: (*a*) a curve, which being repeated could be built up into a fish-scale pattern; (*b*) the tulip, open or in bud, which was not, as might be expected, introduced in compliment to Dutch William after 1688, but is freely found in bindings of fifteen years earlier; in defiance of botany, but with most excellent æsthetic effect, it frequently flowers on the ends of bay-twigs; and (*c*) the "drawer-handle", which has no beauty in itself, representing, more probably, the curved rocker of a cradle, but which is extraordinarily fertile as a basis for the most varied designs. The centre panel was often (not always happily) given a gable at head and foot, thus making what is called the "cottage" pattern; the field was also divided into squares (the "all-over" style), a rather unimaginative basis for a design.

The Restoration style developed into:

(1) *The Harleian.* Until recently these have been regarded as the work of a firm named "Elliot and Chapman". In his *Shrewsbury School Library Bindings* (1943), Mr. J. B. Oldham showed that this was incorrect. There was no such firm, and, indeed, Elliot and Chapman were rival binders and not partners. The style which is known by this name has a strongly marked rectangular centre panel surrounded by a broad border.

(2) *The Scottish.* This exists in two main styles. One which resembles the Harleian, but has for a centre-piece a straight stem from which branch short sprays at regular intervals on either side. The other, a later form, consists mainly of a large wheel pattern.

(3) *The Irish,* which is distinguished by a large centre lozenge of inlaid fawn leather.

These styles flourished throughout most of the eighteenth century, only yielding towards its end to the classical movement.

In the later seventeenth century in France there was a revolt against the over-rich decoration of Le Gascon bindings, and we find in their place bindings of a severe simplicity, in which the excellent morocco is only decorated by a centre-piece (often armorial) and corner-fleurons; these are called the "Jansenist" bindings, and perhaps the most beautiful are those made for the Baron de Longepierre, in which the

222

sole decoration is the quincunx thus formed by the repetition of his emblem of the Golden Fleece. Jansenist bindings have sometimes richly decorated *doublures* (linings) which belie their Quaker-like exteriors.

Two late seventeenth- and eighteenth-century families of French binders were influential: the Padeloups, especially Antoine Michel le jeune, Royal binder from 1733 to 1758; and the Deromes, especially Nicolas Denis le jeune (d. 1788). Padeloup used many styles, and especially bold and free inlay; but the prevailing fashion was for a *dentelle* (lacework) border with a centre field plain except for a (generally rather florid) coat of arms. In the hands of the masters the dentelle could be very beautiful, but less tasteful artists broadened the gold surfaces and ruined the effect; this happened especially in Germany and Italy. There were, however, in the later seventeenth and in the eighteenth centuries some excellent binders in Germany and Scandinavia, when the rather heavy portrait panel and Lyonnese styles of the sixteenth century had yielded to the Le Gascon influence; notable was the Court binder at Heidelberg between 1660 and 1710. The Derome *dentelle* was also delightfully varied in the 1770's by an Austrian binder who to the traditional bay has added "rococo" clusters of grapes and flowering sprays. Italy, which had taught France the art of gold-tooling, in the seventeenth and eighteenth centuries mostly followed French fashions, at some distance in taste as well as in time.

223

The end of the eighteenth century brought the classical movement into all decorative art. Books that were to stand in cases made by Sheraton and in rooms designed by Adam and decorated with ornaments by Wedgwood had to be dressed in harmony with their surroundings; and the same change is found in the bindings of Germany and Scandinavia, and in France during the reign of "Empire" decoration. In England the great binder of the period, probably indeed our greatest binder, was Roger Payne. He was fortunate in working for cultured collectors such as Lord Spencer and Cracherode, who could appreciate his taste. Payne does not use classical detail much, though his swags, whether curved or vertical, are Roman in feeling; but he subtly adapted the *dentelle* to the new manner. If (as seems probable) he designed Cracherode's armorial stamp, he is to be credited with the one perfect example of the kind; it may be based on that used in the late sixteenth century by the French historian and collector, J. A. de Thou, on the bindings made for him before his marriage. Unfortunately, however, like many of his contemporaries, he used straight-grained morocco on his larger books, although it forms a less satisfactory background to the tooling than do the smooth moroccos used by the French binders; but he actually succeeded in finding a russia which has lasted very well. Neither he nor any other good binder used the atrocious calf popular in England for cheaper bindings at that period.

Nineteenth-century binding, like other forms of

224

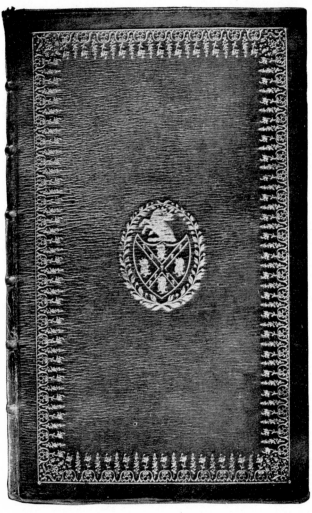

PLATE VII.—BINDING FOR CRACHERODE, BY ROGER PAYNE,
c. 1800

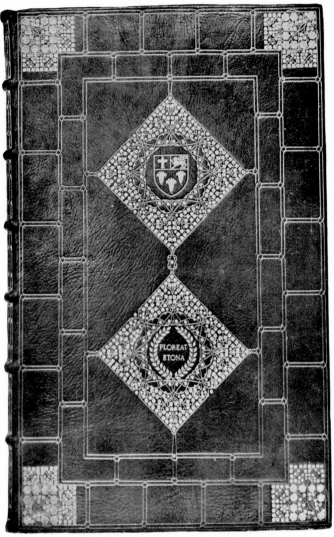

PLATE VIII.—THE ETON ROLL OF HONOUR, BOUND BY
MR. DOUGLAS COCKERELL

decoration, was largely degenerate. Much of it was in imitation of Payne and other eighteenth-century masters but, for the most part, produced unworthy imitations. There are respectable names in plenty, such as Trautz-Bauzonnet, Kalthoeber, Lewis, Bedford, and others but none of real masters. Two little-known London binders of foreign origin, Staggemeier and Welcher, working for some time in partnership, produced some really beautiful bindings in the early part of the century, decorated with classical palmette borders enclosing interlacing geometrical figures in *pointillé* line. In France the Romantic movement produced a short-lived and amusingly ugly "cathedral" style of elaborate Gothic Architectural forms. Towards the latter part of the nineteenth century there were many experiments in appropriate pictorial design; such as a ship on a book of sea-voyages. For the most part they are bad enough to suggest that binding design should be formal.

The real resurrection of leather bindings, however, came in the 1880's with the work of Cobden-Sanderson. Although all his bindings may not be of equal merit, he bound beautifully and was very influential. His work was carried on into the present century by Miss Sarah Prideaux, Katharine Adams and, above all, Douglas Cockerell. In the same manner the designs of Charles Ricketts, another notable designer, were the inspiration of the work of Sybil Pye. Although good binding is still being produced in Europe and in America, in the present economic position of the world there is no longer the same scope as formerly. Some of the loveliest of modern English bindings, for example, were the work of the Gregynog Press. With the closing down of that press, the last remaining real private press in England, in 1940, one of the last channels was closed.

Some large part of the decay of real binding in this century has been due to the development of what was the nineteenth century's chief contribution to this art. In the 1820's the whole position was revolutionized by the use of book cloth as a covering material and the introduction of casing as distinct from binding. The trio of new influences was completed in about 1832 by the discovery of a method of gold-blocking on cloth. From these beginnings there grew a new range of materials and a new tradition of decoration. This soon became the established form of publishers' issue and, although much of the work up to the present day has been uninspired and mechanical, it has shown itself capable of satisfactory work when well used. At any rate, the nineteenth century cannot be considered as a fruitless period when it contributed so important a development to the art.

READING LIST

LIST A.

CHAMBERS' ENCYCLOPEDIA. Article on "Bookbinding".
ENCYCLOPEDIA BRITANNICA. Article on "Bookbinding".

BINDING

LIST B.

BODLEIAN LIBRARY. Gold-tooled bookbindings. (Bodleian picture books No. 2.) 1951.

CARTER, John. Publishers' cloth, 1820–1900. 1935.

COCKERELL, D. Book binding and the care of books. 4th ed. 1939.

HOBSON, G. D. English bindings before 1500. 1929.

HOBSON, G. D. Maioli, Canevari and others. 1926.

HORNE, H. P. The binding of books. 2nd ed. 1915.

HOWE, Ellic. A list of London bookbinders, 1648–1815. 1950.

OLDHAM, J. B. English blind-stamped bindings. 1946.

PLENDERLEITH, H. J. The preservation of leather bookbindings. 1946.

SADLEIR, Michael. The evolution of publishers' binding styles, 1770–1900. 1930.

VICTORIA AND ALBERT MUSEUM. Book bindings. Introduction by John P. Harthan. 1950.

VII

THE COLLATION OF BOOKS

An understanding of the processes of book-building, outlined in the preceding chapters, will enable one to examine and describe books.

The bibliographer, who includes the cataloguing librarian (and to some extent the ordinary reader also), when faced by a volume, has to examine it for the answers to the three questions indicated in Chapter I:

1. What work, or works, does this volume contain?

2. Of what recension and of what edition is it? i.e. by whom is it edited and where, when, and by whom was it printed?

3. Is this a perfect copy of that edition?

IDENTIFYING THE WORK

The mere identity of the work can generally be ascertained from the title-page, or failing that from the colophon, or failing that from the opening words or *incipit*. (*Incipit*, Latin, "here begins": *explicit*, "here ends".) The author's name may be found only as a signature to the dedication, or sometimes half-concealed in an anagram, as in the famous example of the *Hypnerotomachia Poliphili* (Aldus, Venice, 1499), where Francesco Colonna's name, with that

228

of his lady Polia, appears only in this way. Completely anonymous or pseudonymous books may be attributed to their true authors by the aid of several bibliographical dictionaries devoted to them, or sometimes, failing these and similar guides, by much original research. But this belongs to another branch of the subject.

Care must be taken to distinguish between two or more works which are published in one issue, or (as pamphlets often are) simply assembled in one binding for economy's sake. This practice, now generally abandoned in libraries in favour of separate preservation in file boxes or pamphlet covers, was once universal, and "tract-volumes" containing anything from half a dozen to fifty pieces abound on the shelves of old libraries. When two works printed in the same type, without distinctive headlines, pagination, signatures, or title-pages, are bound together, as happened in the first days of printing, the resulting volume needs as careful analysis as one in manuscript. Generally, however, one at least of these guides is present (and the safest is the signatures), since if the second work were intended by the printer himself to be bound with the first, he would give it a distinctive alphabet of signatures, either doubling the letters or using upper-case (if the first book is signed in lower-case), or a combination of upper-case and lower-case. If the division between two works occurs in the middle of a quire, it stands to reason that the two are of one edition and bibliographically inseparable. This fact has not always prevented owners from having such books cut in half and bound as two.

IDENTIFYING THE EDITION

Careful examination of the title-page, colophon, pre-liminaries (dedication, preface, ecclesiastical or secular licence to print), and *incipit* will also normally reveal any facts about the editing, translating, and printing of the edition. Should the printer's name and the place and date, or any of these facts, be omitted or disguised, it will be necessary to hunt them down as closely as possible. Here experience of the printing of various countries and periods is necessary, but there is a whole armoury of books to use in the chase.

A printer's or author's name, like that of a place, may be translated. Among authors the famous case of Desiderius Erasmus stands alone; but there were many writers, especially in the German Renaissance, who Latinized or Græcized their names: examples are Molitor (Müller = miller) and the great reformer Melanchthon (Schwarzerd = black earth). The beginner must be prepared to recognize in Martinus Cæsaris, or even in Martin Emperour, the Antwerp printer Martin de Keyser; and in Henricus Stephanus and also in Harry Stephens (an extreme example of the regular old practice of translating proper names) the scholar-printer Henri Estienne.

Some deliberate mystifications are easily recognized as such, as when a vehement Reformation tract is stated to be printed "before the Castell of Saint Angelo, at the sign of Saint Peter", or "not a mile from a bouncing priest", but experience is necessary to suspect the little books stating themselves as printed at the Sphere in Cologne to be really from Paris or the Low Countries. It may be worth mentioning here that the many English books printed in the Low Countries in the late seventeenth and early eighteenth centuries on account of the paper duty in England which made it cheaper to import the book ready printed, can often be recognized by the tendency of the compositors, setting up a language they did not know, to set *ij* in place of *y*, a letter which did not occur in their language.

To establish the relative dates of two editions is the important duty of the bibliographer, especially if they are rivals for the proud position of *editio princeps*, or first edition.

There is much misunderstanding by the public of the true value of first editions, and the value set on them, often quite unintelligently, in the market has led to an equally unintelligent contempt. In spite of certain notorious but quite occasional malpractices there is, however, much genuine and reputable collecting with an honest regard for the author's text at its heart. At the present day, when proofs of every edition that appears in his lifetime are submitted to the author for his corrections, the authentic definitive text of a book which future editors will have to reprint, and future scholars to study, is most probably the author's last; but even so the first will be of interest, and second only to the original manuscript as showing his first thoughts and the process of his corrections. The practice of submitting proofs to the author is one which began long after the invention of printing; at first it took the form of allowing him to attend at the press while the printing was in progress, but also later by sending proofs. The best general account of proof-reading is Dr. Percy Simpson's "Proof-reading in the 16th, 17th and 18th centuries" published in 1935 as one of the *Oxford Books on Bibliography*.

For the most part in the sixteenth and seventeenth centuries later editions are mere reprints of the first with the addition of fresh printer's errors; the first edition is therefore usually the nearest we can get to the author's own words. A noteworthy example is the First Folio Shakespeare of 1623 which is our primal authority for several of the plays for which no early separate quarto editions survive. The second, third, and fourth folios, which are purchased for large sums in order to make a set on the shelves of collectors, are merely inaccurate reprints, of interest as showing the dates at which the demand created a new edition, but intrinsically of no authority and worthless.

DATING THE EDITION

So much for the importance of the chronological order of editions. Methods of establishing it are many:

(*a*) A date may be concealed in a chronogram.

This tiresome device of the over-ingenious consists in embedding the roman figures of the date in a motto, so worded that these letters occur exactly often enough to add up to the required total, and distinguishing them by printing them in upper-case or a different fount. They are in the process often tortured into almost unintelligible arrangements: the following is an easy example:

gUstaVUs aDoLphUs gLorIose pUgnans MorItUr

U	=	5
V	=	5
U	=	5
D	=	500
L	=	50
U	=	5
L	=	50
I	=	1
U	=	5
M	=	1000
I	=	1
U	=	5

1632, the year of Gustavus Adolphus's death.

(*b*) The dates of the printer's activity, where his name is known, will give the outside limits of date. Occasionally, a deduction will have to be made from the dates of the printer's birth and death. In such cases, it can be assumed that he would not have printed during the first fifteen or twenty years of his life and allowance must be made for books which might appear still bearing his name for about two years after his death.

(*c*) The dates between which the printer is known

to have printed, or the publisher to have published, at a particular address. For instance, Wynkyn de Worde, conveniently for bibliographers, quitted Caxton's old shop at Westminster for the Sign of the Sun in Fleet Street, London, at the end of the year 1500. Some of the undated mid-seventeenth-century English ballads which bear the imprints of several publishers in conjunction can be closely dated to the only few years in which all of them were in business. The most useful tools for tracing English printers and publishers up to 1775 are the series of dictionaries of the book-trade published by the Bibliographical Society.

(*d*) The printer was at first always, and for the next century decreasingly, his own type-cutter and type-founder. The punches cannot have had the durability of those now used, for printers constantly changed their founts. Thus Caxton used eight text-types in seventeen years. By registering chronologically the signed and dated books from a press, the unsigned and undated can be attributed to their printer and approximately to their year. On the special methods of type-study of fifteenth-century books more guidance will be found in the section on the cataloguing of early printed books.

(*e*) The printer also often used, either in addition to his name or as a substitute for it, a woodcut device. These were changed from time to time, either because the block wore out or because its owner tired of it. The appearance of devices in dated books gives us a good foundation for dating undated

234

books. Thus Wynkyn de Worde used successively no fewer than seventeen devices.

(*f*) Devices, borders, initial letters, ornaments and all other forms of woodcut were liable to split from wear in the press or from being kept too dry. They might be attacked by worm and show the holes, though only the less careful or more impecunious printer would use wood-blocks in a worm-eaten state. Metal plates, and especially copper, owing to the softness of the metal, wear down in the course of printing and give inferior impressions. Progressive deterioration in all these ways may be used to arrange undated books, in which wood or metal blocks were used, in a chronological sequence. If, in copy B, the cracks are seen to have widened, the worm-holes to have multiplied, the engraving to have less definition than in copy A, then copy B is safely put down as the later of the two.

(*g*) In the early period of the art every printer made advances in technique which, once made, were not abandoned, and which can therefore be used as evidence of priority or vice versa. A book with a title-page, or with foliation, or with signatures, or with perfect justification of the line-endings, will always be later than one from the same press without these signs of accomplishment. It need not be later than one from another press, since different printers, and printers in different centres, reached the same level of technique at different times. Caxton, for example, is to the end much more primitive than his contemporaries at Paris or Lyons or Venice.

235

Conversely, two books representing the same level of technical advance and from the same press are necessarily close together in date. This is the case noticed in Chapter I, the *Expositio S. Hieronymi in Symbolum Apostolorum* printed at Oxford by Theodoric Rood and bearing the date "1468".

(*h*) There is a general rule that a first edition is printed in a larger and handsomer style, in a larger format, and with more leaves, than a later edition. Thus, a folio will be followed by a quarto, a quarto by an octavo. This does not usually apply to special editions, such as collected editions; for example, the first *folio* edition of Shakespeare's plays came later in date than the *quarto* editions. Other exceptions are found, sometimes with no apparent reason.

(*i*) The printer of a first edition normally starts with the text, leaving the preliminaries to be printed last; the preface is probably not written until the text is all in type. He will sign the first quire of text as B and the preliminaries A, following this up with a, b, etc. if the prefatory material overruns A. Alternatively he may use A as the first signature for the text and allocate an arbitrary symbol, such as an asterisk, for the preliminary matter.

The author does, or at least did, not usually write a new preface for the second edition. There was nothing, therefore, to prevent the printer from starting with the half-title or title and printing straight ahead. The break between preliminaries and text may often occur in the middle of a quire, proving that this has been the case.

Where edition A collates with the preliminaries separate and edition B with the text following on without a break, A is the first edition. A good example is Dryden's *An Evening's Love*, in the first and second editions, both of 1671. The first edition collates, A⁴, a⁴, b²; A–L⁴, M² in 56 leaves; the second edition, A–N⁴, O² in 54 leaves.

It is worth noting that the preliminaries are often a half-sheet with the other half concluding the book; cases are known where the two halves have been left undivided by the binder.

(*j*) The watermark in the paper may sometimes be datable by the aid of such works as Briquet's *Les Filigranes* or Churchill's supplement to that work or one of the several special studies which have appeared. It has to be borne in mind that it is the paper and not the book which is thus dated although there is obviously a relationship between the two. It is a method which is being increasingly used in bibliographical investigation and one famous example of its application, that of the "1619" Shakespeare quartos, is described in the first chapter of this book.

In early nineteenth-century books the watermark will sometimes be found to include a date.

(*k*) Dated manuscript notes of ownership may provide a date after which the book cannot have been printed. The most famous example is the copy in the Bibliothèque Nationale at Paris of the "Gutenberg" or "Mazarin" or "42-line" Bible. In this, Henricus Cremer, Vicar of St. Stephen's, Mainz, stated that he finished rubricating and binding this copy on

24th August, 1456. Copies must, therefore, have been on sale before this date and we are thus provided with a capital landmark in the history of printing.

In certain instances negative evidence of this kind is valuable. One of the tests applied by Carter and Pollard in the Wise forgeries was that in no case was there a contemporary date of acquisition; in one case only was there an author's presentation inscription and that was dated thirty-two years after the alleged date of publication.

(*l*) In every problem regarding the dating of books it must not be forgotten that there have been two important adjustments to the calendar during the age of the printed book.

The present uniform method of beginning the calendar with the first of January ("new style", or "n.s.") was, in this country throughout the seventeenth century, slowly superseding the "old style" (or "o.s.") calendar which began on 25th March. The change was made gradually and without a general ordinance; for a time it was not uncommon for dates from January 1st to March 24th inclusive to be given in the double form, e.g., $16\frac{69}{70}$. But this convenient form is exceedingly rare in imprints and any date on a book may, unless there is evidence that it falls within the period March 25th to December 31st, stand for either of two years. A book printed at any time between March 25th, 1670, and December 31st, 1670, would be dated 1670 according to either style calendar; but if printed between January 1st and March 24th it would be 1669 if the old style

238

calendar were in use and 1670 according to the new style. The possible range of a single year's date is, therefore, not twelve months but fifteen months all but seven days.

Now it is possible that the printer of a first edition appearing in the debatable three first months of the new-style year used new style, and that the printer of the second edition, still before March 25th, used old style, thus making it the close of the previous year, with the result that the first edition bears a date later by one year than that of the second. This fantastic result is found in the early editions of Milton's *Pro Populo Anglicano Defensio*, first edition, Londini, Typis Du-Gardianis, 1651, a handsomely printed 4°, and 3rd edition, Londini, Typis Du Gardianis [Utrecht], 1650, 12°; the true order was first pointed out by Mr. F. F. Madan in *The Library*, 4th ser., vol. iv, pp. 119–145.

King Charles I was beheaded on January 30th, 1649 (n.s.) or 1648 (o.s.). Within a few days there was rushed out the first edition of his prayers and meditations, entitled Εἴκων Βασιλική (*Eikon Basilikē*). No fewer than sixty editions and translations of this popular book appeared before the end of 1649 o.s. (i.e. March 24th, 1650 n.s.); of these twenty-five are dated 1648, a date which has surprised later owners who had been brought up to believe that King Charles was beheaded in 1649, and who had no knowledge of the styles of dating with which to modify that belief. These were, of course (without deducting possible later unaltered reprints of 1648

imprints) produced in the two months before March
25th, 16$\frac{48}{49}$, and so may have been some of those
dated (if dated by new style) 1649. They are, at the
lowest estimate of their number, remarkable evidence
of the strength of the Royalist feeling roused in the
country by the execution of the King. There were,
in fact, so many copies on the market that only one
edition (1662) was called for in the years following
the Restoration, when everyone was eager to show
himself Royalist, and how better than by buying
"the King's Book"?

The other important change was the adjustment
necessary on the introduction of the Gregorian
calendar. The actual length of the solar year is a
few hours more than 365 days and in 1582 Pope
Gregory XIII cancelled ten days from the old Julian
calendar in order to bring the calendar into line with
the seasons again. This reform was adopted by
Roman Catholic countries with the result that
October 4th, 1582, was followed immediately by
October 15th, 1582. In England the change was not
made until 1752, by which time it was necessary to
cancel eleven days, and September 2nd, 1752, was
followed immediately by September 14th, 1752.

COLLATING THE COPY

Satisfied then as to the edition, the bibliographer
turns to the third question, and endeavours to
satisfy himself that the copy before him is complete. The process of doing this is called *collation*.
Collation means a putting side by side or com-

240

parison, and may be used of the investigation of texts, whether manuscript or printed. The 42-line Bible once more provides us with a palmary example. It used to be debated whether the other very early Bible printed in the still larger type associated with the first Mainz press, and called the 36-line Bible, were not the earlier of the two. But it was discovered that the printer of this had skipped a considerable passage in the text of the Old Testament, and that the omitted matter corresponded exactly with a complete leaf of the 42-line Bible. Only two explanations are possible, either that he turned over two leaves instead of one, or that the copy used lacked that leaf. In either case he must have set up from a copy of the 42-line Bible, and the later date of the 36-line Bible, suspected on other grounds, is amply proved. Dr. McKerrow has recorded another case of a reprint from an imperfect copy. The printer of the 1585 edition of *The Secrets and wonders of the world*, working from a copy of *A Summarie of the Antiquities, and wonders of the worlde* [*c.* 1565], perceived the imperfection in his copy-text and filled in the hiatus from his own invention.

Whether a particular copy of a book is or is not complete can only be settled by a thorough examination of its physical structure or "make-up". It is, of course, not necessary to carry out this examination of all new books entering a library. The result would not justify the labour. But an older book should always be collated, for many things may have happened to it since it was new.

FORMAT

Just as bibliography is the biology of the book, collation is its bloodless anatomy. Anatomists must understand the structure they examine. The basis of the structure of the book is the folding of the sheets of paper to form the leaves.

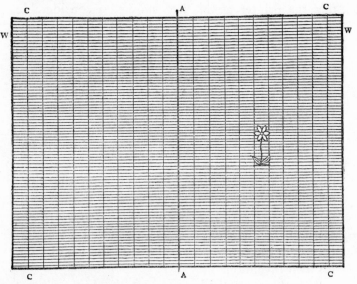

FIG. 10.—TWO LEAVES OF A SHEET FOLDED IN FOLIO.

A whole sheet of paper which has not been folded and which was often used for printing maps, proclamations, and the like, is usually called a *broadsheet* or sometimes a *broadside* or *open sheet*. When half a sheet of paper is used unfolded there seems to be considerable justification for calling it a *half-sheet*,

242

although it has traditionally, but not very accurately, been called a *single-sheet*. Some writers urge that tradition has hallowed this nomenclature, but *half-sheet* is certainly to be preferred.

In a broadsheet the watermark is to be found in the centre of one half of the sheet, which is crossed breadthways by the spaced chain-lines ((c) in Fig. 10) and lengthways by the close wire-lines ((w) in

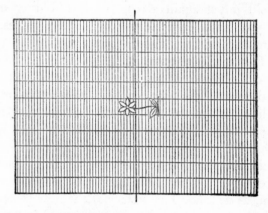

FIG. 11.—TWO LEAVES OF A SHEET FOLDED IN QUARTO.

Fig. 10). Fold the sheet once down the line AA and we get a pair of leaves, or four pages, *in folio*. The watermark is in the middle of one leaf, the first or second according as the printer places the sheet on the press, and the chain-lines still run perpendicularly.

Fold it again across the first fold and we get a *quarto* folding of four leaves or eight pages. The watermark is divided by or close to the fold of one

243

of the pairs of leaves, either the inner or the outer pair according to which way the fold is made. It cannot be found half on one of the inner and half on one of the outer leaves, unless the book has been taken to pieces and wrongly re-bound, or unless a leaf has been supplied from another copy. The chain-lines run horizontally across the leaf, reversing their position in folio.

Fold it yet again across the last folding made, and you have eight leaves or sixteen pages, the commonest format since about 1700, when paper was first made in quantity in sheets of dimensions to yield a fair-sized page in this folding, which is called *octavo*. The proportions of the octavo leaf are not like the square quarto leaf, but are very much those of folio; of course it is smaller, at least in the old hand-made papers, which were not made in such widely varying sizes as are the modern machine-made papers. The chain-lines run perpendicularly again, as in folio. The watermark is now (when the binder's shears allow it to be seen at all) in quarters in the top inner corner of either leaves 1, 4, 5, and 8 (the outer leaves of the quartette on either side of the sewing) or of leaves 2, 3, 6, and 7 (the inner); they can be in no other combination in a sheet that has not been tampered with. Illustrations do not show these multiple foldings easily, but by working them out with a sheet of paper it is not difficult to understand them.

Yet another fold brings the sheet to *sextodecimo* or *sixteens*, a gathering of 16 leaves or 32 pages; the chain-lines are again horizontal as in quarto, the shape is again squarish but small in proportion. The watermark is to be found near the top of the fore-edges and it is rare to find more than traces of it. The 16° has a fold at the foot of the leaf. Further doublings produce 32°, 64°, 128°, but these are rare except in modern pocket-book diaries and the like.

An alternative and much commoner folding, resulting in a small book, is *duodecimo* or *twelves* ("the dear and the dumpy twelves" of Austin Dobson's poem), giving 12 leaves or 24 pages. There are many occasional but only two normal ways of folding. By one method, which was current in England in the late sixteenth, seventeenth, and eighteenth centuries, the sheet was cut into two-thirds and one-third. The larger part was folded as an octavo while the other was folded by two vertical folds and the four leaves so formed were placed within the other folding. By the other method, common during the nineteenth century, the sheet was divided into three and then folded twice across. In both these cases the chain-lines will be horizontal. By the first method, the watermark will be towards the top outer corners of leaves 7 and 8 or 11 and 12; by the second method, towards the top outer corners of leaves 7 and 12 or the foot of leaves 9 and 10. In many instances the watermark will have disappeared in the process of binding, but there is still the shape of the leaf, which is rather narrower than in octavo, to distinguish it from the square leaf in sixteens.

Doubling the duodecimo produces 24°; and a common variation in French books is eighteens. Half-sheets of this last achieve what bibliographers have denied the possibility of, and what one may be allowed to wish were really impossible, an intact section with an odd number of leaves; in this case, nine.

These various terms are written in abbreviated forms:

Broadsheet	=	1° *or* bs.
Folio	=	2° *or* fol.
Quarto	=	4° *or* 4to *or* Q° *or* Q
Octavo	=	8° *or* 8vo
Duodecimo	=	12° *or* 12mo
Sextodecimo	=	16° *or* 16mo
Tricesimo-secundo	=	32° *or* 32mo
Sexagesimo-quarto	=	64° *or* 64mo

In every case the pronunciation should follow the full word.

In the ordinary way nothing more is needed than to note the format of the sections or quires and to run through the book as the binder does, checking them by the signatures. The use of signatures in a modern book is queried by some people in view of the presence of pagination and back marks. If the book is uncomplicated the binder can collate by pagination by remembering that the first pages of the sections should read in an arithmetical progression, such as 1, 17, 33, 49, 65, and so on, though much higher numbers are probably not so ready to the mind. Even so, is it not easier to fan the sections out and read the alphabet at the foot? If the structure of the book is in any way complicated, the work of the binder is still further multiplied for nothing. Each unsigned section of a two-volume book may belong to either volume and may have been put on the wrong pile in the warehouse and so be cased in the wrong volume, until the text has been checked— and that by a binder who may not be able to read the author's language. Then, the arithmetical progression, inferior as it is at its best as a guide to the binder, may be thrown right out in two ways. Firstly, the preliminary leaves may not be separately printed but may be given a separate roman pagination. For example, the text may begin with page 1 before the end of the first section, let us say after page xiv. Sections 2, 3, and 4 will then begin, not on the easily remembered pages 17, 33, 49, but on pages 3, 19, 35. Secondly, if page 7, for example, in the second section and pages 21, 27, and 31 in the third section bear full-page zinco line-blocks, printed with the text, then if these pages are not reckoned in the pagination, page 7 (as we should number it) being preceded by page 6 and followed by page 7, we should find the sections beginning with pages 3, 18, 31. In spite of the attempts made to discard them, including some in certain finely produced modern books, it is still generally considered more really practical to retain signatures; collation will occasionally be needed.

Experience has shown that two apparently impossible errors in collating are habitually made by beginners. One is to reckon the binder's fly-leaves as part of the book. They are, of course, mere accidents, like the rest of the binding. The other is to state that the format can always be ascertained by simply counting the leaves from signature to signature. They who state this are the less to blame in that James Duff Brown in his *Manual of Practical Bibliography* (that able librarian's least satisfactory work) makes just this preposterous statement. One can only reply, *more Socratico*, by a question, "Of what format, then, is a book with six leaves to a section? Of what format one with fourteen? Still more, of what format one in alternate eights and fours?"

The number of leaves to a section is, of course, only a secondary guide, when the shape, the foldings and the waterlines and marks of the paper have been noted. Only in the eighteenth century, and perhaps only in England, has it been usual to make up folios in single-sheet sections of two leaves; in the fifteenth century five sheets were gathered, making a quinternion or quire of ten leaves, often alternating more or less regularly with quaternions, or quires of eight.[1] There is at least one case of a folio quire of fourteen leaves. In England in the sixteenth and seventeenth centuries sixes were the rule for folios. The eighteenth-century practice of making up in two is unexplained; it was immensely wasteful of

[1] This Latin word "quaternio" is the true origin of our word "quire" and of the French *cahier*; the choir of a church, which has been absurdly held to be its origin (the leaves standing on either side of the sewing, as do the singers!) is, of course, from "chorus".

sewing, and avoidance of this is, of course, the motive for gathering several sheets into one quire.

Quartos are fairly often found in eights, i.e. the sheets gathered in pairs; but preliminaries often show a sheet with a half-sheet gathered into it (six leaves), and quarto books habitually end with half-sheets (two leaves).

In octavos the single-sheet section is the norm, and only an experience limited to modern octavos could have occasioned Brown's error. But even here half-sheet sections occur, notably at the beginnings and ends of books.

Sixteens are now habitually so imposed as to be cut in half and made up in half-sheets of eight leaves. These closely resemble octavos, especially since modern machine-made paper does not afford the old guides; if the bolt at the foot has been shorn away in casing it is really indistinguishable from an octavo.

In the eighteenth century duodecimos were very often made up in this way in half-sheet sections of six leaves. Variations of this practice gave, by cutting into two-thirds and one-third, alternate eights and fours (or else, by inserting the four leaves inside the eight, twelves); and by cutting into thirds, continuous fours.

Italian printers of the fifteenth and the first half of the sixteenth centuries had an admirable practice of printing at the end of the book, below the colophon, a registrum—whence the signatures are now sometimes spoken of as the "register"—setting out the quires of which the complete book should be made

up. Before the days of signatures the first or identifying words of each recto before the sewing of each
quire would be set out in due order. The invention
of signatures simplified the registrum, since it was
then only necessary to set out the series of signatures
with a note of the number of leaves to be found in
each, e.g.:

a–z, A–T

omnes sunt quaterniones praeter 1, duernionem;

or,

tutti sono fogli,

the latter meaning that, say in a quarto, all the quires
are single and intact sheets, i.e., in fours.

The registrum fully achieves the frequently expressed bibliographical ideal, that every book should
carry its own collation; but what is meant by the
phrase is generally the more restricted requisite,
that the pagination and signatures should clearly
cover the entire book.

Blank, or possibly blank, first and last leaves must
be reckoned in collating, if only with a query. They
are conjugate with printed leaves and are part of the
book. Besides, they may not be blank. If their blank-
ness is recorded, then the mind of the possessor of a
copy which lacks them is set at rest. The first leaf
may well bear a licence to print, the last leaf a device
or a publisher's list. The modern publisher's list at
the end of a book is normally a quite separate section
or pamphlet, merely sewn-in in the casing, and is no
part of the book it accompanies. Dryden's *Britannia*

Rediviva, 1688, was reprinted by Jacob Tonson in 1691 to complete his collected set of the poet's works. The title-page was reprinted unaltered from that of 1688, but on the spare last leaf Tonson added an advertisement which included the true date. Many copies of this textually valueless edition have been deprived by accident or cunning of their last leaf and have been passed off as the first edition.

In collating it is necessary to be sure that the book is perfect, and has not merely been *"made perfect"*. This latter process consists of supplying the place of a missing leaf by the appropriate leaf from another imperfect copy. Such leaves may be quite useful additions to an imperfect book to fit it to be a "working copy"; but they do not carry authority, and in fact are not infrequently taken from wrong editions.

Great care must be taken to detect the insertion of leaves reproduced in facsimile. As a rule, the difference between the facsimile and genuine leaves is clear from the paper and from the photographic tone, but it is not always so. Copies of complete modern photographic reprints are sometimes stained and passed off as originals. The only test is to examine the paper closely, by touch and by holding it to the light. It need perhaps not be more than lightly indicated that the phrase occasionally seen in the less scholarly dealers' lists "Unique, the title-page in facsimile" is self-contradictory. If the book is unique, whence came the facsimile?

In the absence of signatures and foliation the collator falls back on the evidence of the sheets themselves. He collates by *watermarks*.

But first let it be observed that unwatermarked papers existed from the fifteenth century, and were common in the eighteenth; and that modern machine-made paper does not give the regularly placed markings necessary to this method. The method does, however, work very well for the great mass of books up to 1700 at least; and, of course, those without printed signatures are the products of the first generation of typographers, until the modern American incunabula began to be produced; after that early period signatures rarely fail except in preliminaries.

The way to quire an unsigned book is this:

A. A folio: Look at the first leaf against the light, then the next, and so on, noting whether they have watermarks. Put down on a piece of paper an X or any other symbol for a watermarked leaf, and an O for an unmarked leaf. After four leaves begin to look for the sewing. If the book is tightly bound and the thread is invisible, restrain your impatience; the watermarks will in the end tell their tale and the backs of books must not be broken, even in a good cause; collation is a *bloodless* anatomy. Let us say that you find your sewing. Mark it with a stroke and proceed with the search for watermarks. You have, let us say, now got this down on paper:

X O O X /

As each complete sheet of paper has a watermark in one of its two halves and none in the other (Fig. 10), the next leaf, which will be the pair of (or "conjugate with") that immediately preceding the sewing, must be without a watermark. The next two must have watermarks, since their pairs have none, and the fourth after the sewing will be unmarked. You now have

X O O X / O X X O

which should, if all is well, be a quire of eight leaves, a quaternio, followed by a visible division between it and the next; but only in original bindings can one see easily down to the back. Copies in the tightest late eighteenth- and early nineteenth-century morocco bindings, such as those made for King George III, Lord Spencer, Cracherode, the Duke of Devonshire, and others, were fortunately hot-pressed quire by quire, and the outside pages of the quires can be identified by the gloss. If the quire-ending does not appear after the eighth leaf, but clearly or doubtfully after the ninth, we have to make sure that there is not a leaf missing at the very beginning. It is true that it may be a blank; but, even if it is, it is a part of the book and must be accounted for. The best plan is to suspend judgment and to go on collating the watermarks for another quire, which will probably settle the matter. If neither the second nor the third quire explains the first, it is a hard case, and I have before now in such a pose turned the book upside down and collated it from the end backwards —it does just as well.

B. But suppose our book to be a quarto, a less common case in the earliest period. In the first leaf we may find either no watermark or half a watermark, divided by the sewing, and possibly not easy to see. It may have been placed a little out of the centre and be complete in one leaf or the other: but, even so, it will be quite close to the sewing. Mark the unmarked leaf O and the marked X, as before, the X standing normally for half a watermark. We will, say, get before the sewing

X O /

The leaf following the sewing must be the rest of the unmarked half of the sheet, and the next and last of the quire must bear the remaining half of the watermark, giving us the complete quire as

X O / O X

The curious thing is that the paper-maker did not pile the sheets with the watermarked halves all at one end, or else the pressman did not take them up and put them in the tympan of the press all the same way, for so far from our finding all the watermarked halves (in a folio) before the sewing or all after it, they run in any order. But one thing is certain, barring cancels, made-up copies, and occasional unmarked papers, that every marked half in a folio is paired across the sewing by an unmarked half.

PLATES

The plates as well as the text must be collated. Before the eighteenth century there is rarely a printed collation of plates beyond a numeration; a slip of directions to the binder was often printed, but has nearly always gone the way of all printed slips. These are well named for they are the most elusive and evanescent of printed matters. In modern books the plates can usually be collated from the list in the preliminaries. These are not, however, always strictly accurate and care must be taken to ensure that an apparently "missing" plate is not lurking in some unorthodox part of the book's make-up.

IMPRINTS

The following are a few of the more important and less easily recognized place-names found in imprints. They normally appear in the locative case, but often in adjectival or possessive forms, e.g. *in urbe Maguntina, in alma Parisiensium academia.*

Abbatisvilla	Abbeville
Abredonia	Aberdeen
Andegavum . . .	Angers
Andreapolis	St. Andrews
Aquisgranum . .	Aachen; Aix-la-Chapelle
Argentina, Argentoratum .	Strassburg
Augusta (alone) . . .	Augsburg *or* rarely London
Augusta Taurinorum, Taurinum	Turin
Augusta Trebocorum .	Strassburg
Augusta Treverorum .	Trèves; Trier
Augusta Trinobantum .	London
Augusta Vangionum .	Worms
Augusta Vindelicorum .	Augsburg
Aurelia, Aureliacum .	Orleans
Aurelia Allobrogum .	Geneva

Avenio		Avignon
Babenberga . . .		Bamberg
Barchino, Barcino .		Barcelona
Basilea		Basle
Bisuntia, Vesuntio .		Besançon
Bononia		Bologna
Borbetomagus . .		Worms
Brixia		Brescia
Cadomum . . .		Caen
Cæsaraugusta . .		· Saragossa
Colonia		Cologne
Colonia Agrippina .		Cologne
Colonia Allobrogum .		Geneva
Colonia Claudia . .		Cologne
Colonia Munatiana .		Basle
Colonia Ubiorum . .		Cologne
Complutum . .		Alcalà de Henares: famous for the "Complutensian" polyglot Bible, printed there in 1514–17
Constantinople . .		almost always a fictitious imprint
Cosmopolis . . .		always a fictitious imprint
Crisopolis . . .		Parma
Daventria . . .		Deventer
Divio		Dijon
Dordracum . . .		Dordrecht
Duacum . . .		Douai
Eblana . . .		Dublin
Eboracum . . .		York
Eleutheropolis . .		*literally*, "free city"; a fictitious imprint found on "free" books
Erfordia . . .		Erfurt
Gandavum . . .		Ghent
Gippeswicum . .		Ipswich
Gravionatium . .		Bamberg

Hafnia	Copenhagen
Herbipolis	Würzburg
Hispalis	Seville
Holmia	Stockholm
Leida	Leyden
Lipsia	Leipzig
Lovanium	Louvain
Lugdunum	Lyons
Lugdunum Batavorum . .	Leyden
Lutetia	Paris
Maguntia	Mainz; Mayence
Malborow ("in the land of Hessen")	Marburg. English books with this imprint were, however, probably printed at Cologne
Mancunium . . .	Manchester
Mantua Carpetanorum . .	Madrid
Matritum	Madrid
Mediolanum . . .	Milan
Moguntia	Mainz; Mayence
Monachium . . .	Munich
Mounts	Mons
Mutina	Medina
Norica; Norimberga; Noriberga	Nuremberg; Nürnberg
Panormum	Palermo
Papia	Pavia
Parisius	a peculiar locative plural found regularly in the fifteenth century where Parisiis would be expected
Parthenope (rarer than Neapolis)	Naples
Patavia	Passau
Roan; Roane; Rothomagum .	Rouen
Salisburia	Salzburg
Salmantica	Salamanca
Sanctandrois . . .	St. Andrews

I

Sarisburia; Sarum . . .	Salisbury
Senae	Sienna
Spira	Speier; Speyer; Spires
Striveling	Stirling
Sublacense Monasterium .	Subiaco
Taurinum; Augusta Taurin-orum	Turin
Theatrum; Theatrum Sheldonianum	the first University Press (late seventeenth century) at Oxford
Tigurum	Zurich
Trajectum Ad Rhenum .	Utrecht
Treviri	Trèves; Trier
Tridentum	Trent
Ultrajectum . . .	Utrecht
Ulyssipo	Lisbon
Venetiæ	Venice
Vesuntio; Bisuntia . .	Besançon
Vienna	Vienne
Vindobona	Vienna
Vormatia	Worms
Vratislavia	Breslau
Wigornum	Worcester

VIII

THE DESCRIPTION OF BOOKS

Having examined a book, and learned all that it has to tell of its identity, its contents, and its history as shown by the condition in which it has survived, it will be necessary to record the knowledge so obtained, either for oneself, or for others who have not access to the book itself. It is necessary, in other words, to describe the book.

Every catalogue-entry is a description of the book catalogued; but according to the purpose of the catalogue is the degree of elaboration of the description.

At the lowest it must identify the work; anything short of this is incompetence, as seen in the entry in an auction catalogue of a celebrated illuminated MS. Psalter, which was simply catalogued from its decorated first word as

A big book, "Beatus".

I. Minimum Entry

The minimum catalogue entry would then be represented by

Tasso: Aminta,

which would at least tell the reader the author and the title of the book, and if he had heard of both before would be of some small use, were he indifferent to matters of text and annotation. But if he is advanced enough to wish to select his edition, such an entry is as good as useless. What he will want will be something like this:

II. SHORT ENTRY

TASSO (TORQUATO) Aminta, ristampata da N. Ciangulo. Utrecht, 1725. 12°. Imperfect.

An entry of this type not only tells the reader that the library contains an *Aminta*; it enables him to find its author among others of the same surname (not, it must be confessed, a very difficult matter in this case), to identify the author of the commentary, and to draw what *a priori* conclusions he likes from its date, in other words, its position in the chronological sequence of editions of the *Aminta*, and its probable part in the growing corpus of knowledge of the play and its sources and so forth. The notation of bibliographical format, "12°", which is often accompanied by the pagination as printed, serves little purpose here; but the latter information is useful in many entries to distinguish a pamphlet from a substantial work. In early books where there was perhaps more than one edition in a year, or more than one undated edition, the format is often the handiest distinction. In short catalogue entries of modern books the size-notation, whether strictly bibliographical or by inches or millimetres in the modern style, seems to be entirely useless, unless to warn a reader that a volume is of specially large or small dimensions.

III. SHORT STANDARD DESCRIPTION

There is yet a further need which a catalogue can satisfy, and that is to anticipate as far as possible questions which may be asked about a book's physical and intellectual composition, either by someone who has no access to a copy, or by someone who has a copy which is in imperfect or only dubiously perfect and genuine condition. Such a catalogue entry is a full or standard description; standard, because once competently made it is permanent and can be referred to at any time.

It will be obvious that not all books, nor even many in proportion to the number which exist, would repay the labour of making standard descriptions on a full scale. Yet in any primal and official register of books certain minimum information about any book ought to be found. We cannot be sure what book will become important, or what book will become rare.

The elements of such a minimum standard description are:

1. *Heading:* the author's name, full enough for identification.

2. *Extract:* the title, as found on the title-page, with necessary abbreviations indicated by a three-dot leader (. . .); the edition number, if any. The names of editor, translator, illustrator, to be supplied in square brackets if not given on the title-page.

3. *Collation:* pagination; format; signatures, covering the entire volume; plates.

4. *Imprint:* the publisher's name, place of publication, and date.

In a retrospective bibliography might be added:

5. *The printer's name and place.*

6. *A note of any vital fact (not opinion) bearing on the book's origin or history; such, for example, as that it was suppressed.*

And in a catalogue of a library might also be added:

7. *A note on the copy: binding, MS. notes, previous ownership, if of consequence, and, of course, an exact statement of imperfection or damage.*

In summary form, and for normal purposes, such a description will occupy less space than its analysis as given here. As for example:

TASSO (Torquato) Aminta, favola boscareccia . . . Ristampata . . . da Nicolo Ciangulo, Maestro Italiano in questa celebre Università d'Utrecht.

Per Pietro Muntendam Stampator Italiano. Utrecht. 1725.

12°. *, A–L⁴ (pp. 96), + pl. [Front.] + I–VII.

Dedicated to Sir Francis Head, Bart. Wants C2, 3.

Mottled calf, contemporary. Bookplate of Thomas Philip, Earl de Grey.

[Library press-mark]

This entry will meet many needs. It will show,

(*a*) the identity of the work and edition,

(*b*) the editor's name and the relevant fact that he taught Italian at Utrecht,

(*c*) the date,

(*d*) the number of quires (a preliminary one signed *, and eleven signed A–L for the body of the book),

262

(*e*) the way in which the sheets are folded, a third of a sheet to each quire, as is shown by the arrangement of the wire-lines on the paper combined with the signatures. The watermarks, being cut away, do not contribute their evidence,

(*f*) the total number of pages in the printed sheets,

(*g*) the number of plates and how they are numbered,

(*h*) the fact that the book was (it is indeed very conspicuous) dedicated to an English baronet, though published in Holland.

So far the information given would equally be true of any perfect copy of this edition. What follows, i.e. note of the imperfection, binding and past and present ownership of the volume, is rigidly confined to those matters which concern the copy in hand and that copy only. The more intricate the description, the more necessary it is to observe this division of the details into the two halves, describing firstly all copies, and secondly, the one copy. In short entries we can tolerate collocations like "red morocco, quarto", suggesting that red morocco is of the first essence of the book's production, whereas a binding (other than a publisher's casing of a modern book) is no more a part of the original book than is his coat a part of a man. Both are changeable without affecting the identity of what they cover.

IV. Full Standard Description

But if the researcher on Tasso desires to know what

preliminaries, notes, etc., there may be elucidating
Tasso's text or illustrating his reputation in the
eighteenth century; or if the researcher in the by-
ways of engraving in the place and period would like
to know what the plates are; or if the owner of an
imperfect or suspect copy wishes to settle the
arrangement of the engraved and type-set preliminary leaves, and to know too whether leaf L4
(which is, let us suppose, lacking in his copy) is the
last in the book, or whether it is followed by another
quire or quires; then it will be necessary to expand
the entry again, and we reach the type of description
which aims at mentally laying the book, so far as can
be done without reprinting the text or photographing
the leaves, before the enquirer. This is: Standard
Description.

It falls into much the same headings as the shorter
types of description, but with certain additions,
which will be noted and remarked on afterwards:

1^1. Tasso (Torquato) Aminta, *ed.* N. Ciangulo. Utrecht,
1725.

2. Aminta | Favola Bosca|reccia | di | Torquato
Tasso | Ristampata | *Per uso degli Amatori della* |
Lingua Italiana, | Da | Nicolo Ciangulo | Maestro
Italiano in questa | celebre Università | d'Utrecht. |
[Ornament] | Per Pietro Muntendam | Stampator
Italiano Utrecht | 1725.

3. 12°. $*$, A–L^4. pp. [1–8] + 9–96. Pl. [Front.] +
I–VII. 28 lines + headline and signature and catchword line, 90 (95) × 57 mm.

4. $*1^a$, title-page; $*1^b$, blank; $*2^a$–3^b, Ciangulo's dedication
to Sir Francis Head ("Fancesco [*sic*] Head Baronetto

---

[1] The paragraphs are only numbered here for reference.

d'Inghilterra"), dated 26 Octob. 1725; *4, "In Lode del Medesmo. Ode", signed "Il suo N.C."; A1^a (p. 9)–L2^b (p. 92), text; L3^a–L4^a, tribute to Tasso by Trojano Boccalini; L4^b, another, from Louis Moreri's *Grand Dictionnaire Historique*.

5. Plates: line-engravings:
   (1) arms of Head, facing a conjugate leaf bearing
   (2) the engraved title, supported by angels holding a crown surmounting arms, numbered I;
   (3) numbered II. "Prologue fol. [*sic.* for pag.] 9";
   (4)–(8), numbered III–VII, heading the openings of Acts I–V, and facing pp. ("fol") 13, 37, 54, 66, and 81.

6. [Some note might perhaps be given here upon the dedicatee and his travels, which are vaguely referred to in the dedication, and possibly amounted to no more than the Grand Tour. His christian name is given as "Fancesco" both in the prose dedication and in the ode.]

7. 105 × 58 mm. Imperfect, wanting C2, 3. The last leaf mutilated. Contemporary mottled calf. Armorial book-plate of Thomas Philip, Earl de Grey, cut down to fit so small a volume.

[Library press-mark]

Notes on the Preceding Description.—1. The short-title entry with which this long description is headed is inserted in order to help the eye in turning over manuscript sheets or printed leaves of a special catalogue. If only modern books, say after 1700, are in question, when clear title-pages will be the rule, it may be enough to head the extract from the title-page with the author's name in bold type or upper-case. The method given is, however, preferable, as it shows the edition and date clearly and at once. Any element which is common to a number of books being described together, e.g. place, date, or author, can of course be omitted.

2. (*a*) The title-page (and if one occurs, the colophon) should be quoted exactly and in full, barring any great verbosity or long motto. Any excisions must be indicated with . . ., and, if more than one line be omitted, with the line-end stroke also (see below). Thus, supposing that this title-page were very long, and that the words in italics were to be omitted, the passage would read RISTAMPATA | . . . | . . . | DA | NICOLO, etc. Parts of a line omitted can be indicated similarly, as thus:

Maestro Italiano . . . | . . . Università.[1]

(*b*) In transcribing, upper-case must be reproduced by upper-case, and lower-case by lower-case. It is also allowable, if not essential, to distinguish, either in transcribing or by a note, between the three great divisions of type, roman, gothic, and italic. But attempts to distinguish between sizes of founts employed on title-pages, which are often numerous, such as the Oxford Bibliographical Society's scheme, referred to at the end of this chapter, seem to yield results hardly worth the labour and the increased possibility of error; though it must be said that the method has been well put into use by Miss Gwendolen Murphy in her *Bibliography of English Character Books*, 1608–1700 (Bibliographical Society, 1925). Beginners, at least, do well to reserve this

---

[1] This does not maintain grammar, as omissions should, but will serve to illustrate the principle.

266

complication for later and more experienced days. After all, a facsimile of a title-page in zincograph is not inordinately expensive; while an unobvious word in very large type can be indicated in a short note.

It is not necessary to retain long s (ſ) in transcribing, at least before 1775, when it began to go out. If the long s appears in a book of much later date than this, it may well merit a separate note. It ought not to be necessary to add that ſ should never be confused with f.

(c) Contractions occur and must be represented either exactly, or (since not all printers have them) by spelling out and italicizing supplied letters.

(d) The upright strokes represent line-ends, and help to identify editions and also to bring the title-page's arrangement before the inward eye. Some bibliographers use a double stroke, to avoid confusion with a sloping stroke used by Caxton and other early printers as a comma; others indicate varying leading by varying the number of line-end strokes. But the simple single stroke is preferable.

(e) The ornament (a printer's flower, to be distinguished from a device) is mentioned in brackets. Similarly, a printer's line or "rule" or "double rule" (two lines close together) printed across the page, must be mentioned. If the title-page be framed in rules or in a border made of one large woodcut block (a "compartment"), or of two or three, or of printers' type-ornaments, the fact is to be stated as a note at the end of the transcript.

3. (a) The bibliographical format must be stated,

not as a mere indication of dimensions and shape, but exactly, on the principles laid down in the chapter on Collation.

(*b*) The signatures can most shortly and clearly be stated in the "algebraic" manner as shown. An older method was to say "$*$ A–L in fours". But, with a large book containing varying sequences of signatures this was very cumbrous. Such a sequence as

$$A–K^8 \quad L–N^4 \quad O–T^{8/4} \quad V–Z^2 \quad Aa^4$$

would have had to be stated thus:

A–K in eights, L–N in fours, O–T in alternate eights and fours, V–Z in twos, Aa four leaves.

A totally unsigned quire must be provided with a square-bracketed signature, e.g. $[A^4]B–F^8$.

(*c*) The pagination is shown exactly. In many books it does not cover the whole of the preliminaries, and has to be explained thus: pp. [8] + 87 + [1].

(*d*) The plates are similarly set out, so that the entire physical contents of the book are apparent. Details about them will, if justifying it, form a separate paragraph (*5*).

(*e*) The number of lines to a page, whether in double columns or long lines, whether with headlines, marginal notes, catch-words, etc., and the size of type, are details more suitable to an entry where the interest is at least partly typographical and not purely literary. In descriptions of early books, much detail of the kind, including ornaments, capitals, etc., is given.

268

The measurement of the type-surface in milli-metres (better than inches as being of international use) is the only measurement of old books which pro-vides a norm, since binders will have cut down more or less drastically all surviving copies and no two will measure the same. If the copy is uncut this should be stated, and the measurement of the paper-page given in this place. As given here the type-page is measured both with and without the headline and footline.

(*f*) References to previous bibliographies may be given here.

(*g*) It is occasionally the practice to record the first words of some selected page in the text, often p. 11. These, called the "dictio probatoria" or "justi-ficatory words", were a device of mediæval cata-loguers for identifying the copy of a work belonging to a particular library. They serve some purpose in identifying very similar editions, and indeed any edition where the searcher has only an imperfect copy. For this reason the page chosen should not be too near the beginning, where imperfections most often occur. But the justificatory words, though included in his model forms for Scottish books before 1700 by H. G. Aldis, are in most cases not worth including.

4. The analysis of the contents shows the pages occupied by every part of the book, preliminaries and blank leaves and pages included.

Blanks which are conjugate with printed leaves are a part of the book, and must be reckoned; if not so conjugate, they are binder's fly-leaves and of no consequence, except as carrying MS. notes, which must be dealt with not here but in describing the copy, under paragraph (7).

References to leaves and pages are best made by the signatures, as being generally more comprehensive than the pagination. A reference to the last leaf of quire C is given as C4, not as C⁴, which is the form used to show in setting down the collation that quire C has four leaves. The later and unsigned leaves of a signed quire can be referred to without any brackets. Recto and verso are differentiated as "a" and "b". Some bibliographers use "r" and "v", but these letters are so similar in handwriting that their use leads to misprints and misreadings, and "a" and "b" seem clearly preferable. Thus the recto of the last leaf in quire C is referred to as C4ᵃ, the verso as C4ᵇ.

Any words and phrases transcribed in this and other paragraphs, except the extract from the title-page in (2), may be transliterated into normal lower-case, but *verbatim et litteratim* as before. Indeed, one of the first things a bibliographer has to learn is to copy with minute and absolute accuracy any document put before him.

In transcribing from books printed before about 1640, difficulty will arise from the old use of I and J and of U and V.

In the upper-case the tailed form (our J) was simply the gothic, and the short form (our I) simply the roman form of one and the same letter. As a general rule, therefore, the printer will have used the form appropriate to the fount which he was using. In lower-case in English printing j was only used when following i, especially in roman numerals, as for example "xij" where we should write "xii"; otherwise, i represents both our i and j. The simple rule is to follow the practice of the printer.

Similarly U and V were respectively the gothic and roman forms of the same letter. But the lower-case use was more complicated than that of i and j, for both occurred in roman. In initial positions v only was used, in medial and final positions u only. When this is grasped, the fact that "Juan" and "Ivan" are both forms of the name which we know as "John" becomes clear. Thus a sixteenth-century printer would set the Latin word which we write (or till recently wrote) "UVA" and "uva", if setting in upper-case, "VVA", if setting in lower-case, "vua". Scholarly printers of the Renaissance, especially in Italy, often renounced v altogether in printing Latin and would have set up "uua". They could not have brought themselves to print "uva" or (Mr. Pollard's examples) "Qveene" or "Vniversitie". Yet so excellent a bibliographer as the late Mr. Charles Sayle did so in his catalogue (1904–1907) of the early English books in the Cambridge University Library; and Mr. St. John Hornby has, to an eye practised in books of the period, done something to spoil his noble Ashendene Press edition of Spenser's *Faerie Queene*, in which an Elizabethan air is cultivated, by printing the title as "THE FAERIE QUEENE" (not QVEENE).

We have then

Modern	Elizabethan
UVA	VVA
uva	vua (or uua)
QUEEN	QVEENE
queen	queene
UNIVERSITY	VNIVERSITIE
university	vniuersitie

When transcribing upper-case in upper-case or lower-case in lower-case, the simple rule again is to follow the practice of the printer. When transcribing from upper-case into lower-case it is usual to adopt the form which the printer would have used had he been printing in lower-case.

W and w, which also did not occur in the Latin alphabet, are at first, and freely in England till 1600, represented by VV and vv. It is well to retain this in transcribing.

On every occasion, but especially in setting down collations, it is absolutely necessary to be exact in the use of the words "leaf" and "page", which are much misused in common speech. A page is bibliographically not a piece of paper in a book but one of its sides. Utter confusion in calculating the make-up of a book results from any laxity in maintaining this distinction. Some careful bibliographers even substitute "title-leaf" for "title-page" when it is the leaf they mean.

"Sheet" is also a very confusing word, but one hard to escape; it means the sheet as manufactured, and also the section as folded, if assumed to consist of one sheet. "Section" or "quire" is best used for the latter meaning.

5. Illustrations, or the art collation. The processes of all illustrations should be identified and noted. Sets should be indicated as such, and the number of blocks or plates, and their standard dimensions, set down. In early books woodcuts are often repeated, and this should be observed, e.g. "144 woodcuts, 75 × 120 mm., 36 appearing twice". Unless numerous, the pages on which cuts occur, or which the plates face, should be entered.

If the engraver's and designer's names are known, they are an important point in the book's claim to notice, perhaps the most important point. They should be given in this form: "Plates: I–VII, line-engravings, by Blake after Maria Flaxman, frontispiece and facing pp. . . ."

6. It is sometimes absurdly supposed that the scientific and historical bibliographer does not concern himself with the contents of books, but confines himself to studying their physical construction. The book in hand yields very little material for a note; but any important facts which the describer can glean from examination of the book (he should always read all preliminaries and should at least glance over the text) or from research should be set down. But they must be facts and not mere opinions. The business of bibliography is to record books, not to appraise them. Facts which indicate a book's importance are, of course, not excluded.

7. The description of the individual copy follows

when all points common to all copies have been disposed of, as observed above.

The measurement is that of the leaves as left by the binder. All imperfections and serious damage must be noted. Then follow any important facts in the copy's history, such as the binding, book-plate, and notes of ownership, and lastly the name of the library owning it, the date and source of acquisition (especially if by gift or bequest), and press-mark.

V. DESCRIPTION OF INCUNABULA

In the latter part of the seventeenth century when, after two centuries had elapsed, the earliest products of the printing-press began for the first time to be objects of interest in themselves, a Dutch bibliographer, Cornelius a Beughem, 1688, used this fanciful term *incunabula artis typographicæ*, "swaddling clothes of the typographic art". The term did not pass into common use till it was revived late in the nineteenth century as "incunabula" simply (singular, incunabulum; Anglice, incunable). This replaced, in England, the word "fifteener", which had sometimes been used, and came into general use in various vernacular forms. In Germany, it was freely translated into *Wiegendrucke*, or "cradle-prints".

Incunabula, which are the products of the yet unstandardized printing-press, need to be studied typographically: and for special purposes later books may be so studied. Some of the typographical details given above, such as the mention of the sizes and styles of types used, the number of lines to the page,

274

and the printer's flower on the title-page, which are optional in describing a book of 1725, should be included and elaborated in describing one of 1525, still more of 1475.[1]

The cataloguing of incunabula has now a technique of its own, that serving the so-called "natural history method of bibliography" founded by Henry Bradshaw. Intensive study of the types used before 1500 has made it possible to use their evidence as a basis for dating and attributing to their presses the great mass of books of the period.

Fig. 12 provides an example of a standard description of a late Strassburg incunable, from the press of "the Printer of Jordanus de Quedlinburg", also called "the Printer of the Saints' Days", from his method of dating his books; it is from the British Museum *Catalogue of Books printed in the XVth Century*.

Let us go through the paragraphs as outlined above for a Full Standard Description, and note any points, additional to those dealt with there, which arise.

1. The exact day of printing, if in the colophon, should be mentioned. If given at all by the printer, it is often given either by the ancient roman calendar, by Nones and Ides, or as here (a habit of this printer) by the ecclesiastical year. Reference in any case of

---

[1] The pioneer period ended at different dates in different places. At London it lasted till near 1557, and Gordon Duff insists that all English books up to that date should be so treated; in Venice it ended perhaps by 1490. For convenience 1500 has commonly been used as the closing date for incunabula.

NICOLAUS DE BLONE Sermones de
tempore et sanctis   23 August, 1498.

1ᵇ TITLE Sermones uenerabilis magistri Nicolai de ‖
blony decretorū doctoris. capellani episco‖pi Bosnonien-
sis ualde deseruientes popu≠‖lo. § et clero utcūcʒ docto
eos digne legenti ‖ predicāti. aut audienti. de tempore. et
de scīs 384ᵇ. COLOPHON : Fiuiunt sermones venerabilis
magistri ‖ Nicolai blony decretoʒ doctoris de tem≠‖pore :
impssi Argētine Anno dñi. Mcccc. ‖ xcviij. Finiti ī vigilia
sancti Bartholomei. 385ᵃ. TITLE . Sermones Nicolai ‖
de Blony de sanctis. 477ᵃ. COLOPHON : Finiunt sermones ‖ magistri Nicolai de Blony decreto≠‖rū doctorī.
Capellani episcopi Bos≠‖noniensis. de tempe et sanctī.
Cōscri‖pti ab eodē Anno domini. M. cccc. ‖ xxxviij. vt
videtur capi ex sermone. c≠‖xiij. circa medium membri
ṗmi eius≠‖dem sermonis. Impressi Argentine. ‖ Anno
domini. M cccc. xcviij. In vi‖gilia sancti Bartholomei.

Folio   Part I : Aa⁸ Bb Cc⁶ ; a–c⁸ d–z A–D⁸ ⁶ ⁶ E⁶ F–V⁸ ⁶ ⁶ X Yᵈ
Z⁸ Aa⁶ Bb–Gg⁸·⁶·⁶ Hh⁸   Part II : [∗]⁴ a–f⁸ ⁶ ⁶ g–n⁶ o⁸. 478 leaves,
the last blank. 2 columns, with printed head-lines. 21ᵃ : 52 lines,
204 × 133 mm. Types : 160, title, head-lines, &c. ; 80, text. Spaces
left for capitals, with guide-letters. Hain *3263.

A reprint of the edition of 22 November, 1495.

276 × 193 mm. Capitals and paragraph-marks supplied in red and blue alternately, initial-strokes in red ;
the large capitals on 21ᵃ and 389ᵃ have border decoration
in mauve, green, and gold. A slip containing a note of
ownership has been torn away from the head of the first
title-leaf, which has been mounted. On the first fly-
leaf is the signature of R. G. Mackintosh (1818). From
the library of the Duke of Sussex, with his press-marked
book-plate.

Bought in November, 1844.   IB. 1975.

FIG. 12.—STANDARD DESCRIPTION OF AN INCUNABLE.

doubt should be made to A. Cappelli's *Cronologia e Calendario perpetuo*, 1906.

The printer's name should be given, if known, or, if not (as here), the name given to the anonymous press to which the group of books being described is attributed. In the catalogue from which our example is chosen this is found in the heading to the series of descriptions of books from the press.

If there is more than one work in the book (apart, of course, from any mere binding together of separately published works), then the titles of both must be given.

2. Colophon as well as title-page (if any), and failing the title-page the incipit, and failing the colophon the explicit, must be quoted, with references to show on what page each occurs.

Contractions [1] abound in the fifteenth century, and must be understood. They were a device of the scribe for economizing labour and writing material, and being largely conventional and of regular recurrence, were well understood. In technical books, e.g. of law and scholastic philosophy, they are much more drastic, and are very difficult for the non-expert to decipher.

The printer inherited contractions with the rest of the outward aspect of the mediæval book, but they were no saving to him, since every extra "sort" in a fount means an extra pigeon-hole in the case, and

---

[1] Fuller information must be sought in the handbooks on palæography and archives, and in A. Cappelli's *Lexicon abbreviaturarum*, 2nd ed., 1912, or in Dr. McKerrow.

extra time in composition. Contractions gradually become less frequent (they are relatively sparse in the example chosen, printed in 1498), but survive in stray examples into the seventeenth century. The ampersand ($\mathcal{E} = et$) is the only survivor of what was a great army.[1]

Here is a typical highly contracted incipit of 1486:

Incipiūt titl'i p'ores d' duodecī ḡneralib' qd'lib3 in phetas scī Thome d' Aq'no ordīs frat ᴿ p̄dicato2| īp'ssi p Hānibalē Parmēsem sociosq3 ei9 āno dn̄i MCCCCLXXXVI die v'o vltīo mēsis madij,

which being expanded reads:

Incipiu*nt* titu*li* p*ri*ores d*e* duodeci*m* generalib*us* q*u*odlib*et* in p*ro*phetas *s*an*cti* Thome d*e* Aqu*i*no ord*in*is fratru*m* predi-catoru*m* i*m*pressi p*er* Hannibale*m* Parme*n*sem sociosq*ue* ei*us* anno d*o*m*i*ni MCCCCLXXXVI die v*er*o vltimo me*n*sis madij.

Three stock contractions:

$$\mathcal{Z} = et$$
$$\text{?} = con$$
$$2| = rum$$

are constantly used to follow the signature alphabet before a fresh alphabet is commenced. Almost any omitted letter, but mostly m or n, is represented by a stroke over the preceding letter, e.g. Incipiūt ordis. Other very common contractions are:

$$\underline{p} = per \text{ (or par)}$$
$$\dot{p} = pri$$

[1] It is difficult to believe that "poetaz" in the phrase "narcissus poetaz" is not a nurseryman's version of a mediævalist amateur gardener's "poetarum", written "poeta2|".

278

$\bar{p}$ = pre or prae
$\underset{\sim}{p}$ = pro
9 = us
b' = bus

More elaborate contractions depend on the subject
matter of the book, and the recurrent words which
the original reader was expected to recognize in
shorthand form. Thus in breviaries Om$\bar{p}$s = Omni-
potens; in scholastic treatise ph9 = philosophus, i.e.
(often) Aristotle, and ℞ = respondetur.

3. A case occurs here of an elaborate sequence of
signatures, which for part of the book run in triads
of eight leaves, six leaves, and six leaves; this, for
brevity, is set down as "8.6.6."

A quantity of *typographical evidence* is stated here.

The types are allotted to the purposes for which
they are used in the book, e.g. whether for headlines, text, or commentary. They will be seen in our
example to be differentiated by numbers. Thus the
text-type is entered as 80. This figure is that of
20 lines of type in millimetres, which is taken as the
norm. Sometimes if a type only occurs in single lines,
it is difficult to estimate the figure for 20 lines at all
exactly.

The types can be at least provisionally identified
by the use of Dr. Konrad Haebler's *Typenreper-
torium der Wiegendrucke* (1905–24). This work contains a table of one hundred forms of the gothic M
(the letter most varying in design from fount to
fount) which occur in fifteenth-century types, and a
detailed description of all the types noted under each

279

m, arranged in order of size, and with information as to the presses and dates in which they were used.

Suppose, then, that we have a book manifestly printed before 1501 in a gothic type. We must try to date and "place" the book, and the type gives us our best evidence. In later periods, when the type-founder was well established, types give way to ornaments as evidence of origin. We look through a few pages till we find M; then we compare it with Haebler's table and find, say, that it corresponds most nearly with his M 47. We then measure 20 lines of the type, set solid; if there be any which seems to be cast on a larger body it may make great difficulty in identification. The measurement of the 20 lines in millimetres, combined with its M-form, becomes the notation by which we identify and refer to the type. If a normal text-type, 20 lines may measure 80 mm. It is then described as M 47 : 80. By running over Haebler's descriptions of the types of that measurement and with that M, which descrip-tions are all found together, we can probably pick out ours. Then we go to the shelves or to facsimiles, such as those published by the Gesellschaft für Typenkunde or the Type Facsimile Society, or to the Woolley Photographs, made by George Dunn, and compare closely the various sorts of the type as used by the printer indicated in Haebler's list with those that appear in ours. At this stage great care and discretion are needed, and hasty identification is a snare, particularly after 1480. But with that warn-ing, the method is sound. It can, of course, only be practised in a great library. The similar method with roman types is much less satisfactory, as there is no letter so liable to variation in design as M in gothic; Qu (often a ligature) is the best.

We find then a statement in figures for 20-line measurements of the type or types as part of the description.

If there are any ornamental woodcut *capitals* (again the distinction between capitals and upper-case must be remembered), they should be noticed, and the dimensions given. They will identify the press even better than will types, since they could not then be multiplied like type. The printer, how-ever, very generally left a blank space for the rub-risher (or it might be, the illuminator) to fill the capitals in, and it is the practice to state this, and to note whether "guide-letters" have been printed in the spaces in order to save the rubrisher from making mistakes, which he sometimes did. When we come to the description of the individual copy (and only then) we must note whether, and if so, in what style, the capitals have been painted in by hand, for this will vary from copy to copy, and in many copies will not have been done at all.

Any other points should be noted which show the printer's practice and stage of development; these may be useful, either to "place" this book, or by its aid, if it is one that tells its own story, to place others that do not. Uneven line-endings (long a thing of the past by 1498) are one of these points, since they are a mark of an early stage in technical skill.

281

It may be mentioned here that in many of the best and most recent bibliographies of incunabula our paragraphs 2 and 3, the transcript and the collation, are transposed. So long as consistency is maintained in any one catalogue, the point is immaterial.

4. This is a book of simple composition and hardly needs a contents paragraph.

5. Similarly it is without illustrations.

6 and 7 seem to raise no points not already dealt with.

READING LIST

LIST A

DUNKIN, Paul S. How to catalog a rare book. 1951.

GUPPY, Henry. Rules for the cataloguing of incunabula. 2nd ed. 1932 (reprinted 1947).

POLLARD, Alfred W., *and* GREG, W. W. Some points in bibliographical descriptions. (A.A.L. Reprint No. 3.) 1950. (Reprinted from the *Transactions of the Bibliographical Society.*)

LIST B

BOWERS, Fredson. Principles of bibliographical description. 1949.

BÜHLER, Curt F. *and others*. Standards of bibliographical description. 1949.

COWLEY, J. D. Bibliographical description and cataloguing. 1939.

IX

BIBLIOGRAPHIES: SOME CLASSES AND EXAMPLES

PRIMARY BIBLIOGRAPHIES

Primary bibliographies are those which are the original record of the whole or part of their contents, while secondary bibliographies are those in which material registered elsewhere is rearranged for the convenience of research. Bibliographies of bibliography are, of course, secondary but seemed to be more conveniently treated of at the opening. For this reason they have been given pride of place in this list.

In any research the first duty of the scholar, and also of the bibliographer, is to know what has been written before upon the subject of his inquiry. As a step towards that he should know, or be able to find, the appropriate bibliography in which what has been written has been recorded. This may be in one of the attempts at universal bibliographies; in the current lists of new publications, mainly made by and for the book trade; or in special lists of the writings in particular arts or sciences.

Select lists, such as abound and are very useful for helping to choose books for libraries of moderate size, are of little service here. They mention nothing that is not recorded elsewhere, and the object of the type of researcher we have now in mind is not to find the best books but to find all that has been written or printed on a subject, or by an author, or in a period, or from a press. Excellent works, like Sonnenschein's *Best Books*, or Nelson's *Standard Books*, are accordingly ruled out. Lists of collectors' books, however, such as those of Watt, Lowndes, and Brunet, remain in as recording books unrecorded elsewhere.

Although the student may make his first acquaintance with these bibliographies by means of a list such as that which follows, he must do everything he possibly can to enable him to handle the books themselves. He must know the names by which they are commonly called, such as "Courtney", or "Proctor" or "S.T.C.". Above all he must make himself familiar with the scope and arrangement of these tools, upon the skilled use of which his efficiency will so largely depend.

The number of examples given in this book has been kept down to an absolute minimum, so that it should not be outside the power of the student to become acquainted with them. Titles are given as briefly as is consistent with clearly identifying them. Further details, such as publisher and place of publication, together with fuller notes, can be found in the bibliographies of bibliography.

BIBLIOGRAPHIES OF BIBLIOGRAPHIES

The oldest which is still of any service is

1. PETZHOLDT (Julius). Bibliotheca bibliographica. 1866.

But this, with its successors,

284

2. VALLÉE (L.). Bibliographie des bibliographies. 2v. 1883–1887

which is primarily an author list, and

3. STEIN (Henri). Manuel de bibliographie générale. 1897,

which is arranged by subjects, have been largely superseded by

4. COURTNEY (William P.). Register of national bibliography. 3v. 1905–1912

which is a large (and, in spite of its title, international) subject list of bibliographies.

The most modern work of this nature is

5. BESTERMAN (Theodore). A world bibliography of bibliographies. 3v. 1947–1949.

Of particular value is the

6. BIBLIOGRAPHIC INDEX, published by H. W. Wilson, Co., of New York.

This is an index of bibliographies which appear as separately published books, as parts of books, pamphlets, or in periodicals. From its foundation in 1938, it appeared quarterly, with annual and five-yearly cumulations, but from mid-1951 onwards its publication became semi-annual.

Another work which attempted to cover the periodical lists of books was

7. GODET (M.) *and* VORSTIUS (J.). Index bibliographicus. 2nd ed. 1931.

Under the same title, but now published under the

auspices of Unesco, it has been completely revised and is being issued in parts,

> 8. BESTERMAN (Theodore). Index bibliographicus. 3rd
> ed. 1952. (In progress.)
> Vol. 1. Science and technology.
> Vol. 2. Social sciences, education, humanistic
> sciences.

Other useful tools are those which provide lists of reference books of all sorts, among which bibliographies will be found. The best known of these is probably

> 9. WINCHELL (Constance M.). Guide to reference books.
> 7th ed. 1951. (Supplement, 1954.)

This is published by the American Library Association and based on the 6th edition of the work with the same title edited by Miss I. G. Mudge. The Library Association began the publication of a very similar work which was abandoned after the first supplement

> 10. MINTO (John). Reference books. 1929. With Supple-
> ment. 1931.

A number of other handbooks exist such as those catalogues which have been published by many of the large libraries of the books contained on their reference shelves. There are also guides for students which record the most important books, such as,

> 11. SCHNEIDER (G.). Handbuch der Bibliographie. 4th ed.
> 1930.

12. VAN HOESEN (H. B.) *and* WALTER (F. K.). Bibliography, practical, enumerative, historical; an introductory manual. 1928.
13. ROBERTS (A. D.). Introduction to reference books. 2nd ed. 1951.
14. COLLISON (Robert L.). Bibliographies, subject and national. 1951.

UNIVERSAL BIBLIOGRAPHIES

There is, naturally, no universal bibliography, nor will there ever be one worthy of the name. The material is too vast. This has not prevented attempts from being made, and these, even in their incompleteness, are frequently of great value. In the main, the most useful avenue of approach is through the national, period, subject or other special bibliographies.

Hopeful attempts at world bibliographies soon began to be made. The father of our craft was Conrad Gesner, physician of Zurich, a man as amiable as he was learned. Although he died before he was fifty, he became a *doctor universalis*, master not only of the natural sciences but also of much of the general learning of his day by reading and by maintaining friendly relations with scholars of all countries. His book is

15. GESNER (Conrad). Bibliotheca universalis, sive catalogus omnium scriptorum locupletissimus, in tribus linguis, Latina, Græca, et Hebraica. 1545.

Modern vernaculars were then despised by the learned, to our great loss, which accounts for the limitation expressed in the title.

Gesner was contemporary with the foundation of the first of two annual international lists of new books, the *Messkataloge* of the great book-fairs of Frankfurt and Leipzig, which ran from 1564 to 1749 and from 1595 to 1860 respectively, and were gathered up and indexed as

16. Codex nundinarius Germaniae literatæ bisecularis, ed. Gustav Schwetschke. 1850–97.

But the fairs were not only (as Schwetschke suggests in his title) chiefly used by German publishers; they were largely confined to the learned works likely to achieve an international sale, and, like Gesner, excluded the vernacular and local works which are now the hardest to trace and in some ways (certainly so far as market value is evidence) the more valuable.

In the first half of the eighteenth century, two single-handed attempts were made at a world list,

17. GEORGI (Gottlieb). Allgemeines europäisches bücher-lexikon.
5 parts (covering 1501–1739). 1742–1753.
3 supplements (covering 1739–1757). 1750–1758.

18. MAITTAIRE (M.). Annales typographici ab artis inventæ origine ad annum 1664. 5v. 1719–1741; with 2v. supplement (covering period 1549–1599) by M. Denis. 1789.

Lists of standard or rare books, often unrecorded elsewhere, began with

19. BURE (G. F. de). Bibliographie instructive: ou traité de la connaissance des livres rares et singuliers. 7v. 1763–1768.

288

De Bure's book is a large repertory, and is classified, and was once very useful. It was largely superseded in the nineteenth century by the famous

20. BRUNET (J. C.). Manuel du libraire et de l'amateur de livres. 5th ed. 6v. 1860–1865.
    3v. supplement. 1870–1880.

Brunet gives us, beside the main author list, a subject index, the arrangement of which in its time was a standard and is still used with some modifications in many large libraries. The three supplementary volumes include one which is a *"Dictionnaire de géographie ancienne et moderne"*, being a list of place-names found in imprints. Brunet, first published in 1810, was imitated and supplemented, but has not been superseded, by

21. GRAESSE (J. G. T.). Trésor de livres rares et précieux. 7v. 1859–1869.

Out-of-the-way books will also naturally be traceable by their appearances in the auction-room, often the only evidence of their existence. These can be found recorded in such works as

22. BOOK AUCTION RECORDS. Annual from 1902.
23. BOOK PRICES CURRENT. Annual from 1886,

both of which cover English and American sales, or

24. AMERICAN BOOK PRICES CURRENT. Annual from 1895

which covers American sales only, or

25. JAHRBUCH DER BÜCHERPREISE

which covered many European countries from 1906 to 1938.

K   289

Mention should also be made of the important part played by the book catalogues issued by the great booksellers. Details given are frequently very full and, in the cases of the best examples, of meticulous accuracy.

But if, as seems reasonable, a universal bibliography is regarded as one which is not limited by language, period, or subject, then naturally, the printed catalogues of the great libraries of the world will be among the nearest approaches to this ideal. The number of such catalogues is considerable but the following are among the best known.

26. BRITISH MUSEUM. General catalogue of printed books. 95v. 1881–1900.
13v. supplement. 1900–1905.
Now being superseded by a new edition which commenced publication in 1931 and, by 1952, had reached v. 49 (covering up to "Degt").

27. BRITISH MUSEUM. Subject index of the modern works added to the library.

This is commonly called by the name of its first editor G. K. Fortescue. The period 1881–1900 is dealt with in three volumes, and the period since 1900 in five-yearly supplements. Earlier than 1881 it has never been found possible to push the Subject Index, but some assistance is given by the four series of

28. PEDDIE (R. A.). Subject index of books published before 1880. 1933–1948.

Peddie is not a library catalogue nor the official publication of a library but much of his material was taken from the British Museum collection.

29. OXFORD UNIVERSITY. Bodleian Library. Catalogus librorum impressorum bibliothecæ Bodleianæ in Academia oxoniensi. 4v. 1843–1851.

30. FACULTY OF ADVOCATES, Library. Catalogue of the printed books. 7v. 1857–1879.

31. EDINBURGH UNIVERSITY, Library. Catalogue of the printed books. 3v. 1918–1923.

32. JOHN RYLANDS LIBRARY, Manchester. Catalogue of the printed books and manuscripts. 3v. 1899.

33. LONDON LIBRARY. Author catalogue. 2v. 1913–1914.
    First supplement (covering 1913–1920). 1920.
    Second supplement (covering 1920–1928). 1929.
    Third supplement (covering 1928–1950). 1953.
    Subject-index. 1909.
    First supplement (covering 1909–1922). 1923.
    Second supplement (covering 1923–1938). 1938.

There is also one very remarkable private library whose catalogue is of use as a general storehouse of out-of-the-way as well as standard books.

34. BIBLIOTHECA LINDESIANA. 4v. 1910–1913.

This is the collection formed at Haigh Hall, Wigan, by successive Earls of Crawford.

In America, there is the

35. LIBRARY OF CONGRESS, Washington. Catalog of books represented by Library of Congress printed cards. 209v. 1942–1948.

Supplements to this are published as the

36. CUMULATIVE CATALOG OF LIBRARY OF CONGRESS PRINTED CARDS

which has been issued monthly from 1947 onwards,

with quarterly and annual cumulations. There is also

37. LIBRARY OF CONGRESS, Washington. Subject catalog: a cumulative list of works represented by Library of Congress printed cards.

This work, which began in 1950, is published quarterly with annual cumulations.

In France, there is the

38. BIBLIOTHÈQUE NATIONALE, Paris. Catalogue général des livres imprimés: auteurs,

publication of which began in 1900, and by 1950 had reached volume 178 (covering up to "Stos").

The searcher for scarce literature will often find that, short of recourse to one of these national centres, there are directories of libraries and institutions of higher learning which will put him on the right track. Such are,

39. INDEX GENERALIS

which appeared annually from 1919 until publication was interrupted by the Second World War.

40. MINERVA: JAHRBUCH DER GELERHTEN WELT

which since its origin in 1891 has had its annual publication interrupted during the period of two world wars.

41. WORLD OF LEARNING

which has been appearing annually since 1947.

For the special collections and special libraries of this country there is the

42. ASLIB [Association of Special Libraries and Information Bureaux] DIRECTORY. 1928,

the usefulness of which is somewhat limited until a new and revised edition appears.

INCUNABULA

The ideal of a complete bibliography has been approached for one period only, and that is the pioneer period of printing, reckoned for convenience as ending at the end of the fifteenth century. So early as the end of the eighteenth century Georg Panzer produced his annals of the presses of this and the next generation.

43. PANZER (Georg W. F.). Annales typographici ad annum 1536. 11v. 1793–1803.

In 1812–15, T. F. Dibdin, with much enthusiasm and splendour of printing, catalogued the fine library of early books collected by Earl Spencer. This, the Althorp, library passed in 1897 into the John Rylands Library, Manchester. It is in the catalogue of books of this library, compiled by Gordon Duff, then librarian there, rather than in Dibdin, that instructed information as to presses and dates must be sought.

A quarter of a century later than Panzer followed the famous work of Ludwig Hain,

44. HAIN (Ludwig F. T.). Repertorium bibliographicum ad annum MD. 2v. in 4. 1826–1838,

to which can be added a series of supplements:

> BURGER (K.). Register. Die drucker des XV.
> jahrhunderts. 1891.
> COPINGER (W. A.). Supplement. 2v. in 3. 1895–
> 1902.
> BURGER (K.). Supplement zu Hain und Panzer.
> 1908.
> REICHLING (D.). Supplement. 7v. 1905–1911.
> REICHLING (D.). Supplement and general index of
> authors. 1914.

Based largely on the collections of the Munich Hof-
bibliothek, then greatly enriched by books from the
Bavarian monasteries, Hain's is an author-list; and
it is noted for its extreme accuracy, at least in the
entries which he distinguished with an asterisk as of
books seen by himself. He gives the number of
leaves, and some other typographical notes, in a code
of abbreviations which needs some practice to
decipher: but though he mentions the presence of
signatures he does not collate by them. Nor does he
attempt to attribute books to their printers. His
descriptions of some 16,000 incunabula, however,
put the knowledge of early printing on a new basis,
and Burger's index of printers paved the way for
Proctor. The Supplements to Hain by Copinger and
Reichling are unfortunately not nearly so accurate as
their original.

The work of Henry Bradshaw, Holtrop, and
Campbell on the early productions of the Low
Country presses gave a new method of study of these
monuments. As a consequence, the catalogue of the

incunabula in the public libraries of France made for the Ministry of Public Instruction is, though an author-list like Hain's, much more expert on the typographical side.

45. PELLECHET (Marie L. C.). Catalogue général des incunables des bibliothèques publiques de France (continued by Louis Polain). 3v. 1897–1909.

Unfortunately, this was left unfinished at "Gregorius Magnus". But the full fruits of the "natural history method", taught by Bradshaw, appeared in

46. PROCTOR (Robert). Index to the early printed books in the British Museum ... to 1500, with notes of those in the Bodleian Library. 4v. 1898–1899.

This was a marvellous piece of work, achieved in ten years by a short-sighted man with other duties, in which not far short of ten thousand books (perhaps a third of them bearing no printer's name) are sorted out on typographical evidence under their countries, towns, presses, and dates—an arrangement which has ever since been spoken of as "Proctor order". Indexes of authors are, of course, provided. Part II of Proctor's work was designed to take the work down from 1501 to 1520, a period in which woodcut illustrations and ornaments are more salient features than types, since types were by now being made wholesale by type-founders and therefore used at unconnected presses. The date 1520 was chosen as stopping short of the flood of Lutheran pamphlets. Proctor lived to complete only Section I, covering Germany, of this second part. Sections 2 and 3, covering Italy, Switzerland, and Eastern Europe, were completed by Frank Isaac and published in 1938.

Proctor's short-title Index is expanded and worked over, and his method carried further, in

> 47. BRITISH MUSEUM. Catalogue of books printed in the XVth century now in the British Museum. 1908–.

This is fully illustrated with facsimiles of types. German and Italian printing was finished in the first seven volumes, with France and French-speaking Switzerland covered in the eighth volume which was published in 1949. The Low Countries, Spain, Austria, England, and Scandinavia remain for later volumes.

In 1912 the Prussian Government projected a definitive author catalogue of incunabula. The Commission then formed for the purpose under Konrad Haebler later became independent of the State. The result of their exhaustive census of the surviving copies of known incunabula was

> 48. GESAMTKATALOG DER WIEGENDRUCKE.

Publication of the parts began in 1925 and the last to appear was Part I of Volume 8 in 1940, covering up to "Fredericus". Although it was discovered, after the Second World War, that much of the material gathered by the Commission, together with the slips ready for printing, was still in existence, it now seems improbable that any further progress can be expected with this great project.

National Literatures

The phrase "national literature" is perhaps liable to be misunderstood. In the sense in which it is meant here it includes all books produced in the language of the country, and all books produced in the country, whatever their language. No limitation to poetry, plays, novels, or to the authors mentioned in histories of literature, can be accepted by the bibliographer; these may be the mountain-peaks, or the flowery fields, of the national literature, but they are not more a part of it than are the arid tracts represented by scientific or theological or educational writings.

A separate list of most of the more general bibliographies of national literatures is

49. PEDDIE (Robert A.). National bibliographies; a descriptive catalogue of the works which register the books published in each country. 1912.

A more recent list is found in

50. HEYL (Lawrence). Current national bibliographies; a list of sources of information concerning current books of all countries. 1942.

Further lists will also be found in the general guides such as Winchell.

Catalogues of manuscripts will not be included in the select lists which follow; but it must be remembered that books in manuscript, whether remaining unprinted or existing as the sources and tests of the printed editions, are a vital part of a national literature.

ENGLISH LITERATURE

The would-be editor of an English author, or the would-be historian of English literature or life has two or three guides to his sources:

    51. NORTHUP (C. S.). A Register of the bibliographies of the English language and literature. 1925,

a rather overloaded compilation, but superseding any other general list of the kind; and

    52. ESDAILE (A.). The Sources of English literature. 1928,

being lectures on the Sandars foundation in Cambridge University, and designed to provide an easy introduction to the most important bibliographies and catalogues of English books.

The chief repertory of English books is of course the general catalogue of authors of the British Museum Library. The "B.M.'s" proud position in this respect is due to two causes, both of which have operated for over a century. One is the purchase grant allowed by Parliament—now terribly inadequate, but throughout the latter half of the nineteenth century very good. The other is the right accorded by Copyright Acts and first effectively by that of 1842, of receiving free all books published in the United Kingdom. The right of free deposit was given by the Act of 1709 to nine libraries, the Royal Library, the University libraries of Oxford (the Bodleian), Cambridge, Edinburgh, Glasgow, St. Andrews, and Aberdeen, the Faculty of Advocates at Edinburgh and Sion College, London. King's

Inns and Trinity College, Dublin, were added in 1801, the year of Union. In 1836 the four Scottish Universities, King's Inns, and Sion College were bought out for small annual payments, equivalent to the poor use they had made of the right; and in 1911 the National Library of Wales was added. After the separation of the Irish Free State the existing rights were reciprocally continued.

In one form or another most nations now have a law of deposit. In England, the Act of 1663, which made deposit in the Royal Library, the Bodleian and Cambridge University Library legally binding, and in itself doubtless an imitation of the French decree of 1617, had been preceded by an arrangement made at the beginning of the seventeenth century between Sir Thomas Bodley and the Company of Stationers in favour of the newly founded Bodleian Library. The Bodleian was for at least a century and a half in effect the national library; and it is correspondingly rich in rare English books. Its published catalogue was, at the time of its issue in 1843–1851, "the largest presentation of printed literature which had ever been issued". Now, as a record of that great library's holdings, it is, naturally very incomplete, but there are several special catalogues. Cambridge University Library, likewise rich in English books, has no published general catalogue. The greatest contributions of the other "copyright" libraries and their catalogues are in the literatures of Scotland, Wales, and Ireland respectively, and they will be mentioned later in those connections.

Two general works incidentally contain considerable, though very uneven, bibliographies of English authors.

53. STEPHEN (Leslie) *and* LEE (Sidney). The dictionary of national biography. 63v. 1885–1900 (re-issued in 21v.).
    1st supplement. 1901.
    2nd supplement (1901–1911). 1912.
    3rd supplement (1912–1921). 1927.
    4th supplement (1922–1930). 1937.
    5th supplement (1931–1940). 1949.
54. WARD (Sir A. W.) *and* WALLER (A. R.). The Cambridge history of English literature. 15v. 1907–1927.

The bibliographies in the latter, which were omitted from the cheaper edition of 1932, formed the basis for what has come to be the major bibliographical work on English literature:

55. BATESON (F. W.). Cambridge bibliography of English literature. 4v. 1941.

The first three volumes of the Cambridge bibliography are arranged in chronological order, while the fourth volume is an index. It is an indispensable reference work and is one of the major achievements of the learned press by whom it was published.

English books passing through the auction rooms form a large part of the *Book Auction Records, Book Prices Current* and *American Book Prices Current*, already mentioned. Those desiring to pursue rare English books through successive sales have as guides

56. BRITISH MUSEUM. List of catalogues of English book sales, 1676–1900, now in the British Museum. 1915.

57. DE RICCI (Seymour). English collectors of books and manuscripts (1530–1930), and their marks of ownership. 1930,

being Sandars Lectures by this author, who had an unrivalled knowledge of the migrations of rare books.

A general list of rare books after the manner of Brunet, but less accurate, and confined to English authors, is the celebrated

58. LOWNDES (William Thomas). Bibliographer's manual of English literature. 6v. in 11. 1858–1864.

Although Lowndes was first published in 1834 it is best known through the considerably enlarged edition edited and published by H. G. Bohn in the middle of the century.

For the better-known English and American authors Lowndes is now reinforced by

59. DE RICCI (Seymour). The book-collector's guide; practical handbook of British and American bibliography. 1921,

which is a very exact record of the migrations of copies, and also notes existing bibliographies. The prices which are given in Lowndes and De Ricci are now irrelevant except as historical record. The element which brought both books into existence is thus curiously the first to lose consequence.

Mediæval English literature must be sought in catalogues of manuscripts; but a remarkably full analytical bibliography is also to be found in the work of an American scholar,

60. WELLS (John Edwin). Manual of the writings in Middle English (1050–1400). IV. and 8 supplements. 1916–1941.

The period of the beginnings of printing in England has of course been the field of typographical bibliographers from Joseph Ames and William Herbert down.

61. AMES (Joseph). Typographical antiquities, 1471–1600. 1749.
        Augmented by William Herbert. 1785–1790.

Caxton's work was first studied by a typographical expert in

62. BLADES (William). The life and typography of William Caxton. 2v. 1861–1863,

which Blades revised in

63. BLADES (William). Biography and typography of William Caxton. 1877.

The best accounts of Caxton, however, are given in the short life by

64. DUFF (E. Gordon). William Caxton. 1905,

written for the Caxton Club of Chicago, and unfortunately not easy to obtain, and in the introduction to

65. CROTCH (W. J. B.). Caxton's prologues and epilogues. 1928.

A complete account of the copies of Caxton's books is

66. DE RICCI (Seymour). A census of Caxtons. 1909.

For ordinary purposes the whole output of English presses to 1500 (except for stray later discoveries) has been adequately described by

67. DUFF (E. Gordon). Fifteenth century English books. 1917.

Since its foundation in 1892 the Bibliographical Society has aimed at helping forward the bibliography of English literature as one of its main tasks. To this end it has published series of handlists of the works of English printers, such as:

68. HANDLISTS OF BOOKS PRINTED BY LONDON PRINTERS, 1501–1556, by E. G. Duff, W. W. Greg, R. B. McKerrow, H. R. Plomer, A. W. Pollard, R. Proctor. 4 parts in IV. 1895–1913.

69. DUFF (E. Gordon). A century of the English book trade. Short notices of all printers, stationers, bookbinders and others connected with it, 1475–1557. 1905.

70. McKERROW (R. B.). A dictionary of printers and booksellers in England, Scotland and Ireland, and of foreign printers of English books, 1557–1640. 1910.

71. PLOMER (H. R.). A dictionary of the booksellers and printers at work in England, Scotland and Ireland from 1641 to 1667. 1907.

72. PLOMER (H. R.) *ed.* A dictionary of the printers and booksellers who were at work in England, Scotland and Ireland from 1668 to 1725, by Henry R. Plomer. 1922.

73. PLOMER (H. R.), BUSHNELL (G. H.), *and* DIX (E. R. McC.). A dictionary of the printers and booksellers who were at work in England, Scotland and Ireland from 1726 to 1775. 1932.

303

But the major contribution of the Bibliographical Society to this field, and possibly the most influential single work yet published by them, is the well-known "S.T.C".

> 74. POLLARD (A. W.) *and* REDGRAVE (G. R.). A short-title catalogue of books printed in England, Scotland, and Ireland, and of English books printed abroad, 1475–1640. 1926.

This is an author-list, a new edition of which is in preparation, while the plans for a chronological list of the same period, under the proposed title of "The annals of printing", are still receiving attention.

A useful index to the S.T.C. has been published by the University of Virginia Bibliographical Society as

> 75. MORRISON (Paul G.). Index of printers, publishers and booksellers in A. W. Pollard and G. R. Redgrave: Short-title catalogue . . . 1950.

The period immediately following what has now come to be known as "the S.T.C. period" has now been covered in a similar manner by

> 76. WING (Donald G.). Short-title catalogue of books printed in England, Scotland, Ireland, Wales and British America and of English books printed in other countries, 1641–1700. 3v. 1945–1951.

Like Morrison, Wing is an American publication, being published by Columbia University Press for the Index Society.

Many catalogues of English books printed before 1641 (in some cases before 1600) had appeared before the S.T.C., and some are still of importance as giving fuller information than a short-title catalogue can.

Two stand out:

77. BRITISH MUSEUM. Catalogue of books in the library of the British Museum printed in England, Scotland, and Ireland, and of books in English printed abroad, to 1640. 3v. 1884,

which is arranged by authors, and has indexes of titles (including some class headings such as "Plays") and of printers, the latter hard to use.

78. CAMBRIDGE UNIVERSITY LIBRARY. Early English printed books in the University library, 1475–1640, edited by C. E. Sayle. 4v. 1900–1907.

Commonly known as Sayle, though largely the work of the University Librarian, Francis Jenkinson; it is arranged by presses, with author and other indexes.

The contemporary record of new publications began earlier in England than in any other country, a few years earlier than even the fair catalogues of Germany. In 1557 the Company of Stationers of London, which had existed since the beginning of the fifteenth century, was granted Incorporation. Attached to the rights of that state were duties, by which the Company practically became the Crown's instrument in controlling the press. A monopoly of printing was given to the members of the Company, and extended rather later to the Universities of Oxford and Cambridge. By the *Injunctions* of 1559 nothing was to be published without licence by the

Crown, Privy Council, Archbishops or Bishop of
London and the licences were to be entered in a
register for the keeping of which the Company was
responsible. By this ingenious plan the Crown
secured a very real, if never quite complete, control
over printing. Provincial printing, of which there
had, in fact, been but little before 1556,[1] disappeared, with the exception of the Universities and
of the Royalist presses of the Civil War period,
until after the desuetude of the licensing Acts in
1695. The period at which the Company was incorporated was so stormy both in dynastic and in
ecclesiastical politics, and the right of every Government to control opinion so universally practised and
allowed, that the action of the Marian Government
was merely natural, and was, moreover, in its method
one of the very few signs shown by Mary of the
statecraft of her father and sister.

The Register of the Stationers' Company was kept
at first fully, but in the seventeenth century the
entries decline, in spite of the obvious convenience
of having a record of copyrights, and by 1911, when
the Copyright Act tacitly abolished it, the Register
was very little used. Up to the date of the first Copyright Act (1709) it is accessible in print: the rest
may be consulted at Stationers' Hall.

79. STATIONERS' COMPANY. Transcript of the registers of
the company . . . 1554–1640, edited by Edward
Arber. 5v. 1875–1894.

[1] See E. Gordon Duff: *The English Provincial Printers, Stationers, and
Bookbinders to* 1557 (Sandars Lectures), 1912.

Continued for 1641–1708, edited by G. E. B.
Eyre, transcribed by H. R. Plomer. 3v. 1913–
1914.

For the last sixty years of the seventeenth century we
have two other contemporary sources, which are
much fuller than the declining Stationers' Register.

In 1641, at the outbreak of the Civil War, George
Thomason, a Scottish bookseller in London, per-
ceiving the value which the fugitive literature of a
disturbed time would have if methodically collected
and carefully preserved, procured so far as he could,
everything published, other than folio volumes, and
on most of the pieces he noted the day of receipt.
His collection, which he ceased to make in 1661,
after the Restoration of Charles II, failed for a
century to find a purchaser: but on his accession
George III bought it for £300 and presented it to the
newly founded British Museum, where in consequence Thomason's 22,000 books, pamphlets, and
sheets long bore the title of "the King's Tracts".
They have been catalogued chronologically, as
Thomason's written dates allow, an arrangement
which has obvious advantages in dealing with historical sources, and which might well be adopted
for similar catalogues for other periods:

80. BRITISH MUSEUM. Catalogue of pamphlets, books,
newspapers, manuscripts relating to Civil War,
Commonwealth, and Restoration (1640–1661),
collected by G. Thomason and edited by G. K.
Fortescue. 2v. 1908.

In 1668 began to be published a current classified

list of new books, pamphlets unfortunately being excluded, which appeared once in each law term (Hilary, Easter, Trinity, and Michaelmas); it originally bore the title of *Mercurius Librarius*, and was the venture of the booksellers Starkey and Clavell: it has been republished, although with an inadequate index, as

81. ARBER (Edward). The Term catalogues, 1668–1709, with a number for Easter term, 1711. 3v. 1903–1906.

During a long life W. C. Hazlitt, grandson of the essayist, collected and periodically published titles of English books, mostly of the literary and popular type, of the period ending at 1700.

82. HAZLITT (William Carew). Handbook to the popular, poetical and dramatic literature of Great Britain from the invention of printing to the Restoration. 1867.

This was continued by

Bibliographical collections and notes, 1474–1700. 6v. 1876–1903,

and a general index was provided by G. J. Gray in 1893.

Most of the great private collections have been chiefly composed of books printed before the eighteenth century; among many may be mentioned those of Richard Heber (sold 1834–1837), Henry Huth (catalogued 1880, sold 1911–1920), and the Christie Miller or Britwell (sold 1910, 1916–c. 1925). This last was largely founded from the

Heber, and much of it has passed into the Henry E. Huntington, now endowed and public, at Pasadena, California. Of the many other great American collectors the chief are perhaps Robert Hoe, the printer (catalogued 1903–1905, sold 1912), and Pierpont Morgan (father and son), whose collection is now endowed and public in New York. Even the most random thoughts on English book-collecting would not be complete without some mention of the stormy career of Sir Thomas Phillipps (1792–1872) which resulted in the splendours of his collection— mainly notable for its manuscripts.

In every country the bibliographically darkest period is that intermediate between the early period, the slightest productions of which are collected for their rarity and historical interest, and the contemporary period, in which the trade makes current lists of new publications for its own use, and in which the national libraries gather by privilege the output of the press. In England the eighteenth century is ill served, except by special bibliographies of the greater writers, which are numerous. The London Catalogue, which began in 1773 nominally providing a trade list of books published since 1700, is for its earlier issues entirely worthless, and the best source we have is certainly

83. WATT (R.). Bibliotheca Britannica, or, a general index to British and foreign literature. 4v. 1824.

Watt was a Glasgow doctor, who originally intended a medical and scientific catalogue, but whose appetite grew with what it fed on till he aimed at universality. The British part, however, is much larger and more valuable than the foreign. The work is in two parts, Authors and Subjects, Anonyma being entered in the latter. Efficient trade lists, which lapsed with the Term Catalogues, began again with the gradual improvement in the first half of the nineteenth century of the London Catalogue and the foundation in 1853 of a rival, the British Catalogue. These were amalgamated by Sampson Low in 1864 into

84. The English Catalogue of Books, 1835–1863.

A retrospective volume, covering 1801–1836, edited by R. A. Peddie and Q. Waddington was published in 1914. The period after 1863 is covered by a series of cumulative volumes up to those of our own time. The present practice of the *English Catalogue* is an annual volume with a five-yearly cumulation. It is drawn largely from the weekly lists in

85. The Publishers' Circular, 1837–.

A similar compilation, but including classified lists, is

86. Whitaker's Cumulative Book List, 1924–,

which appears quarterly, annually, and, from 1939 onwards, with four- or five-yearly cumulations. As *English Catalogue* is to *The Publishers' Circular*, so is the *Cumulative Book List* to the weekly

87. Bookseller, 1858–.

The most recent arrival in this field, and undoubtedly the most important, is the

88. BRITISH NATIONAL BIBLIOGRAPHY, 1950–.

This is issued weekly by the Council of the British National Bibliography, representing a number of interested associations, in conjunction with the Copyright Department of the British Museum. It is arranged in classified order according to the Dewey Decimal Classification and catalogued fully in accordance with the Anglo-American Code. It cumulates quarterly, with an annual bound volume, providing the necessary indexes.

Thomason in the seventeenth century secured most of the London books, but few from provincial presses; and today the national libraries do not get all provincially printed books. For records of these we have to fall back on local bibliographies and on the catalogues of local collections, which are found in all considerable, and in many small, public libraries.

The separate countries of the United Kingdom stand apart and have their own bibliographies. For Scottish books the great centre is the National Library of Scotland. This was formerly the Advocates' Library and so has as its foundation catalogue the one published for the Advocates Library in 1857–1879. But there are also the catalogues of the four Universities, especially that of Edinburgh University. The books before 1700 are set out in an admirable short-title list printed for the Edinburgh Bibliographical Society:

89. ALDIS (H. G.). A list of books printed in Scotland before 1700, including those printed furth of the realm for Scottish booksellers, with brief notes on the printers and stationers. 1904.

Fuller information than is given in Aldis, though not so recent, for the earlier Scottish presses is to be found in

90. DICKSON (R.) *and* EDMOND (J. P.). Annals of Scottish printing from 1507 to the beginning of the 17th century. 1890.

Welsh bibliography is mainly found in two works, the first historical,

91. ROWLANDS (William). Cambrian bibliography: containing an account of the books printed in the Welsh language or relating to Wales from the year 1546 to the end of the 18th century, with biographical notices, edited and enlarged by D. S. Evans. 1869.

The literary output of Wales for the nineteenth century must be sought in library catalogues, such as,

92. CARDIFF PUBLIC LIBRARY. Catalogue of printed literature in the Welsh department by John Ballinger and J. I. Jones. 1898,

and, more particularly, in the series published by the National Library of Wales at Aberystwyth,

93. BIBLIOTHECA CELTICA: a register of publications relating to Wales and the Celtic peoples and languages. 1909–.

Of this, author-lists appeared annually for the years 1909 to 1913 inclusive; then cumulations covering the following periods, 1914–1918; 1919–1923; 1924–1926; 1927–1928. After this date the new series takes over, as subject lists, one covering 1929–1933, and the most recent one, to date, covering 1934–1938 was published in 1952. The later material is on cards in the National Library and will be published in due course.

The chief repository of Irish books is similarly the "copyright" library of that country.

> 94. TRINITY COLLEGE, DUBLIN. Catalogus librorum impressorum. 1864–1867.

There is a very large collection in the University Library of Cambridge, which came to it from Henry Bradshaw's family. It was catalogued by C. E. Sayle,

> 95. CAMBRIDGE UNIVERSITY LIBRARY. Catalogue of the Bradshaw Collection of Irish books. 1916.

An important class of Irish books, starting with the first press set up in the country, is recorded in

> 96. DIX (E. R. McC.). Catalogue of early Dublin printed books, 1601–1700, with an historical introduction and bibliographical notes by C. Winston Dugan. 4v. in 2 and suppl. 1898–1905,

while the same bibliographer has, single-handed, produced bibliographies of most of the Irish provincial presses.

Many English counties and cities have bibliographies, which generally record the earlier products of the local presses. An interesting list of some of them can be found in Winchell and will give some idea of the range available. They vary considerably in quality and completeness. As an example, one may be mentioned which was compiled by an eminent bibliographer for a city of no mean printing importance.

97. MADAN (Falconer). Oxford books; a bibliography of printed works relating to the University and city of Oxford, or printed or published there (up to 1680). 3v. 1895–1931.

Pieces recorded nowhere else may also be found in bibliographies of literary classes, mostly in particular periods. For example, for English drama, the range extends from the series of play-lists of Kirkman and Langbaine in the seventeenth century, through

98. HAZLITT (William Carew). Manual for the collector and amateur of old English plays; edited from the material formed by Kirkman, Langbaine, Downes, Oldys, and Halliwell-Phillipps. 1892,

to more recent lists such as

99. HARBAGE (Alfred). Annals of English drama, 975–1700; an analytical record of all plays, extant or lost, chronologically arranged and indexed by authors, titles, dramatic companies, etc. 1940,

and the lists which are included in Allardyce Nicoll's several volumes on the history of English drama. In this field there is, however, one work which is of such outstanding bibliographical merit that it should be studied carefully by the student as a model:

100. GREG (*Sir* Walter Wilson). A bibliography of the
English printed drama to the Restoration.
To be complete in three volumes. v. 1, 1939; v. 2,
1951.

Pieces can also be traced in special bibliographies of
other kinds, such as lists of the writings of members
of religious bodies, monastic orders, and so forth,
which are perhaps best treated as part of the bibliography of history.

Another class of bibliographies, which experience
proves to be essential, is that of anonymous and
pseudonymous books. Most of the books recording
and revealing the secrets of concealed or disguised
authorship are limited to particular languages, and
those that are so limited are fuller within their limits.
Two of wider scope, dealing with disguised authorship and disguised imprints respectively, are

101. WELLER (Emil). Lexicon pseudonymorum: wörterbuch
der pseudonymen aller zeiten und völker. 2nd ed.
1886,

and

102. WELLER (Emil). Die falschen und fingierten druck-
orte. 2nd ed. 2v. 1864.

The chief one for English writings is

103. HALKETT (Samuel) *and* LAING (John). Dictionary of
anonymous and pseudonymous English literature.
Enlarged edition by James Kennedy, W. A. Smith,
and A. F. Johnson. 7v. 1926–1934,

while a strong American element will be found in

315

104. CUSHING (William). Anonyms: a dictionary of revealed authorship. 1889,

and

105. CUSHING (William). Initials and pseudonyms: a dictionary of literary disguises. 2v. 1886–1888.

Current guides to the field are provided mainly by

106. MODERN HUMANITIES RESEARCH ASSOCIATION. Annual bibliography of English language and literature. Annually from 1920,

and

107. YEAR'S WORK IN ENGLISH STUDIES, edited for the English Association. Annually from 1919/1920.

Small, but useful, general guides to the whole field, particularly valuable to students, are

108. CROSS (Tom Peete). Bibliographical guide to English studies. 10th ed. 1951,

and

109. KENNEDY (Arthur Garfield). A bibliography of writings on the English language from the beginnings of printing to the end of 1922. 1927.

BRITISH EMPIRE AND COMMONWEALTH

Outside the United Kingdom, the Empire and Commonwealth is not rich in bibliographical records, except in so far as they are provided by the Royal Empire Society's "Subject catalogue".

Australia has one general list in

110. FOXCROFT (A. B.). Australian catalogue; a reference index to the books and periodicals published and still current in the Commonwealth of Australia. 1911.

A larger work, as yet incomplete, is

111. FERGUSON (John Alexander). Bibliography of Australia; survey of books, pamphlets, periodicals and newspapers printed in, or relating to, Australia from 1784 onwards. *To complete in 5v.*
v. 1 (1784–1830). 1941.
v. 2 (1831–1838). 1945.
v. 3 (1839–1845). 1952.

The very early years are included in

112. SPENCE (Sydney A.). A bibliography of selected early books and pamphlets relating to Australia, 1610–1880. 1952.

Much background material for Canadian bibliography is provided by

113. MORGAN (Henry James). Bibliotheca canadensis; or a manual of Canadian literature. 1867,

which is an alphabetical list of works by authors who were native to those provinces "now constituting the Dominion of Canada".

114. DIONNE (Narcisse E.). Inventaire chronologique. 4v. and suppl. 1905–1912

is a chronological list under broad headings published by the Royal Society of Canada.

Current material is catered for by the annual publication of

115. TORONTO PUBLIC LIBRARY. Canadian catalogue of
  books published in Canada, about Canada, as well
  as those written by Canadians. 1921/1922–,

which will be reinforced by the new national bibliography,

116. CANADIANA,

published monthly by the newly founded Canadian
National Library.

South Africa is covered mainly by the

117. SOUTH AFRICAN CATALOGUE OF BOOKS. 3rd ed.
  (1900–1947). 2v. 1948,

which is continued by monthly supplements cumu-
lating into an annual volume.

AMERICAN LITERATURE (U.S.A.)

Printing began in what is now the United States
of America in the middle of the seventeenth century, and for a long time was slender in bulk; but
American patriotism has left very little of its early
productions to be discovered, and still less to be
easily acquired. The beginnings of American printing are dealt with in a bibliography which is as yet
incomplete:

118. EVANS (Charles). American bibliography: a chronological dictionary of all books, pamphlets, and
  periodical articles printed in the United States of
  America from the genesis of printing in 1639 down
  to and including the year 1820; with bibliographical and biographical notes. v. 1–12. 1903–1934.

The twelfth volume takes the record as far as 1799. This is followed chronologically by one of the series of contemporary trade records that are still current,

119. ROORBACH (Orville Augustus). Bibliotheca Americana, 1820–1861. 4v. 1852–1861.

Roorbach is arranged alphabetically by author and title; much the same kind of information (publisher, date, size, price) is given in its continuation,

120. KELLY (James). American catalogue of books published in the United States from Jan. 1861 to Jan. 1871. 2v. 1866–1871.

The next in sequence is

121. AMERICAN CATALOGUE OF BOOKS, 1876–1910. 9v. in 13. 1876–1910.

From this point onwards the main record is the

122. CUMULATIVE BOOK INDEX,

which has appeared monthly, with frequent cumulations, finishing in a five-yearly cumulation, since 1898. In its origins it was simply a record of American publications but the scope has widened with the years. From 1930 onwards it has included books published in Great Britain, Canada, South Africa, and British dominions and colonies generally. It indexes material under a wide variety of headings and justly sub-titles itself "a world list of books in the English language".

The C.B.I. also acts as a supplement to

123. UNITED STATES CATALOG. 4th ed.; books in print,
        Jan. 1st, 1928,

the first three editions of which had recorded the
books in print on 1st January of 1899; 1902; and
1912.

The library carrying the right of receiving a copy
of every book published in the U.S.A. is the Library
of Congress. Its printed catalogue cards are sub-
scribed to by a large number of libraries and its
"Catalog of books represented by Library of Congress printed cards", while not limited to American
books, is a valuable record of them.

For the select literary output of the United
States, apart from bibliographies of individual
authors, there are

124. ALLIBONE (Samuel Austin). Critical dictionary of Eng-
        lish literature and British and American authors,
        living and deceased, from the earliest accounts to
        the latter half of the nineteenth century. 5v.
        1858–1891,

which, while not very critical, is valuable for minor
American authors.

125. CAMBRIDGE HISTORY OF AMERICAN LITERATURE,
        edited by W. P. Trent, J. Erskine, S. P. Sherman,
        Carl van Doren. 4v. 1917–1921,

has, in its full edition, useful select lists. But the best
bibliography combined with a literary history is in
the more recent

126. LITERARY HISTORY OF THE UNITED STATES, edited by
        Robert E. Spiller, and others. 3v. 1948,

of which the third volume is entirely devoted to a bibliography.

In addition, covering the field from a literary as well as an historical viewpoint there is Sabin's *"Bibliotheca Americana"*.

Other national literatures will be found to have bibliographical records and books falling into much the same classes, except that only England has a Stationers' Register. There is in most countries:

(1) A library with a fairly complete collection of the modern books, due to the legal right to deposit, but rarely with a printed catalogue;

(2) A retrospective bibliography founded in the nineteenth century (Watt for England, Quérard for France, Brinkman for Holland, Hidalgo for Spain);

(3) Studies of the earliest productions of the printing press (Duff for England, Haebler for Spain, Claudin for France);

(4) Catalogues of private libraries;

(5) Special bibliographies and lists for collectors;

(6) Current Trade lists:—

    (*a*) weekly or monthly;

    (*b*) annual; and

    (*c*) quinquennial or the like.

There is no need to enumerate the apparatus for all countries; the titles can be found in Winchell, Schneider, etc. This book is intended for English students and therefore English bibliography has been dealt with at more length than that of other lands; but it will be well to include a more restrained selection of the chief bibliographies of the nations

which have been most important to England—
France, Germany, and Italy.

French Literature

In a consideration of the bibliographies of French
literature, mention must first be made of the catalogue of the Bibliothèque Nationale. The right of
deposit, dating from a decree of 1617 but not effec-
tive till the mid-seventeenth century, has brought
two copies to the national library—one from the
publisher, one from the printer. Of these, one copy
was retained by the Bibliothèque Nationale while the
duplicates were distributed among special libraries
in Paris. The literary duplicates, for example, have
always gone to the Arsenal Library. The result has
been the creation of an outstanding collection of
national literature, of which the catalogue, when
complete, will be an author-list. The position has
been substantially changed by the law of June 1943,
but this does not affect the status of this catalogue.

Another comprehensive record, of recent origin
and also incomplete, is

127. Répertoire de Bibliographie Française, contenant
tous les ouvrages imprimés en France et aux
colonies et les ouvrages français publiés à l'étranger,
1501–1930. 1937—*in progress.*

The outstanding general bibliography of French
literature is

128. Lanson (Gustave). Manuel bibliographique de la littérature française moderne, 1500–1900. New edition.
1921.

This is supplemented for the period since 1800 by

129. THIEME (Hugo Paul). Bibliographie de la littérature
française de 1800 à 1930. 3v. 1933,

and by the, as yet, unfinished

130. TALVART (Hector) *and* PLACE (Joseph). Bibliographie
des auteurs modernes de langue française (covering
from 1800 up to the year of publication of each
volume). 1928—*in progress.*

A work which was designed as a more general supplement to Lanson, recording primarily books
written on the earlier periods but published between
1921 and 1935, is

131. GIRAUD (Jeanne). Manuel de bibliographie littéraire
pour les XVIe, XVIIe, XVIIIe siècles français.
1939.

The beginning has been published by the Syra-
cuse University Press of a work which promises to
be of great value in this field.

132. CABEEN (D. C.) *ed.* Critical bibliography of French
literature.
Designed in seven volumes. v. 1 (The Medieval
period, *ed.* U. T. Holmes). 1947.

It will be remembered that Brunet's *Manuel* is
specially rich in rare and important French books
up to 1800. The French bookman has always been
a bibliophile, and a remarkable library, containing
many unique items of French literature, is that of

133. ROTHSCHILD (N. James E. de), *Baron, and* PICOT (E.).
Catalogue des livres composant la bibliothèque de

323

feu M. le baron James de Rothschild. 5v. 1884–1920.

The real corner-stones of the literature, the first editions of the great French classics, are described, with facsimiles, in

134. LE PETIT (Jules). Bibliographie des principales éditions originales d'écrivains français du XVe au XVIIIe siècle. 1888.

This same kind of bibliophile bibliography has been carried down to more recent times by

135. VICAIRE (Georges). Manuel de l'amateur de livres du XIXe siècle, 1801–1893. 8v. 1894–1920.
136. CARTERET (Léopold). Le trésor du bibliophile romantique et moderne, 1801–1875. 3v. and index. 1924–1928.
137. CARTERET (Léopold). Le trésor du bibliophile; livres illustrés modernes, 1875 à 1945. 5v. 1946–1948.

Finally, the one to which such frequent reference is found in catalogues,

138. TCHEMERZINE (Avenir). Bibliographie d'éditions originales et rares d'auteurs français des XVe, XVIe, XVIIe, et XVIIIe siècles contenant environ 6000 fac-similés de titres et de gravures. 10v. 1927–1934.

The French have no repertory of their early printed books to be compared with Duff's *Fifteenth Century English Books*, or *S.T.C.*, which is curious for such a race of bibliophiles; but most French incunabula (whether in French or in Latin) would probably have been found in Pellechet, had her work been completed; as it is, the French have an old bibliography of their vernacular incunabula:

139. BRUNET (Gustave). La France littéraire au XVᵉ siècle, ou, catalogue raisonné des ouvrages en tout genre imprimés en langue française jusqu'à l'an 1500. 1865,

and although the British Museum's French books cannot be more than a fraction of those in the Bibliothèque Nationale, it includes some uniques and many extreme rarities, and there is therefore use even in France for:

140. BRITISH MUSEUM. Short-title catalogue of books printed in France and of French books printed in other countries from 1470 to 1600, now in the British Museum. 1924.

This was the first of a projected series of special lists of countries and periods, of which that for sixteenth-century Spain and Portugal is the only other published.

As in England, the intermediate period is the darkest, and the more so that there was neither Stationers' Register nor Term Catalogues, nor, curiously enough, has any exhaustive work been since done on a period which, after all, included the glories of the Grand Monarque. The fifth volume of Georgi (above, No. 17) is about all there is until the French contemporary and counterpart of Watt, the bookseller Joseph Marie Quérard, produced his first great work:

141. QUÉRARD (Joseph Marie). La France littéraire: ou,
dictionnaire bibliographique des savants, historiens
et gens de lettres de la France, ainsi que des littéra-
teurs étrangers qui ont écrit en français, plus par-
ticulièrement pendant les XVIIIe et XIXe siècles.
12v. 1827–1864.

But though he throws light on the eighteenth century, he does not go further back, and he is less
hospitable to small and unknown writers than is
Watt.

Quérard followed up his big book with one which
recorded the literature of his own time, but he did
not himself complete it:

142. QUÉRARD (Joseph Marie) *and others*. La littérature
française contemporaine, 1827–1849. 6v. 1842–
1857.

The main period following Quérard is covered by

143. LORENZ (Otto) *and others*. Catalogue général de la
littérature française. 1840–.

This is a list mainly by author and title with very
full detail, with briefer entries in classified order.
The early volumes cover up to as many as 25 years
in one sequence, the more recent ones are of much
more limited periods—of about three years. Lorenz
will cover up to the year 1933, after which date the
main record will be the annual volumes of

144. BIBLIO,

a monthly record, with authors, titles, and subjects
in one list, of books published in France and French
books published elsewhere.

326

Books deposited officially in the Bibliothèque Nationale are recorded, together with trade announcements of new books, in the weekly,

145. BIBLIOGRAPHIE DE LA FRANCE. 1811–.

French anonyma and pseudonyma are dealt with by

146. QUÉRARD (Joseph Marie). Les supercheries littéraires dévoilées. 2nd ed. 7v. 1869–1879.

This edition includes A. A. Barbier's "Dictionnaire des ouvrages anonymes" as v. 4–7. It is supplemented by

147. BRUNET (Gustave). Dictionnaire des ouvrages anonymes [de Barbier], suivi des Supercheries littéraires dévoilées [de Quérard]: supplément à la dernière édition de ces deux ouvrages. 1889.

It should be remembered that many French books appear in Belgium and Switzerland, and that some of these are not announced in Paris but must be sought in the Belgian and Swiss lists.

GERMAN LITERATURE

Since Germany had no political unity until 1870 and since the position subsequent to the Second World War has been very confused, there is no single and central source for German books such as obtains in many other countries for their national literatures. Each State library had the right to the books produced in that State; the Royal Library of Berlin obtaining it, in imitation of the French as it were, in

327

the late seventeenth century. Two unifying attempts made some progress in the period between the World Wars. In 1913 the German book-trade organization, the "Börsenverein", established a library at Leipzig, the town where it had its headquarters. This library, the "Deutsche Bücherei", received the voluntary deposit of all German books. There was also the highly organized Auskunftsbureau or Information Office in the State Library of Berlin, which united about 800 libraries in an interlending organization and began the publication of a union catalogue.

The middle centuries of German literature are as imperfectly covered by bibliographies as the nineteenth and twentieth centuries are well covered by the very thorough current trade bibliographies. That is perhaps because the Thirty Years War devastated the country and reduced it to a state of misery and even of savagery which has few parallels in Western history, and which allowed of little leisure for the arts of literature.

The period from the invention of printing to the outbreak of Lutheran pamphleteering is in a large measure explored. The chief bibliographies and catalogues of incunabula describe the books printed before 1501, while the first twenty years of the sixteenth century are dealt with in the first section of Part II of Proctor's *Index*, and in Panzer's *Annales*. Books in the German language up to 1526 were also described in

148. PANZER (Georg Wolfgang F.). Annalen der altern
     deutschen Literatur. 2v. 1788–1805,

to which much was added for the fifteenth century by Hain's *Repertorium* (1826–1838) and for the sixteenth by

149. WELLER (E. O.). Repertorium typographicum. 1864.

The fair catalogues, and the universal bibliographies such as Gesner and Georgi, carry on the story; but we reach firm ground again in the eighteenth century with

150. HEINSIUS (Wilhelm). Allgemeines Bücher-Lexikon, 1700–1892. 19v. 1812–1894.

Like Heinsius, the two other founders of modern German current bibliography were contemporaries of Watt and Quérard.

151. KAYSER (Christian G.). Index locupletissimus; vollständiges Bücherlexikon, 1750–1910. 36v. 1834–1911,

which began with six volumes covering 1750–1832, published between 1834 and 1836, and continued with five-yearly volumes, with indexes of subjects. The second founder was

152. HINRICHS (J. C.). Hinrichs Halbjahrs-Katalog,

which, beginning in 1797, appeared in two slim six-monthly volumes, one of authors, one of subjects. After 1916, it changed to the "Halbjahrsverzeichnis der Neuerscheinungen des deutschen Buchhandels", coming to a finish in 1944 with a total of 292 volumes.

The German weekly corresponding to the *Publishers' Circular* was

153. Wöchentliches Verzeichnis der erschienenen und der vorbereiteten Neuigkeiten. 1842–1930,

which was continued and enlarged from 1931 as

154. DEUTSCHE NATIONALBIBLIOGRAPHIE,

which was suspended in 1945. At the present time the material is being covered in two separate publications, one for Western Germany and one for the Russian Zone.

Anonymous and pseudonymous German books are well dealt with by

155. HOLZMANN (M.) *and* BOHATTA (H.). Deutsches Anonymen-Lexikon, 1501–1910. 7v. 1902–1928,

and

156. HOLZMANN (M.) *and* BOHATTA (H.). Deutsches Pseudonymen-Lexikon. 1906.

General bibliographies of German literature for students, comparable to Lanson's of French, are

157. ARNOLD (R. F.). Allgemeine Bücherkunde zur neueren deutschen Literaturgeschichte. 3rd ed. 1931.
158. GOEDEKE (K.). Grundriss zur Geschichte der deutschen Dichtung aus den Quellen. 2nd ed. 13v. 1884–1934; of which v. 11 has not yet appeared.

ITALIAN LITERATURE

Italy (like Germany, and until exactly the same date) was "a geographical expression", and what is more important, a racial and linguistic expression, but not a political unit. The unification of the State was thorough when it came, however, and that is reflected in its book-organization; we find a single official monthly list of new books, of which the annual index makes a series of convenient volumes.

159. FLORENCE, BIBLIOTECA NAZIONALE CENTRALE. Bollettino delle pubblicazioni italiane ricevute per diretto di stampa. 1866–.

The early period in Italy is so vast that its bibliography has never been attempted as a whole, though special studies, as of books illustrated by woodcuts (notably the collections of Prince d'Essling and C. W. Dyson Perrins), and of special presses, as Renouard's of the Aldine, abound. Large histories of literature, like Tiraboschi's, contain bibliographical material, and there are two old collections of titles of rare and important Italian books, in the style of Lowndes for English.

160. GAMBA (Bartolommeo). Serie dei testi di lingua e di altre opere importanti nella italiana letteratura, scritte dal secolo XIV al XIX. 4th ed. 1839.
161. HAYM (Nicola Francesco). Biblioteca italiana, ossia Notizia de' libri rari italiani divisa in quattro parti cisè istoria, poesia, prose, arti e scienze già. 4v. in 2. 1803.

From the mid-nineteenth century there is a work on the lines of Kayser; one long period covering author and title with a subject index, followed by supplements covering ten-year periods,

162. PAGLIAINI (Attilio). Catalogo generale della libreria italiana, 1847–1899. 6v. 1901–1922. (3v. author

and title, 1901–1905 *and* 3v. subject index, 1910–1922).

1st supplement (covering 1900–1910). 2v. 1912–1914.

2nd supplement (covering 1911–1920). 2v. 1925–1928.

3rd supplement (covering 1921–1930). 2v. 1932–1940.

There is also an Italian counterpart to the "Cumulative Book Index", in one series of author, title, and subject entries, which appears quarterly, half-yearly, and with annual cumulations,

163. LA SCHEDA CUMULATIVA ITALIANA, diretta e redatta da T. W. Huntington; indicatore bibliografico per autore, titolo e soggetto delle nuove pubblicazioni italiane. Pubblicato con l'autorizzazione del Ministero dell' educazione nazionale. 1932–.

There are also good bibliographies at the end of each chapter of the Italian counterpart to the "*Cambridge history of English literature*".

164. STORIA LETTERARIA D'ITALIA. 3rd ed. 9v. in 13. 1897–1934.

The chief Italian list of anonymous and pseudonymous literature is

165. MELZI (Gaetano). Dizionario di opere anonime e pseudonime di scrittori italiani. 3v. 1848–1859. With supplements by G. Passano (1887) and E. Rocco (1888).

GOVERNMENT PUBLICATIONS

GENERAL

The publications of governments world-wide are increasing in bulk and importance yearly. Two small manuals, both American, which provide guides to this material, including League of Nations and United Nations publications, are

166. CHILDS (James Bennett). Government document bibliography in the United States and elsewhere. 3rd ed. 1942,

and

167. BROWN (Everett S.). Manual of government publications: United States and foreign. 1950.

GREAT BRITAIN

Useful guides are

168. COWELL (Frank Richard). Brief guide to government publications. 1938.
169. HORROCKS (Sidney). The State as publisher. 1952.
170. LEES-SMITH (H. B.). A guide to parliamentary and official papers. 1924.

Among the main lists of the government publications themselves, a start can best be made with

171. KING (P. S.) *and* SON. Catalogue of parliamentary papers, 1801–1900, with a few of earlier date. 1904.
    To this can be added two supplements covering the periods 1901–1910; and 1911–1920.

For the more recent years there is

333

172. CONSOLIDATED LIST OF GOVERNMENT PUBLICATIONS

which has appeared annually since 1922 and which
is augmented by monthly and daily lists of government publications.

Mention should also be made of the Stationery
Office's

173. SECTIONAL LISTS

devoted to the publications of individual depart-
ments and revised at reasonably frequent intervals.

UNITED STATES OF AMERICA

The best general guides are

174. BOYD (Anne Morris). United States government publications. 3rd ed. revised by Rae Elizabeth Rips.
1949.
175. HIRSHBERG (Herbert S.) *and* MELINAT (Carl H.).
Subject guide to United States government publications. 1947.
176. SCHMECKEBIER (Laurence F.). Government publications and their use. 2nd ed. 1939.

The main catalogues of the publications themselves are

177. UNITED STATES DOCUMENTS OFFICE. Check list of
United States public documents, 1789–1909. 3rd
ed. 1911.
178. POORE (Benjamin P.). A descriptive catalogue of the
government publications of the United States,
September 5, 1774, to March 4, 1881. 1885.
179. AMES (John Griffith). Comprehensive index to the
publications of the United States government,
1881–1893. 2v. 1905.

334

180. UNITED STATES DOCUMENT OFFICE. Catalog of the
public documents of Congress and of all depart-
ments of the government of the United States for
the period March 4, 1893 to December 31, 1940.
25v. 1896–1945. Commonly referred to as
"Document catalog".

181. UNITED STATES DOCUMENT OFFICE. United States
government publications: monthly catalog. Commonly known as "Monthly catalog", it has
appeared since 1895.

For many other countries there are guides and
lists similar to those described for Great Britain and
the United States of America. The main requirements are handbooks to act as a general guide to the
whole field, together with lists of the documents
themselves. The latter usually need to be approached
from chronological, subject, and from numbering or
reference angles. A useful aid to the publications of
countries not so far mentioned is

182. GREGORY (Winifred). List of the serial publications of
foreign [i.e. *not* American] governments, 1815–
1931. 1932.

This is a union list on a similar plan to the same
editor's work on periodicals.

PERIODICAL PUBLICATIONS

The periodical has added a new terror to research.
A century ago there were few, and all but a handful
of those that existed were insignificant, though the
most worthless literature, if it be popular, is in time

of value as an index to social habits and ideas. Now the periodical contains a very large proportion of the first appearances of important literature of the imagination, criticism, essays, and the like, and practically the whole of the original work done in science. A bibliography which ignores articles in periodicals is a one-eyed leader of the blind.

Yet they are very elusive. No library catalogue except the highly specialized ones can enter articles as if they were books, for they are too numerous and largely too worthless, and selection would be a laborious and uncertain business. The titles of the periodicals themselves can be found in such catalogues, but in the current national bibliographies only the first numbers will be found entered; it would be too much to re-enter them all every year.

Periodicals also include the most heterogeneous publications, from cheap daily local newspapers up to weighty annuals, and indeed anything which appears at more or less regular intervals with a running title and numeration. Some academic series are on the borderline, and cause great difficulty.

The range of periodical publications can be most easily appreciated if they are approached in some logical order. The following is suggested as one method:

1. (*a*) lists of current periodicals;
   (*b*) retrospective lists of periodicals.
2. Subject indexes to periodicals. These may be indexes to individual periodicals, general subject indexes to periodicals, or special subject indexes.
3. Location and finding lists of periodicals.

336

The first group will indicate the periodicals which are being, or have been, published. Through the subject lists contained in them, periodicals dealing with particular subjects can be identified. The second group will help to locate an article on a given topic in the range of periodicals covered. The third group will help to locate a run of a periodical once the individual issue which is required has been determined.

1 (*a*). *Lists of current periodicals*

The best known of this group are:

183. ANNUAIRE DE LA PRESSE FRANÇAISE ET ÉTRANGÈRE, ET DU MONDE POLITIQUE

has appeared annually since 1878. Covers mainly French publications but some from abroad.

184. AYER AND SON'S DIRECTORY OF NEWSPAPERS AND PERIODICALS

has appeared annually since 1880. Covers the United States and possessions; Canada; Bermuda; Cuba and Philippines.

185. NEWSPAPER PRESS DIRECTORY

has appeared annually since 1846. Commonly known as "Mitchell's" after former publisher. Covers Great Britain; Northern Ireland; Eire; with some from Commonwealth and foreign countries.

186. ULRICH (Carolyn F.). Ulrich's periodicals directory; a classified guide to a selected list of current periodicals, foreign and domestic [American]. 7th ed. 1953.

187. WILLING'S PRESS GUIDE; a comprehensive index and handbook of the press of the United Kingdom of Great Britain, Northern Ireland, and Eire, together with principal Dominion, colonial and foreign publications.

has appeared annually since 1874.

1 (*b*). *Retrospective lists of periodicals*

Important examples are:

188. CRANE (R. S.) *and* KAYE (F. B.). A census of British newspapers and periodicals, 1620–1800. 1927.

189. MILFORD (R. T.) *and* SUTHERLAND (D. M.). A catalogue of English newspapers and periodicals in the Bodleian Library, 1622–1800. 1936.

190. THE TIMES. Tercentenary handlist of English and Welsh newspapers, magazines and reviews. 1920. Edited by J. G. Muddiman and covers the period 1620–1920. Based mainly on the British Museum collection.

France has a much older work:

191. HATIN (Louis Eugène). Bibliographie historique et critique de la presse périodique française. 1866.

While Germany has

192. KIRCHNER (Joachim). Die Grundlagen des deutschen Zeitschriftenwesens mit einer Gesamtbibliographie der deutschen Zeitschriften bis zum jahre 1790. 2v. 1928–1931.

2. *Subject indexes to periodicals*

Many periodicals publish their own indexes and a useful bibliography of such indexes is contained in

193. NEW YORK PUBLIC LIBRARY. A check list of cumulative indexes to individual periodicals in the New

York Public Library, compiled by Daniel C. Haskell. 1942.

One of the most important of individual indexes is

194. PALMER'S INDEX TO THE TIMES NEWSPAPER

which covers from 1790 and was published quarterly. It is augmented in the later years by the much more detailed

195. OFFICIAL INDEX TO THE TIMES,

which now also appears quarterly and covers from 1906.

Of the general subject indexes to periodicals, the following are the most widely available:

196. POOLE'S INDEX TO PERIODICAL LITERATURE, 1802–1881. 2v. 1891.
   5v. supplements (covering 1881–1906). 1887–1908.
197. READERS' GUIDE TO PERIODICAL LITERATURE. Covers from 1900. Published by the H. W. Wilson, Co., in their usual cumulative form.

There is also an

198. ABRIDGED READERS' GUIDE TO PERIODICAL LITERATURE, covering from 1935, which selects about 30 periodicals from the main "Readers' Guide".

A start has been made on a retrospective supplement designed to cover the nineteenth century, but, so far, only the last decade of the century has been covered by

199. NINETEENTH CENTURY READERS' GUIDE TO PERIODICAL LITERATURE, 1890–1899. 2v. 1944.

Another index published by the H. W. Wilson, Co., is

200. INTERNATIONAL INDEX TO PERIODICALS

covering from 1907 and devoted chiefly to the humanities and science.

The main general index published in this country is the

201. SUBJECT INDEX TO PERIODICALS.

This covers from 1915 and is now published annually by the Library Association. There were no issues for the years 1923, 1924, and 1925.

There is a great range of indexes to periodicals covering special subjects, of which the following provide important examples:

202. PUBLIC AFFAIRS INFORMATION SERVICE. Bulletin

is an American publication which has appeared weekly since 1915, with annual cumulations, and provides a useful index to periodicals, books, pamphlets, etc. in the social sciences. More than a thousand periodicals are used to make the basis of selection for the articles indexed.

There is also the range of subject indexes published by the Wilson Co., such as

203. AGRICULTURAL INDEX, from 1916.
204. ART INDEX, from 1929.
205. EDUCATION INDEX, from 1929.
206. ESSAY AND GENERAL LITERATURE INDEX, from 1900.
207. INDUSTRIAL ARTS INDEX, from 1913.
208. INDEX TO LEGAL PERIODICALS, from 1908.

3. *Location and finding lists of periodicals*

The largest union list of periodicals is certainly

209. GREGORY (Winifred). Union list of serials in libraries
of United States and Canada. 2nd ed. 1943,

which lists some 120,000 titles and the holdings of
600 libraries. Two supplements have already been
published to bring the record down to December
1949 and further supplements will appear in due
course.

Within a specialized field one of the best known
is

210. WORLD LIST OF SCIENTIFIC PERIODICALS, published
in years 1900–1950. 3rd ed. 1952,

which lists over 50,000 journals and the holdings of
250 libraries.

211. UNION CATALOGUE OF PERIODICAL PUBLICATIONS IN
UNIVERSITY LIBRARIES OF THE BRITISH ISLES

was published by the National Central Library in
1937, having been compiled by Marion C. Roupell
on behalf of the Joint Standing Committee on
Library Co-operation. It contained over 23,000
titles and excluded those listed in the "W.L.S.P."

Many areas of this country now have union lists
of varying complexity covering the holdings of
libraries in those regions; among such instances have
been the recent lists of the Liverpool, London, and
Sheffield areas. These are not the sole examples and
students should investigate the position in their own
regions.

In the past, Germany used to have two very famous lists,

212. GESAMT-ZEITSCHRIFTEN-VERZEICHNIS (GZV). 1914,

which was a union list of mainly German periodicals in the libraries united in the Auskunftsbureau in Berlin; while the

213. GESAMTVERZEICHNIS DER AUSLÄNDISCHEN ZEIT-SCHRIFTEN 1914–1924 (GAZ). 1929

was a list of non-German periodicals in a wider circle of libraries. While neither has much usefulness now as a location list, they are both still of service as bibliographies.

Looking to the future, the publication is awaited with interest of the

214. BRITISH UNION CATALOGUE OF PERIODICALS,

which is being prepared by Aslib with the aid of a grant from the Rockefeller Foundation.

LEARNED SOCIETIES

These have increased considerably in our own time and some of the guides to them, such as *"Minerva"*, *"Index Generalis"*, and *"World of Learning"*, are mentioned elsewhere. The publications of these societies frequently contain some of the most important writings on their subject, being written with authority for a specialist audience. The chief guide to the field in this country is

215. SCIENTIFIC AND LEARNED SOCIETIES OF GREAT
   BRITAIN; a handbook compiled from official
   sources.

This has appeared annually since 1884, with an in-
terruption during the Second World War. It gives
material information relating to the Society, with
titles of the publications and, in many cases, details
of the publications for the year under review. The
original issue of 1884 is an important volume since
it gives considerable historical information regarding
the societies which were in existence at that time.

The United States has a list which, while originally a very good one, suffers by being out of date,

216. CARNEGIE INSTITUTION OF WASHINGTON. Handbook
   of learned societies and institutions. 1908.

France is well equipped since the Ministry which
is concerned with public education has for many
years interested itself in the publications of learned
and scientific societies. The result has been the publication of two large bibliographical series, one for
history and archæology, and one for science.

217. LASTEYRIE DU SAILLANT (Robert Charles), *Count.*
   Bibliographie générale des travaux historiques et
   archéologiques publiés par les sociétés savantes de
   la France, dressée sous les auspices du Ministère de
   l'Instruction Publique. 6v. 1888–1918.

This important work covers writings published up to
1900 and is continued by

218. BIBLIOGRAPHIE ANNUELLE DES TRAVAUX HISTOR-
   IQUES ET ARCHÉOLOGIQUES publiés par les sociétés
   savantes de la France. 3v. 1906–1914,

which covered the first decade of the twentieth century.

This in its turn was continued by another series of volumes designed to cover the period 1910 to 1940, which began publication in 1944 and is still in progress. The title of the present series remains the same.

The companion volume to Lasteyrie, which was designed to do the same service for scientific societies, is unfortunately unfinished.

219. DENIKER (Joseph) *and* DESCHARMES (René). Bibliographie des travaux scientifiques (Sciences mathématiques, physiques et naturelles) publiés par les sociétés savantes de la France depuis l'origine jusqu'en 1888.

Publication in parts began in 1895, but nothing has appeared since 1922.

The profusion of German societies is, unhappily, inadequately represented in the work which was another victim of the First World War:

220. MÜLLER (Johannes). Die wissenschaftlichen Vereine und Gesellschaften Deutschlands im neunzehnten Jahrhundert. 2v. issued in parts. 1883–1917.

Italy has

221. MAYLENDER (Michele). Storia delle accademie d'Italia. 5v. 1926–1930.

ACADEMIC WRITINGS

Theses, dissertations, etc., used not to be very numerous in England: when printed they mostly are published and recorded like other books; but they normally repose in typescript in the University library.

In many other countries, they are a recognized part of a University career, and large numbers are (or were up to the First World War) printed and exchanged between University libraries. A dissertation, if of any merit at all, must when new contain data inaccessible elsewhere. Even in after years its contents may not have been entirely absorbed into books; or it may have importance as the earliest work of a famous man.

In the United States, although there is no general retrospective list, there are numerous guides, the basic one being

222. LIBRARY OF CONGRESS. List of American doctoral dissertations printed in 1912–1938. 26v. 1913–1940.

The coverage is now largely continued by

223. DOCTORAL DISSERTATIONS accepted by American Universities; compiled for the Association of Research Libraries,

which is an annual publication covering from 1933.

Many dissertations in America are now available on microfilm and copies are available through University Microfilms. To provide a guide to this material, abstracts of the dissertations are published in a work to which extra volumes have been issued at intervals since it began in 1938. This is

224. MICROFILM ABSTRACTS.

As a further guide to the vast field of American dissertations there is

225. PALFRY (Thomas R.) *and* COLEMAN (Henry E.).
   Guide to bibliographies of theses, United States
   and Canada. 2nd ed. 1940.

In France, where theses are of great importance,
there is an official annual list:

226. MINISTÈRE DE L'EDUCATION NATIONALE. Catalogue
   des thèses et écrits académiques,

which commenced in 1885.

There are also French lists for the nineteenth century of doctorate theses in letters and science respectively:

227. MOURIER (A.) *and* DELTOUR (F.). Notice sur le doc-
   torat és lettres, suivie du catalogue et de l'analyse
   des thèses françaises et latines admises par les
   facultés des lettres depuis 1810. 4th ed. 1880.

This is supplemented by the annual volumes of

   Catalogue et analyse des thèses latines et françaises. 21v. 1882–1901.

228. MAIRE (Albert). Catalogue des thèses de sciences
   soutenues en France de 1810 à 1890 inclusive-
   ment. 1892.

Germany, and likewise other continental countries, also has an official annual list,

229. JAHRESVERZEICHNIS DER DEUTSCHEN HOCHSCHUL-
   SCHRIFTEN.

This has appeared under various titles and from a
number of publishers since its first appearance in
1885. An incomplete work which lists theses, with
accompanying biographical data, back to the seventeenth century is

230. MUNDT (Hermann). Bio-bibliographisches Verzeichnis
     von Universitäts-u.
     Hochschuldrucken von Ausgang des 16. bis Ende
     des 19. Jahrhunderts,

which began publication in 1936.

In England, various Universities had published
lists or abstracts of dissertations and theses, and
some lists had appeared relating to specific subjects.
No large list, however, has yet been produced
although an increasing interest has been shown in
the problem of recent years. A direct result of that
concern has been seen in the publication of

231. RECORD (P. D.). A survey of thesis literature in British
     libraries. 1950,

which has been followed by the first volume of Aslib's

232. RECORD (P. D.). Index to theses accepted for higher
     degrees in the universities of the British Isles.

PRIVATELY PRINTED BOOKS

Privately printed books are numerous, particularly
in local history and genealogy and modern "fine"
printing. It cannot be said that in any country there
is a good recent guide to them. In countries like
France, where the law of deposit is incumbent upon
the printer as well as upon the publisher, the catalogue of the national library should contain them.
Many are, in fact, presented to the national libraries
and are thus traceable. Many private and fine
presses have bibliographies of their own such as,

233. HAZEN (Allen Tracy). A bibliography of the Straw-
    berry Hill Press. 1942,

or the series published as a personal record by

234. GOLDEN COCKEREL PRESS
    Chanticleer.   1936.
    Pertelote.   1943.
    Cockalorum.   1949,
or

235. ASHENDENE PRESS. A chronological list, with prices,
    of the forty books printed at the Ashendene Press,
    1895–1935. 1935.

The one important early substantial list is

236. MARTIN (John). Bibliographical catalogue of books
    privately printed. 1854. (1st ed. 1834.)

This was augmented by the catalogue of a collection
formed by a bookseller:

237. DOBELL (Bertram). Catalogue of books printed for
    private circulation. 1906.

Later lists have been compiled by a man who is
himself concerned directly with the private press
movement,

238. RANSOM (Will). Private presses and their books. 1929,

and the much more detailed, but as yet incomplete

239. RANSOM (Will). Selective checklists of press books: a
    compilation of all important and significant private
    presses, or press books which have been collected.
    (12 parts which, when complete, will be corrected,
    correlated, re-arranged and published as a 3-volume
    work.)

348

X

BIBLIOGRAPHIES: SOME CLASSES AND EXAMPLES

SECONDARY BIBLIOGRAPHIES

So far the bibliographies we have been running over have been primary; that is, they are either in whole or in part the original, and it may be the contemporary, record of books.

We have now to consider the secondary bibliography, i.e. that in which works already recorded in primary bibliographies are selected, recombined, analysed, in manners which will make them throw light on each other, either by subject-matter, or authorship, or period, or typography. Something will be said of methods of arrangement in another chapter.

Bibliographies good and bad, complete and fragmentary, new and out of date, current and retrospective, exist for every branch of human knowledge and activity. We can here but run over a few outstanding examples, and so suggest what the apparatus bibliographicus of research should be.

LIBRARIANSHIP

Librarianship is given its pride of place here only because it may be regarded as of some special concern to the readers of this book. The main bibliography of the subject is

240. CANNONS (H. G. T.). Bibliography of library economy; a classified index to the professional periodical literature . . . from 1876 to 1920. 1927.

This has been continued by the quarterly and cumulative volumes of

241. LIBRARY LITERATURE,

which gathers material from 1921 onwards.

An English publication conceived and executed on a smaller scale was

242. BURTON (Margaret) *and* VOSBURGH (Marion). A bibliography of librarianship: a classified and annotated guide to the library literature of the world. 1934.

Another bibliography which attempted to cover the universal writings on librarianship in the form of an annual publication was

243. HOECKER (R.) *and* VORSTIUS (J.). Internationale bibliographie des buch und bibliothekwesens,

which ran from 1922 to 1938 and continued the work which had been done by

244. HORTZSCHANSKY (Albert). Bibliographie des bibliotheks- und buchswesens. 1904–1912.

A series of useful abstracts began in 1950 and has been published quarterly by the Library Association as

245. LIBRARY SCIENCE ABSTRACTS.

350

Natural Science

In science, as we generally call the natural sciences, knowledge advances and theory changes with extreme rapidity. Nearly all original work appears in journals, transactions, memoirs, and other periodicals; and by the time a discovery appears in the books it may well be overlaid or superseded by a new layer of knowledge. It is apparent, therefore, that a guide to the periodical literature is of prime concern.

The one great attempt at a universal list of scientific periodicals is "The World List of Scientific Periodicals" of which mention has already been made. It is an alphabetical list of over 50,000 journals, with details of the files in the libraries of Great Britain. The titles are repeated in forms abbreviated on a scheme which was designed for universal adoption. The periodicals listed are those which existed in the period, not merely those which commenced in it. It may profitably be compared with the published list of the scientific periodicals indexed under the auspices of the Royal Society.

246. Royal Society. Catalogue of scientific papers, 1800–1900. 19v. 1867–1925.

This was an author-list and was continued by the annual numbers of

247. International Catalogue of Scientific Literature, first to fourteenth annual issues. 1902–1919,

each year being divided into seventeen class lists. The

First World War killed the "International Catalogue" and, although much manuscript material for its continuation existed, nothing more has ever appeared. Equally unfortunate was the project to provide a subject index to the "Catalogue of scientific papers", because this never progressed beyond the first three volumes published between 1908 and 1914.

A number of smaller guides of some importance exist, such as

248. ASLIB. Select list of standard British scientific and technical books. 3rd ed. 1946.

249. HAWKINS (Reginald R.). Scientific, medical and technical books published in the United States of America, 1930–1944; a selected list with annotations, 1946.
Supplements: 1945–1948   (1950),   1949–52 (1953).

As in almost every subject field a major bibliographical tool will be the lists and printed catalogues issued by large or specialist libraries. Here the following are outstanding:

250. BRITISH MUSEUM (NATURAL HISTORY) LIBRARY. Catalogue of the books, manuscripts, maps and drawings in the British Museum (Natural History). 8v. 1903–1940.

251. SCIENCE LIBRARY. Handlist of short titles of current periodicals. 7th ed. 1953.

252. SCIENCE LIBRARY. Classified list of bibliographies in the Science Library bibliographical series. 1946. With supplements.

253. ROYAL SOCIETY. Catalogue of periodical publications in the Library. 1912.

Useful guides to current publications are

254. NEW YORK PUBLIC LIBRARY. New technical books. 1915–.
255. ASLIB BOOK LIST. 1935–.
256. TECHNICAL BOOK REVIEW INDEX. 1917–.

All three are published at intervals throughout the year.

The history of science is catered for by

257. JOHN CRERAR LIBRARY. A list of books on the history of science. 1911.
258. BOLTON (Henry C.). Catalogue of scientific and technical periodicals, 1665–1895. 2nd ed. 1897.
259. SCUDDER (Samuel H.). Catalogue of scientific serials of all countries, 1663–1876. 1879.

The number of abstracts in the field of science has reached a quantity and degree of complexity which makes guides to them essential. Examples of these are

260. SCIENCE LIBRARY. Bibliography of current periodical abstracts and indexes. 1939.
261. ROYAL SOCIETY. A list of periodicals and bulletins containing abstracts published in Great Britain. 1949.

MEDICINE

Medicine is half a science and half an art; but its matter, and so the matter of its bibliographical apparatus, is that of science. By far the largest bibliography, now ceased publication, is

M

262. UNITED STATES. SURGEON-GENERAL'S OFFICE
LIBRARY. Index catalogue.
Commonly called "The Surgeon-General's Catalogue", it was published in four series, each complete in itself.
1st series. 16v. 1880–1895.
2nd series. 21v. 1896–1915.
3rd series. 10v. 1918–1932.
4th series. 10v. 1936–1950.

The current bibliography of periodicals is

263. QUARTERLY CUMULATIVE INDEX MEDICUS, 1927–,

which was preceded by

264. QUARTERLY CUMULATIVE INDEX TO CURRENT MEDI-
CAL LITERATURE. 12v. 1916–1926,

and

265. INDEX MEDICUS, a classified list of the current medical
literature of the world. 1879–1927.

Sir William Osler was an historian of medicine and
a man of wide and human interests; he was also at
one time President of the Bibliographical Society.
These interests are reflected in

266. OSLER (*Sir* William). Incunabula medica; a study of
the earliest printed medical books, 1467–1480.
1923,

and

267. OSLER (*Sir* William). Bibliotheca Osleriana; a catalogue of books illustrating the history of medicine
and science; edited by W. W. Francis, R. H. Hill
and A. Malloch. 1929.

This was the catalogue of his own collection, now in McGill University, in which the books of real importance, those that have influenced later medical thought, are given prominence.

GENERAL HISTORY

The field is too large for any exhaustive general bibliography; but

268. LANGLOIS (Charles Victor). Manuel de bibliographie historique. 2v. 1901–1904,

though growing out of date, is still of value. It is now reinforced by

269. DUTCHER (George M.) *ed*. A guide to historical literature. 1931.

For the mediæval period in particular there is

270. PAETOW (Louis John). A guide to the study of medieval history. 1931.

For periodicals, there is a work similar to the W.L.S.P. in

271. CARON (P.) *and* JARYC (M.). World list of historical periodicals. 1939.

For much general older material mention should be made of the bibliographies which are included in works such as

272. CAMBRIDGE ANCIENT HISTORY. 12v. 1923–1939.
273. CAMBRIDGE MEDIEVAL HISTORY. 8v. 1911–1936.
274. CAMBRIDGE MODERN HISTORY. 13v. 1902–1911.

For current material, recourse may be had to the following:

275. INTERNATIONAL BIBLIOGRAPHY OF HISTORICAL SCIENCES. Annual from 1926. It is now being revived under the auspices of Unesco after its cessation at the beginning of the Second World War.

276. ANNUAL BULLETIN OF HISTORICAL LITERATURE. Annual from 1911.

Covering the major part of the period of the 1939–1945 War there is

277. FREWER (Louis B.). Bibliography of historical writings published in Great Britain and the British Empire, 1940–1945. 1947.

There is a useful general guide to bibliographies in

278. COULTER (Edith M.) *and* GERSTENFELD (Melanie). Historical bibliographies, a systematic and annotated guide. 1935.

ENGLISH HISTORY

An early attempt at providing a general repertory on English history was

279. GROSS (Charles). Bibliography of British municipal history, including gilds and parliamentary representation. 1897.

The same editor inaugurated a task which, when completed, will give us the best general bibliography.

280. GROSS (Charles). Sources and literature of English history from earliest times to about 1485. 2nd ed. 1915.

356

This is being followed by the volumes of the "Bibliography of British History", issued under the direction of the American Historical Association and the Royal Historical Society.

281. READ (Conyers). Tudor period, 1485–1603. 1933.
282. DAVIES (Godfrey). Stuart period, 1603–1714. 1928.
283. PARGELLIS (Stanley) *and* MEDLEY (D. J.). The Eighteenth Century, 1714–1789. 1951.

Current material is dealt with in

284. MILNE (Alexander Taylor). Writings on British history: a bibliography of books and articles on the history of Great Britain from about 450 A.D. to 1914 published during the year.
Annually from 1934.

Two bibliographies of English topography are

285. ANDERSON (John Parker). The book of British topography: a classified catalogue of the topographical books in the library of the British Museum relating to Great Britain and Ireland. 1881.
286. HUMPHREYS (Arthur Lee). A handbook to county bibliography; being a bibliography of bibliographies relating to the counties and towns of Great Britain and Ireland. 1917.

Of especial importance on the social and economic side is the great union catalogue of the London School of Economics and other London libraries:

287. BRITISH LIBRARY OF POLITICAL SCIENCE. A London bibliography of the social sciences, compiled under the direction of B. M. Headicar and C. Fuller. 4v. 1931–1932.

357

With supplements as follows:
1st supplement (covering 1929–1931). 1934.
2nd supplement (covering 1931–1936). 1937.
3rd supplement (covering 1936–1950). Part covering A–F. 1952.

For material relating to the British Commonwealth and Empire there is the large catalogue of the

288. ROYAL EMPIRE SOCIETY. Subject catalogue of the Royal Empire Society, formerly Royal Colonial Institute, by Evans Lewin. 4v. 1930–1937.
v. 1. British Empire generally and Africa.
v. 2. Commonwealth of Australia, Dominion of New Zealand, South Pacific.
v. 3. Dominion of Canada, Newfoundland, West Indies.
v. 4. Mediterranean colonies, the Middle East Empire, Burma, Ceylon, British Malaya, East Indian Islands and Far East.

As in the other historical fields considerable material will be found in the

289. CAMBRIDGE HISTORY OF THE BRITISH EMPIRE. 7v. in 8. 1929– (v. 3 not yet published).

Law also will be regarded as only one manifestation of national political life; the greatest special English law library is that of Harvard; and on it were based (1) the only list of English law books of any extent:

290. BEALE (J. H.). A bibliography of early English law books. 1926.
With a supplement by R. B. Anderson. 1943,

and (2) a useful guide to the historical student of the subject,

358

291. WINFIELD (P. H.). Chief sources of English legal history, 1925.

The best general published repertories of English law books will be the catalogues of the libraries of the Inns of Court; and the most recent and largest of these is

292. MIDDLE TEMPLE. Catalogue of printed books, by C. E. A. Bedwell. 3v. 1914.
Supplement (covering 1914–1924). 1925.

Scottish law is not represented by any up-to-date work; but the great law libraries of Scotland (the Advocates' and the Signet at Edinburgh, and the Procurators' at Glasgow) have catalogues of various dates.

As a source of both legal and political history, proclamations are of great value, and also of great rarity; and an immense private collection of them is in the library of the Earls of Crawford (the *Bibliotheca Lindesiana*); the Hanoverian and later section has been catalogued, in two volumes in 1910, and the earlier Tudor and Stuart proclamations in what calls itself, and is, not a catalogue but a bibliography, in 1913 by Robert Steele. The collection in the University of London's library has also been very well catalogued.

The importance of the Thomason Civil War and Commonwealth Tracts as original historical sources for their period must not be forgotten; it is to be wished that we had similar collections, similarly catalogued by date of publication, for other periods.

359

Carlyle said of them that they are "greatly to be preferred to all the sheepskins in the Tower and other places, for informing the English what the English were in former times".

AMERICAN HISTORY

There are several important tools for the study of American history of which the following are merely a selection.

293. BRADFORD (Thomas Lindsley). Bibliographer's manual of American history, containing an account of all state, territory, town and county histories relating to the United States of North America, with verbatim copies of their titles and useful bibliographical notes, together with the prices at which they have been sold for the last forty years, and with an exhaustive index by titles, and an index by states. 5v. 1907–1910.

294. BEERS (Henry Putney). Bibliographies in American history: guide to materials for research. 1942.

295. LARNED (Josephus N.). The literature of American history, a bibliographical guide. 1902.

One of the finest catalogues produced on early Americana is that of the Church library which is now in the Huntington Library (San Gabriel, California).

296. CHURCH (Elihu Dwight). Catalogue of books relating to the discovery and early history of North and South America, forming a part of the library of E. D. Church, compiled and annotated by George Watson Cole. 5v. 1907.

360

"*Bibliotheca Americana*" or "*Sabin*" is the name normally used to refer to what is probably the most frequently consulted of bibliographies in this field:

297. SABIN (Joseph). Dictionary of books relating to America from its discovery to the present time. 29v. 1868–1936.

The main guide to current material is

298. WRITINGS ON AMERICAN HISTORY,

which has appeared annually since 1906, with the usual war-time interruptions.

FRENCH HISTORY

There exists a better provision of bibliographies for French than for English history. The cornerstone is the one which the Bibliothèque Nationale began to produce in the middle of the nineteenth century.

299. BIBLIOTHÈQUE NATIONALE. Catalogue de l'histoire de France. 11v. with index and 6 supplementary parts. 1855–1905.

Up to 1715 there is also a series of bibliographies of sources to which we can find no parallel in this country:

300. LES SOURCES DE L'HISTOIRE DE FRANCE. 18v. 1901–1935.
Part 1. Origins to 1494, by A. Molinier.
Part 2. 1494–1610, by H. Hauser.
Part 3. 1610–1715, by E. Bourgeois and L. André.

N

There are several other good bibliographies of special periods or localities with, naturally, the Revolutionary period attracting a great deal of the attention. Of this special period the two chief guides are

301. TOURNEUX (Maurice). Bibliographie de l'histoire de Paris, pendant la révolution française. 5v. 1890–1913,

and the very detailed

302. MONGLOND (André). La France révolutionnaire et impérial, annales de bibliographie méthodique et description des livres illustrés. 6v. 1930–1949, with index.

It is worth noting that the British Museum possesses nearly, if not quite, the finest collection of French Revolution tracts, leaflets, newspapers, and so forth, but that the "list of contents" compiled by G. K. Fortescue and printed in 1899 is merely a summary description of the collection and not a catalogue.

GERMAN HISTORY

German history, like French, is covered by several books; but there is one for the whole period, covering through the First World War, which is so well known and valuable that it shall stand alone here:

303. DAHLMANN (Friedrich Christoph). Quellenkunde der deutschen Geschichte. 9th ed. 2v. 1931–1932.

By means of this selection of bibliographies it is hoped that the student will have been enabled to deduce the principles on which bibliographical works are built into their places in the ideal structure of knowledge. From these beginnings he should be able to trace any of the numerous classes or any of the manifold titles not mentioned here. To know them he must use and compare them, but, at the time of his first acquaintance with them, he will help himself considerably by keeping accurate notes regarding them. He will be wise to procure (if he can) and interleave a copy of Winchell's "Guide to Reference Books"; or to use a series of loose-leaf note books or catalogue cards on which he can enter new titles and new editions as they appear. Important new bibliographies appear at frequent intervals and he will see them reviewed in the bibliographical and literary journals. A careful watch must be kept, for he must always aim at the well-nigh impossible ideal of keeping himself absolutely up to date.

XI

THE ARRANGEMENT OF BIBLIOGRAPHIES

When the bibliographer of a subject has assembled his material from existing bibliographies, mainly the primary national and other records of publication, he must find a scheme of arrangement.

Some bibliographers have simply sorted the titles into the alphabetical order of authors; but that is mere intellectual laziness or want of imagination (perhaps the same thing); for while the alphabet enables the searcher to get access in a library to a particular book of whose existence he is aware, or, it may be, to refresh his memory as to a title or date, or other detail in the title, it serves no other purpose. The alphabet does nothing to collocate material bearing on the same or a closely allied side of the subject; it serves you up impartially the prunes and prisms together.

So while the alphabet is reserved for an index to serve the subsidiary purposes mentioned, the main arrangement has to be sought by "fundamental brainwork" in distinguishing the essence of the subject-matter and the point of view of the normal inquirer.

The universal ready-made schemes of the library-classifiers may be profitably glanced at as a first step, but only as a first step. When a bibliographer, armed with the special knowledge acquired in the process of collecting his material, turns to them for guidance, he always finds them entirely inadequate beyond a few first suggestions. That, of course, is not to say that they are not very useful for their own purpose. But the real bibliographer has still his own thinking to do.

Let us take a few broad classes and find the leading principle which should govern the arrangement of each.

A. A BIBLIOGRAPHY OF AN AUTHOR

(1) The "library catalogue arrangement", as prac-tised in the British Museum, is, with variations and elaborations according to the needs of particular cases, as follows:

(*a*) Collected works, complete or nearly so.

(*b*) Smaller collections of two or more works published together.

(*c*) Single works, in alphabetical order, each fol-lowed by references to books dealing with the particular work.

(*d*) Supposititious works, if any; they abound in the authors popular in the Middle Ages.

(*e*) Selections.

In (*a*)–(*e*) translations follow editions in the original tongue. Where that tongue is not English, the translations into English head those into other tongues.

(*f*) Works of other writers translated or edited by the author.

(*g*) Then follows the "Appendix", i.e. references to books dealing with the author and his works in general, but not containing any continuous or considerable text. This may be undivided or divided. Natural divisions will be Criticism and Biography; special cases produce special subheadings, such as "Authorship Controversy" and "Centenary and other Celebrations" under Shakespeare. "Miscellaneous" must be used for all general matter that cannot be got into one of the other headings.

The object of all this is obviously to make quick reference to a known or half-known title easy. But the bibliographer wants to do something more. He wants to elucidate some aspect of his author, to make kindred titles throw light on each other and suggest thought; and in this he is at one with the library classifiers, merely differing in carrying his special process to a higher power.

(2) Very probably a leading aspect which will strike him as to be brought into the light is that of time, the chronological development of his author, and then of his author's posthumous reputation. This is the basis of the short bibliography of John Evelyn, the Diarist, which H. B. Wheatley made for the Bibliographical Society in its early days as a specimen for a bibliography of English literature,[1] and the

---

[1] *Transactions of the Bibliographical Society*, vol. i, 1893.

principle is very commonly adopted for bibliographies of authors.

He begins with the one collected edition, and then
with the first work which Evelyn published. We can
put ourselves back into his time, and see him as the
author not of a famous Diary, but of *Fumifugium* and
a few other topical pieces by 1661, of the *Kalendar-
ium Hortense*, *Sculptura*, and *Sylva* by 1664, and so on.

Later editions than the originals, however, and
also translations, are dealt with by Wheatley more
summarily than is really justifiable, since they can be
of considerable importance.

After the work published by Evelyn himself there
follow in a separate section those posthumously published; then in order, Translations by Evelyn, Works
edited by him, Papers and Letters of his published in
various works and collections, MSS. surviving in
accessible collections, and (since he was an artist as
well as a writer) Drawings and Etchings. This ends
Evelyn's own productions, and there follow Lives of
him, Engraved Portraits, and an Index.

Wheatley, in drawing up this specimen bibliography, intended it as a model for general application, but not of course for mechanical imitation, since
few authors present quite the same problems. Thus if
we turn to the admirable little *Bibliographie Moliéres-
que*, 1872, of Paul Lacroix ("le bibliophile Jacob")
we find there, too, the chronological list of original
editions, near the front; but we find also sections
special to Molière, or at least to French writers of his
day, such as one of seventeenth-century piracies of his

plays printed in the Low Countries. Translations of Molière are naturally more important and numerous than of Evelyn, and they get a separate section, instead of being entered separately under the particular originals. Similarly in the *Essai bibliographique sur les œuvres de Alain René Lesage*, 1910 (a diversion of the learned bibliographer of China, Henri Cordier), we find the two plays separated from the more famous novels, and this is paralleled in the British Museum's division of the Dryden heading into Poems, Plays, and Prose Works. But while a division of this kind by literary genre may in some cases be better for a bibliography than the single chronological arrangement, it is surely better in a library catalogue, where quick reference, and not suggestive collocation, is the object, to keep to the strict alphabetical arrangement.

A very valuable element in a bibliography of a famous early writer, which would be out of place in a library catalogue, is a chronological list of contemporary and later allusions to his works. For Shakespeare and Chaucer these have been made the matter of substantial separate works, and treated on a scale which would overbalance a bibliography.[1] Yet passing allusions by contemporary or other early writers may be of far greater significance in helping us to estimate the rise of the author's reputation than complete works devoted to him by later critics, to which alone references would be found in the

---

[1] C. M. Ingleby: *A Shakespeare Allusion Book*; Caroline F. E. Spurgeon: *Five Hundred Years of Chaucer Criticism and Allusion.*

ordinary bibliography. We have only to remember Lydgate on Chaucer or Ben Jonson on Shakespeare (to take the two poets already mentioned) in order to see the force of this.

A modern writer will probably have first published many of his short pieces (and his novels, too, in serial form) in magazines: the text of these may differ widely from that of the volume publication which followed. The former must be hunted out (they will not be found in the Indexes to periodicals) and recorded in their proper places, preferably in a single chronological series with the volumes, but somehow typographically distinguished from them, a trick which is easily accomplished. They should also be tabulated in order of separate appearance, with reference to their later appearance in volumes and in collected works. Thus, in this extract from a table of George Meredith's poems [1] (see page 370), the lines headed P contain references to appearances in periodicals in the years indicated, while the numbered lines between them contain references to the volumes, of which a list is, of course, given at the beginning of the table. We see that *Phantasy* was published in a periodical in 1861, reprinted on p. 157 of the volume of 1862 (*Modern Love*), and again in vol. iii of the complete *Poems* of 1898, which contained various juvenilia, omitted from vols. i and ii; but that *Phœbus with Admetus*, a later poem, of which Meredith thought better, first appeared in a periodical in 1880, and reappeared in *Poems and Lyrics of the Joy of Earth*,

---

[1] A. Esdaile: *A Bibliography of George Meredith*, 1907.

1883, and was chosen for the *Select Poems*, 1897, and included in vol. i of the *Poems* in both the New Popular and Complete Editions of 1898. On referring to 1861 and 1880 in Section I (the main body of entries) we find the exact references for the appearances in periodicals, which could not be crowded into

	Phantasy.	Phœbus with Admetus.	Pictures of the Rhine.	Progress.
P.—'51 . . .	—	—	—	—
I. '51 . . .	—	—	154	—
P. '52–'62 . .	['61]	—	—	—
II. '62 . . .	157	—	—	—
P. '63–'83 . .	—	['80]	—	—
III. '83 . . .	—	71	—	68
P. '84–'88 . .	—	—	—	—
IV. '87 . . .	—	—	—	—
V. '88 . . .	—	—	—	—
P. '89–'92 . .	—	—	—	—
VI. '92 . . .	—	—	—	—
VII. '92 . . .	—	—	—	—
VIII. '92 . .	—	—	—	—
P. '93–'97 . .	—	—	—	—
IX. '97 . . .	—	77	—	—
X. '98 . . .	—	—	—	—
XI. '98 . . .	—	i. 116	—	i. 196
XII. '98 . . .	iii. 243	i. 144	iii. 212	i. 220

tabular form. Similarly, if there are many editions of a single work to record, and it is decided to record them immediately after the original edition, and not in a separate section (as Lacroix does), it may be very confusing to the reader who opens the bibliography; he does not know which way to turn, finding page after page of a single work. A good example of this difficulty is to be found in Joseph Smith's Quaker bibliography, where the many editions of a single favourite tract by George Fox or William Penn frequently occupy pages on end. The headlines or "shoulder-pieces" should be used as signposts to the arrangement.

B. A Bibliography of an Historical Person

Here, too, we must seek in the hero's career the basis for our division of the literature gathering round his name.

He will, however, have written something, if only letters and dispatches; but these may well be regarded as sources for his biography rather than as literature.

He may have had more than one distinct sphere of activity, and in both have given rise to literature. Thus Napoleon was great not only as a soldier but also as a lawgiver. In the careers of many great men their private lives, and notably their loves, can be isolated from their public lives and separately written, so that here we get another possible principle of arrangement.

But all men have one quality in common; between birth and death they exist in the dimension of time. They are first young, and then old. All literature dealing with special episodes in a life should, therefore, be arranged in the chronological order of those episodes; for example, in the case of Napoleon we should have:

1. General Biography
2. Periods and Phases

   (a) *Early Years*
   (b) *Military Career*
   (c) *Political Career*
   (d) *Family Life and Marriages*
   (e) *St. Helena.*

3. Episodes

   1796–97. *Italian Campaign*
   1798–99. *Egypt and Syria*
   1799. *Coup d'Etat*
   1800. *Campaign of Marengo*
   1801. *Concordat*
   1802. *Consulate Election*
   1803. *Plan to invade England*
   1804. *Coronation*

[and so on, down to:]

   1815. *Waterloo*
   1815. *Voyage to St. Helena*
   1821. *Death*
   1840. *Second Funeral.*

Satires and caricatures of "the Corsican Ogre" would make a section by themselves.

C. A BIBLIOGRAPHY OF A LOCALITY

Local collections flourish in most local libraries, and the classification of the material on the shelves and the preparation of printed catalogues is an important and attractive (if not a very large) part of the duties of the library staff.

Topography and chronology together are clearly the main principles.

Sir Francis Hyett, the Gloucestershire antiquary and bibliographer, contributed to the *Transactions of the Bibliographical Society* [1] a discussion of the classes of material to be included in such a collection and their arrangement, with suggestions for organizing the work. He does not include MSS. (as Wheatley does for Evelyn); prints and maps he doubtfully rejects. Works merely written by inhabitants and speeches or sermons on general subjects delivered in the county, which load some older bibliographies, he very rightly rejects. Locally printed works he is undecided about; but a record of the early presses at work in the locality and their products seems to be clearly worth including. Brought down too late, such an addition would overweigh the rest and be of doubtful value; the dividing line must differ in different cases; 1800 has been suggested as generally suitable. Biographies of inhabitants must depend for admission on the closeness of those inhabitants' connection with the locality. A bibliography of Warwickshire which included all the literature on Shakespeare would be a lop-sided monstrosity.

Sir Francis Hyett's scheme is as follows:

1. Works relating to the County generally:
   - (*a*) Works the whole of which relate to the County
   - (*b*) Works containing substantive references to the County
   - (*c*) Periodicals
   - (*d*) County administration
   - (*e*) Acts of Parliament.

[1] Vol. III, part 1, 1895.

2. Works relating to well-defined districts of the County.
3. Works relating to parishes and towns.
4. Biographies of Inhabitants.

There seems to be little need for the distinction between 1 (*a*) and 1 (*b*) here, but otherwise it is lucid enough.

One or two points may be picked up by comparison with an old County bibliography, John Russell Smith's *Bibliotheca Cantiana*, 1837, which, of course, has not to deal with the great output of the last century. Smith's scheme is:

1. Historians of the County.
2. Principal Maps.
3. Heraldic Visitations.
4. Tracts printed during the Civil War and Commonwealth from 1640 to 1660.
5. Acts of Parliament.
6. Books relating to the County in General.
7. Books relating to the particular parishes and events.
8. Index.

Maps are surely rightly included; and Heraldic Visitations are a class of record apart and worth treating as such. But the insertion of 4, Civil War and Commonwealth Tracts, makes one wonder why that period alone, however rich in such pieces, should be so singled out, and whether a chronological arrangement (or cross-arrangement in an appendix) should not be made of all pieces dealing with single events. Smith's distinction between historians of the County and writers about the County at large (who would now include the writers of picturesque guide-books) is obviously sound.

374

D. A Bibliography of an Art

Writings on an art will fall naturally into Eastern and Western, and perhaps also that of primitive races in other parts of the globe; and those on Western art will fall into classical, mediæval, and modern, and again into national schools; while there may also be cross-divisions by material, as between stone statuary and ivory carving, and by purpose, as between religious and secular music, between landscape and portrait painting, between the architecture of bridges and that of offices and flats. And, as always, the early books will be best arranged, if only in a supplementary and alternative arrangement, by the dates of their production.

E. A Bibliography of a Science

Many of the same considerations will apply to the planning of a bibliography of a science as to that of an art, except that science has no frontiers, and national schools will disappear.

Biographies of artists and men of science are matter for inclusion in these two types of bibliography. In most library classifications biography is absurdly treated as a class apart. The life of Darwin is obviously part of the history of biology, and the life of de Lesseps part of the history of engineering.

In all these classes, and in any others, the references may be made as normally, only one apiece to each

375

book or article, with as much effort as possible at putting them in their proper places. But obviously every book consists of chapters or articles dealing with different aspects or episodes of the subject. A Life of Napoleon will contain, among others, a chapter on the Concordat, a chapter on St. Helena. Why should not these chapters be found entered alongside of the complete books on the Concordat and on Napoleon at St. Helena? Why, in fact, should the bibliographer not analyse his material and index it as closely as leisure, funds, and a sense of proportion permit?

An analytical bibliography made on these lines is generally called "topical"; and there are examples of it in the bibliography of English literature, the most notable being Miss E. P. Hammond's *Chaucer*, 1907 (the earliest of the class) and Professor J. E. Wells's *Manual of the Writings in Middle English*, 1916.[1]

The bibliographer is in this matter in a happier position than the library classifier. He can enter a single and physically individual book in two or many places; while on library shelves it can stand in only one place, unless the librarian uses reference dummies, as is done in the British Museum for volumes containing two or more incunabula—or unless he emulate the judgment of Solomon, a plan which Buckle adopted with his books, and which is legitimate enough with temporary material, as in commercial libraries, but is quite incompatible with the preser-

[1] See A. Esdaile: *Sources of English Literature*, 1928, pp. 92–7.

vation of books, and so with the bibliographical conscience.

Under any of these schemes of classification, the internal arrangement of the ultimate subdivisions at least should be chronological and not alphabetical. While, as already observed, the alphabet merely directs the inquirer to an author he already knows, the order of time satisfies the two largest classes of student, the antiquary, who wants the oldest book, and the modernist, who wants the newest.

F. A BIBLIOGRAPHY OF PERIODICALS

Where all the periodicals can be seen by the bibliographer, there is no reason why they should not be given the same classification as would be given to books or articles. The frequent difficulty of seeing all when they are scattered has in two notable cases, *The World List of Scientific Periodicals* and "*GAZ.*", caused a plain alphabetical arrangement of titles to be preferred, and this is obviously right for a finding list, in so far as it concerns periodicals which are not published by corporate or official bodies.

Not that an alphabetical arrangement is really plain. In the *World List*, where there are about 50,000 titles registered, elaborate modifications of exact alphabetization have had to be made, omitting the unimportant and throwing weight on to the important words.

The difficulties of any alphabetical order of titles become far worse when the publications of corporate bodies, official or academic, enter in. "Report", "Bulletin", "Journal", "Proceedings", "Transactions", to take only English words, will each fill pages upon pages and break the heart of the seeker. The form of the title, too, is often impossible, e.g. "State of Iowa. Annual Report. Dairy and Food Division of the Iowa Department of Agriculture". It is clear that the alphabet, like other good things given for our use, was intended to be used in moderation.

Considered as a main principle of arrangement, place of publication is quite valueless, except for newspapers; and it is a pity that the British Museum should by its headings of Academies and Periodical Publications (the latter excluding newspapers) have given authority to a bad system.

It seems clear that the name of the publishing body should be the heading, and that words and phrases like "of", "for", "for the promotion of", should be disregarded in arrangement. Moreover, where the name of a country, district, or place figures in the name of the body, as in the example from Iowa cited, that the geographical name should be thrown to the front and should govern the order, as:

> Iowa, Dept. of Agriculture.—Dairy and Food
> Division. Annual Report.

Otherwise the place of publication or headquarters will merely be useful to distinguish bodies with the same name, such as "Académie des sciences (Paris)", "Société historique et archéologique (Lyons)".

The massed repetitions of common title-words and

378

place-names will thus be largely broken up and will not impede identification of the title wanted.

Where the title of the periodical does not include the name of the publishing body, as e.g. *The Journal of Hellenic Studies*, which is the organ of the Society for the Promotion of Hellenic Studies, there must be a cross-reference, and we shall find:

> Society (for the promotion of) Hellenic Studies. Journal of Hellenic Studies,

and

> Journal (of) Hellenic Studies. *See* Society (for the promotion of) Hellenic Studies.

A last word. Compiling a bibliography is not paste and scissors work. No book that has not been seen should be included without a note to that effect, and no title should be copied from another bibliography without necessity, except, of course, as a preliminary note. As a precaution it is wise to use slips of two colours, one for preliminary titles, taken from any source, and the other for final titles, taken from the books themselves. Thus plagiarism will be avoided. If no copy of a book can be found, and the title must be transcribed from another bibliography, do it, but say so, giving the full and exact reference. And neither in compiling bibliographies nor in describing individual books may the bibliographer conjecture beyond necessity, or (if constrained by necessity to conjecture) disguise his conjecture as ascertained fact. He is where he is not for his own glory, but for the advancement of knowledge.

READING LIST

LIST A

POLLARD, Alfred W. The arrangement of bibliographies.
    (A.A.L. Reprint No. 2.) 1950. (Reprinted from
    The Library.)

INDEX

INDEX

and examples of, 283–363; universal, 287–92; national, 297–332; secondary, 349–63; arrangement of, 364–79

Bibliography, analytical, 23–5; historical, 25–32; systematic, 32–4

Binding, styles of decorated, 211–26; origin of, in Roman tablets, 211; mediæval enamelled and jewelled, 211–12; mediæval incised and tooled, 212–13; 15th–16th cent., stamped, 214; Oriental, influences Western, 215; Italian renaissance, 216–17; gold-tooled, 215–26; French renaissance (Grolier, Mahieu, Tory, Eve, Lyonnese, Le Gascon), 217–20; lettering on spine and fore-edges evidence of position on shelf, 220; English Restoration (Mearne), 220–2; Harleian, 222; Irish 18th cent., 222; Jansenist, 222–3; Scottish 18th cent., 222; French 18th cent., dentelle, etc., 223; German 18th cent., 223; rococo, 223; Roger Payne and Empire styles, 224; 19th and 20th cent., 224–6

Black letter, *see* Gothic type

Blank leaves at beginning and end of books, 102; when to be noted, 269–70

Blind-tooling and stamping, 207

Block books, 105–6

Blooteling, Abraham, 174

Bodoni, Giambattista, 147; his greek type, 157

Book, the parts of, 94–103

Book of the Dead, The, 160

Bowyer, William, 146

Bradshaw, Henry, 26–7

Brant, Sebastian, 128

British Museum, incunabula in the, arranged by R. Proctor,

26–7; catalogue of, 290, 298; arrangement of sub-headings in catalogue, 365

Brocar, Arnald Guillen de, prints polyglot Bible, 130, 156

Bruges, Caxton's press at, 121

Buckram, 205–6

Bulmer, William, 147

Bunyan, John, *The Pilgrim's Progress*, Pt. I, 1st ed., 1678, variant in copies of, 90

Burin, 169

Burr, 169, 171–2

Byzantine book-decoration, 161

Calf, 201–2; as vellum, 205

Callimachus, his dislike of large books, 93

Cambridge, early printing at, 124

Canadian books, bibliographies of, 317–18

Cancels, 91–2

Canevari bindings, 216–17

Caroline minuscules, the basis of Roman type, 143–4

Carolingian book-decoration, 161

Cases, upper and lower, 65

Casing, publishers', 199–200; first issued by W. Pickering, 137

Caslon, William, 146, 148

Catchwords, 76

Caxton, William, 121–5; types of, 142–3; possible portrait of, 170; bindery of, 214–15

Cellulose (fibre), percentage of, in paper materials, 45

Censorship, in 17th-cent. England, 133

Chain lines, 50

Chancery type (italic), 152

Charles II of England, bindings made for, 220–1

Chase, 79

Chepman, Walter, 125

China, paper invented in, 42

382

INDEX

INDEX

INDEX

INDEX

INDEX

INDEX

INDEX